AF327917

The Photographer's Image

SELF = PORTRAYAL

edited by
James Alinder

101 contemporary self-portraits
with essays by
Peter Hunt Thompson
Dana Asbury
R. Duncan Wallace, M.D.

The Friends of Photography
Carmel, California

ACKNOWLEDGMENTS

This book began over three years ago, initiated in title and concept by Peter Hunt Thompson. Help in funding the project was then sought by Jim Enyeart during his tenure at The Friends of Photography. When I came to The Friends in December of 1977, I was delighted to have the opportunity to carry the project to completion. In March of 1978 a mailing requesting self-portraits was sent to over 2000 photographers; letters were sent to a number of photographers known to have made self-portraits. The response was overwhelming as more than 3000 self-portraits were received from some 600 photographers. There were many more exciting photographs of self than we could use. I was helped in the process of selecting these 101 images by David Featherstone and Peter Andersen, with Peter Turner joining us during the sequencing. The essays were written over the summer and the whole project went to the printers in the late fall.

I would like to thank all those who contributed to the book — the photographers who have provided us with fascinating interpretations of self; the essayists (Dana Asbury, Peter Hunt Thompson, R. Duncan Wallace) who have added another dimension to the book, and my staff, David Featherstone who was responsible for the editorial aspects; Peter Andersen, who saw the book through the production phase and Nancy Ponedel, my secretary.

This publication was supported in part by a grant from the National Endowment for the Arts, Washington, D.C.   J.A.

Type: Helvetica Condensed
Paper: Flokote, 100 lb.
Typography: Graham Graphics, Pacific Grove, California
Printing: Herald Printers, Monterey, California
Binding: Cardoza-James Binding, San Francisco, California

Library of Congress Catalogue Card No.: 78-71591
ISBN: 0-933286-00-7
$9.95

SELF = PORTRAYAL

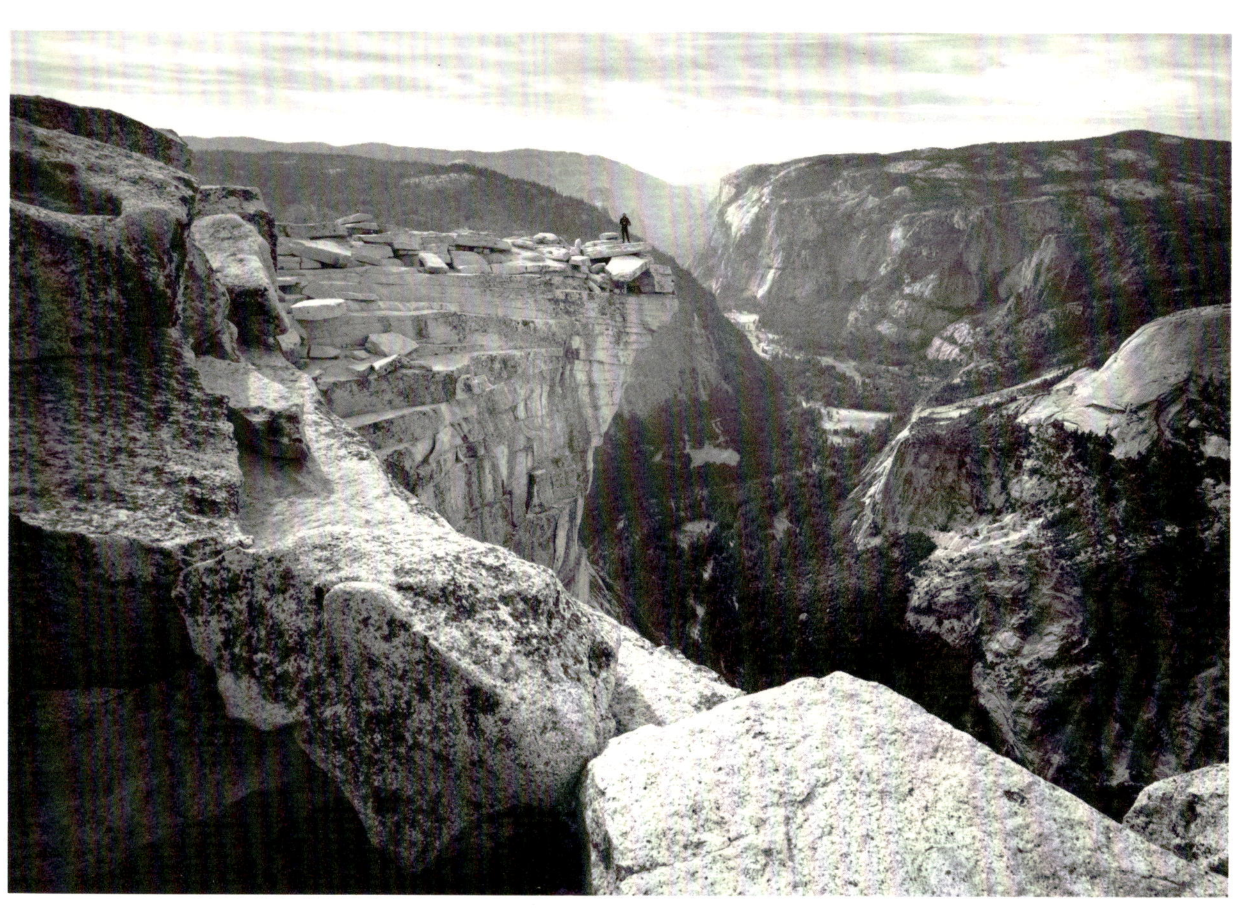

TED ORLAND
Ben Lomond, California
Self-Portrait in an American Landscape, 1977

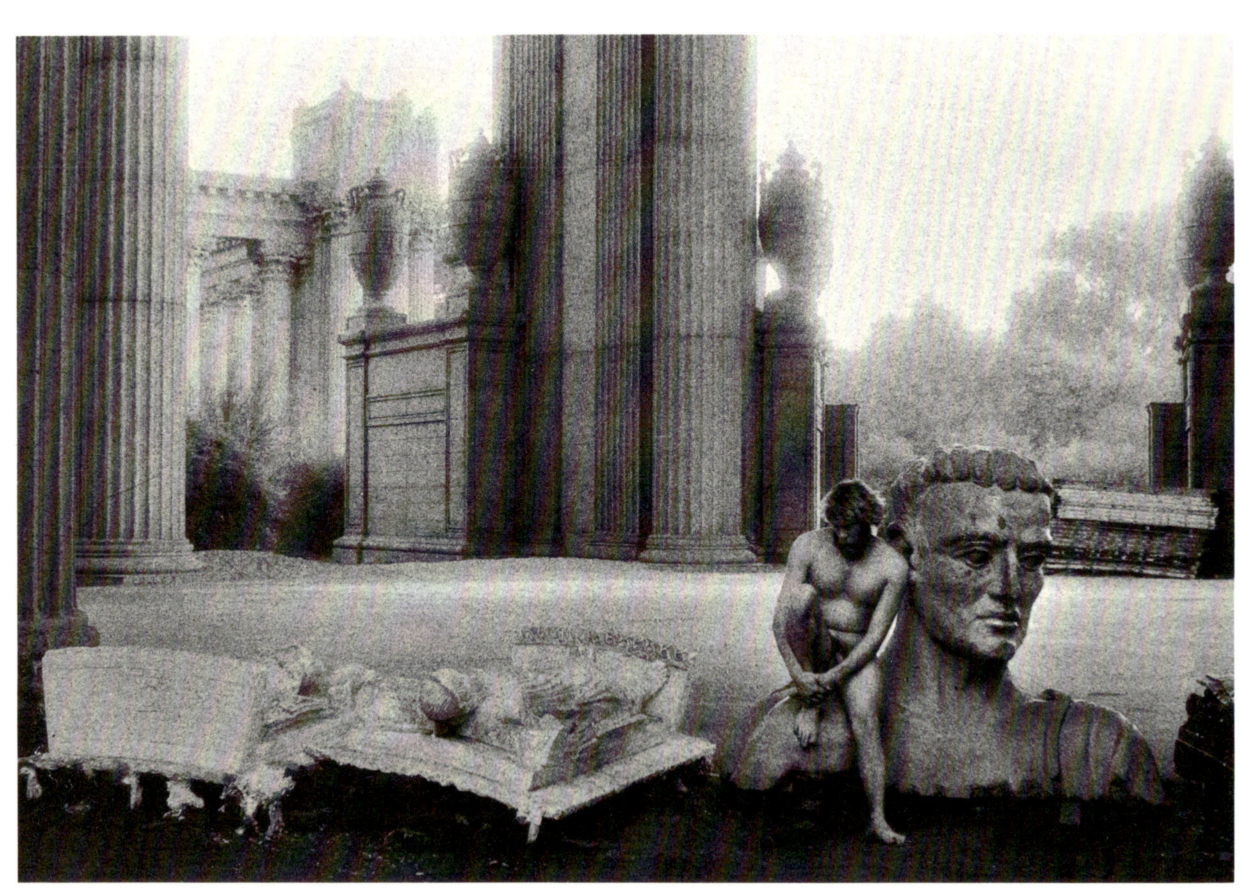

R. VALENTINE ATKINSON
San Francisco, California
Palace of Fine Arts, San Francisco

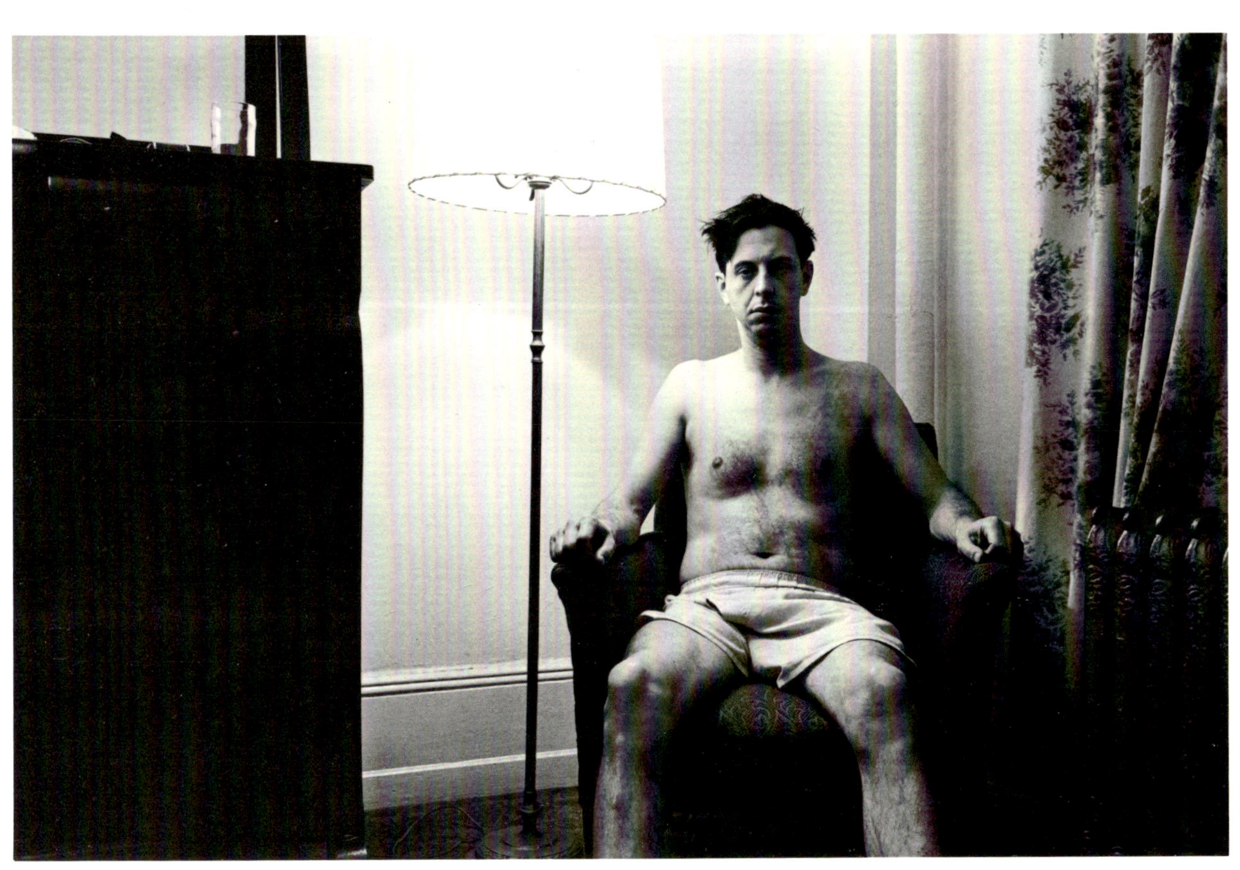

LEE FRIEDLANDER
New City, New York
Self-Portrait, 1965

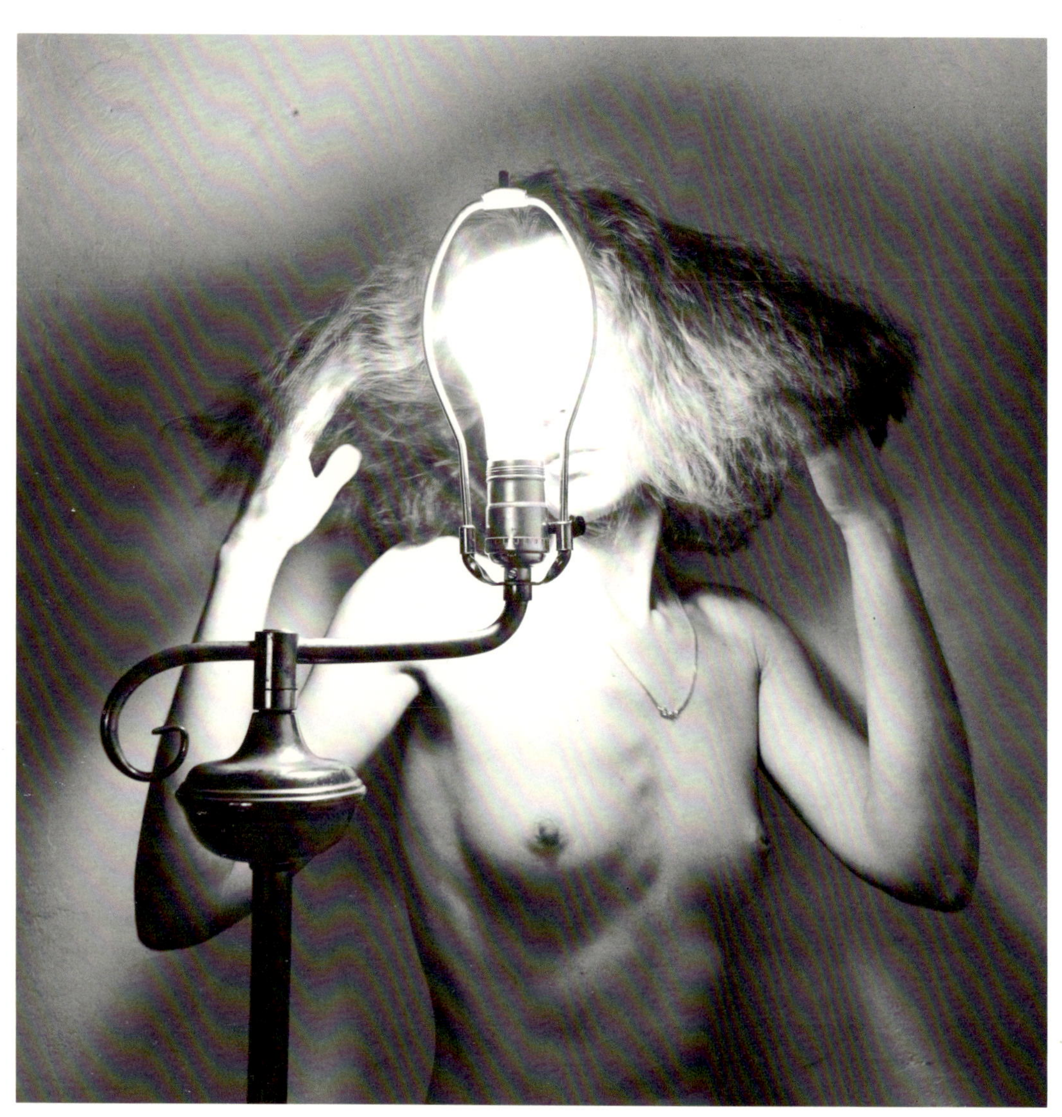

BONNIE F. SCHENKENBERG
Salt Lake City, Utah
Self-Portrait, 1978

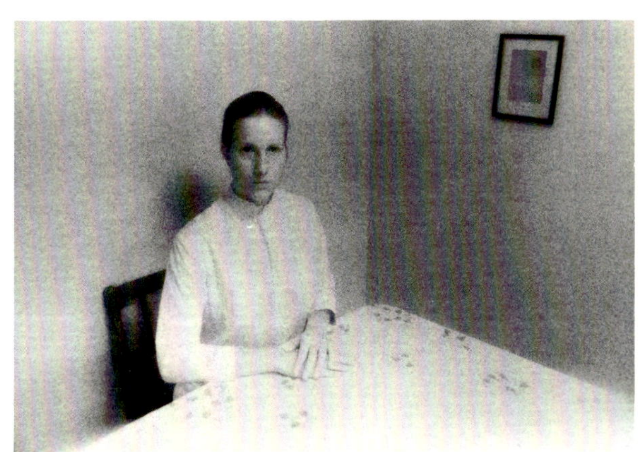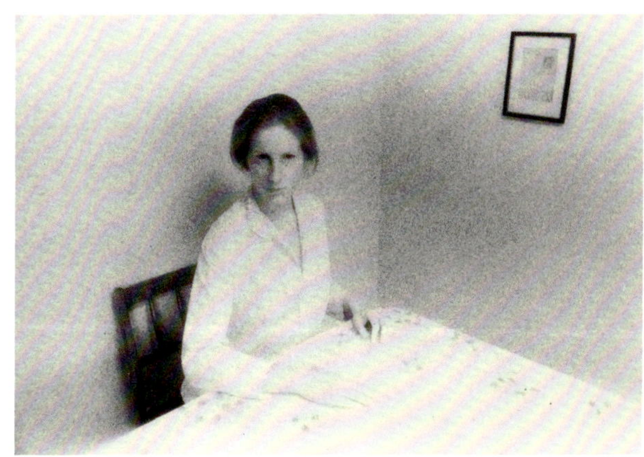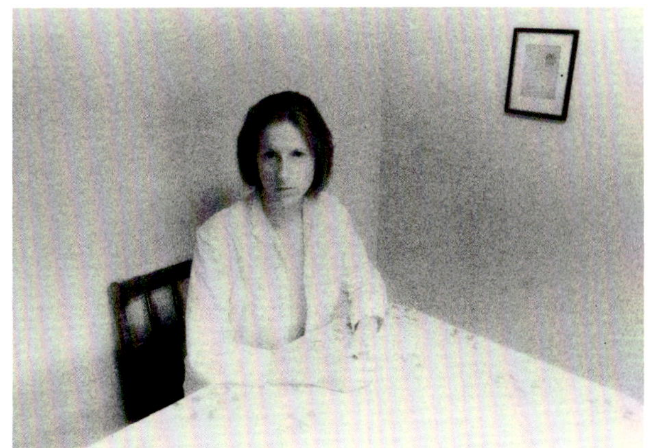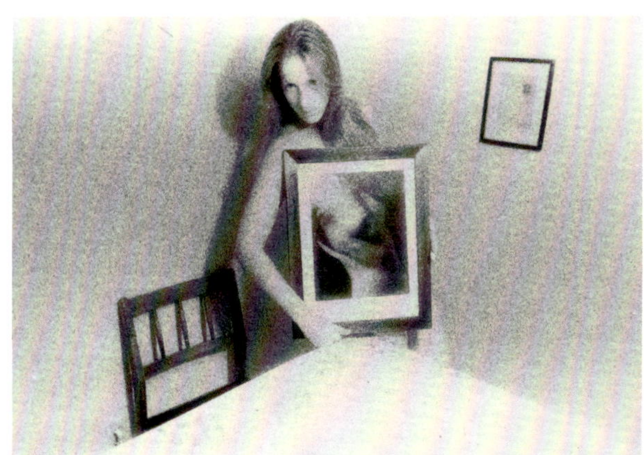

KAREN ANDERSON
Tampa, Florida
Self-Portrait, 1977

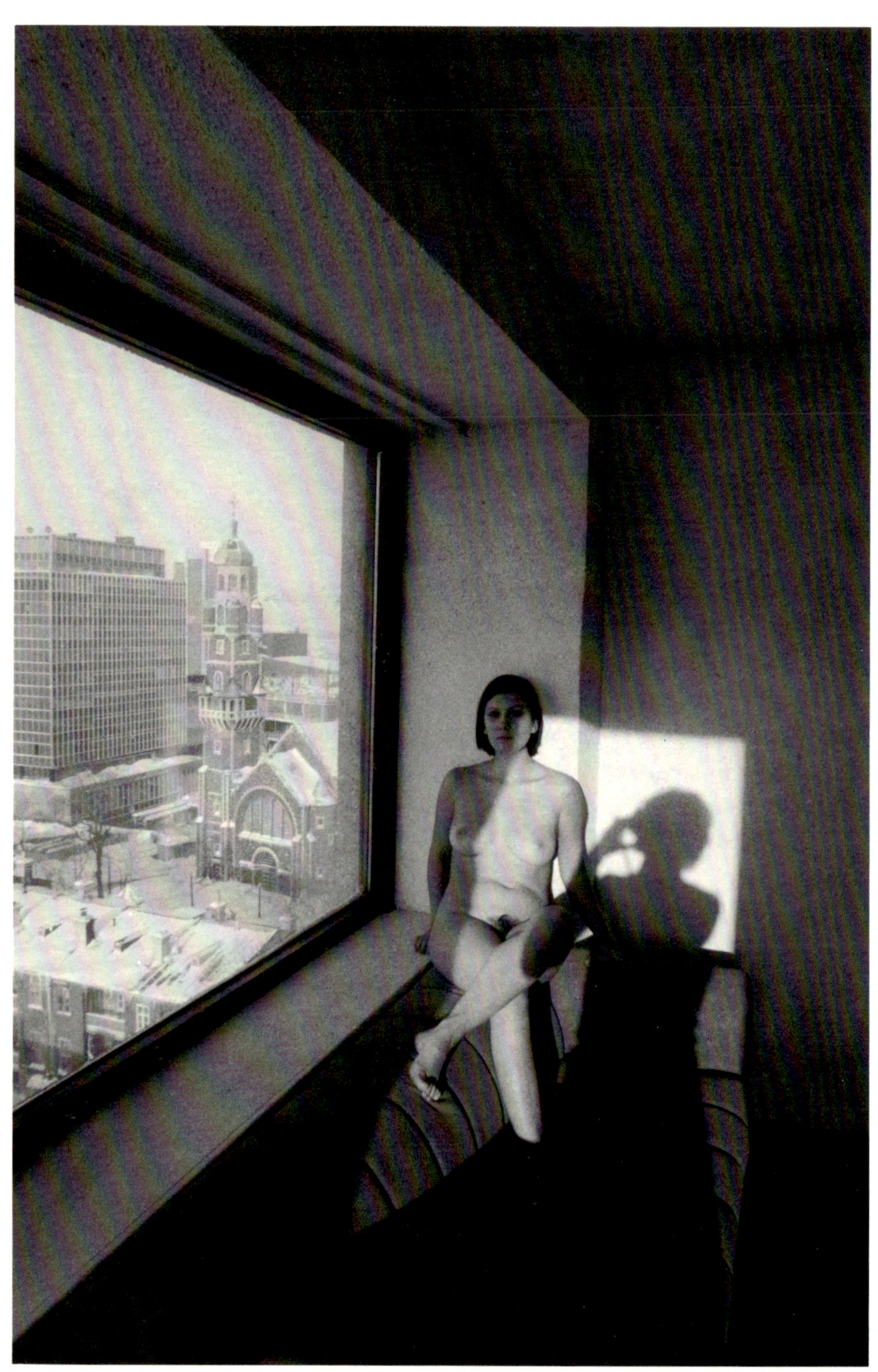

LUCIEN CLERGUE
Arles, France
Self-Portrait in Quebec, 1977

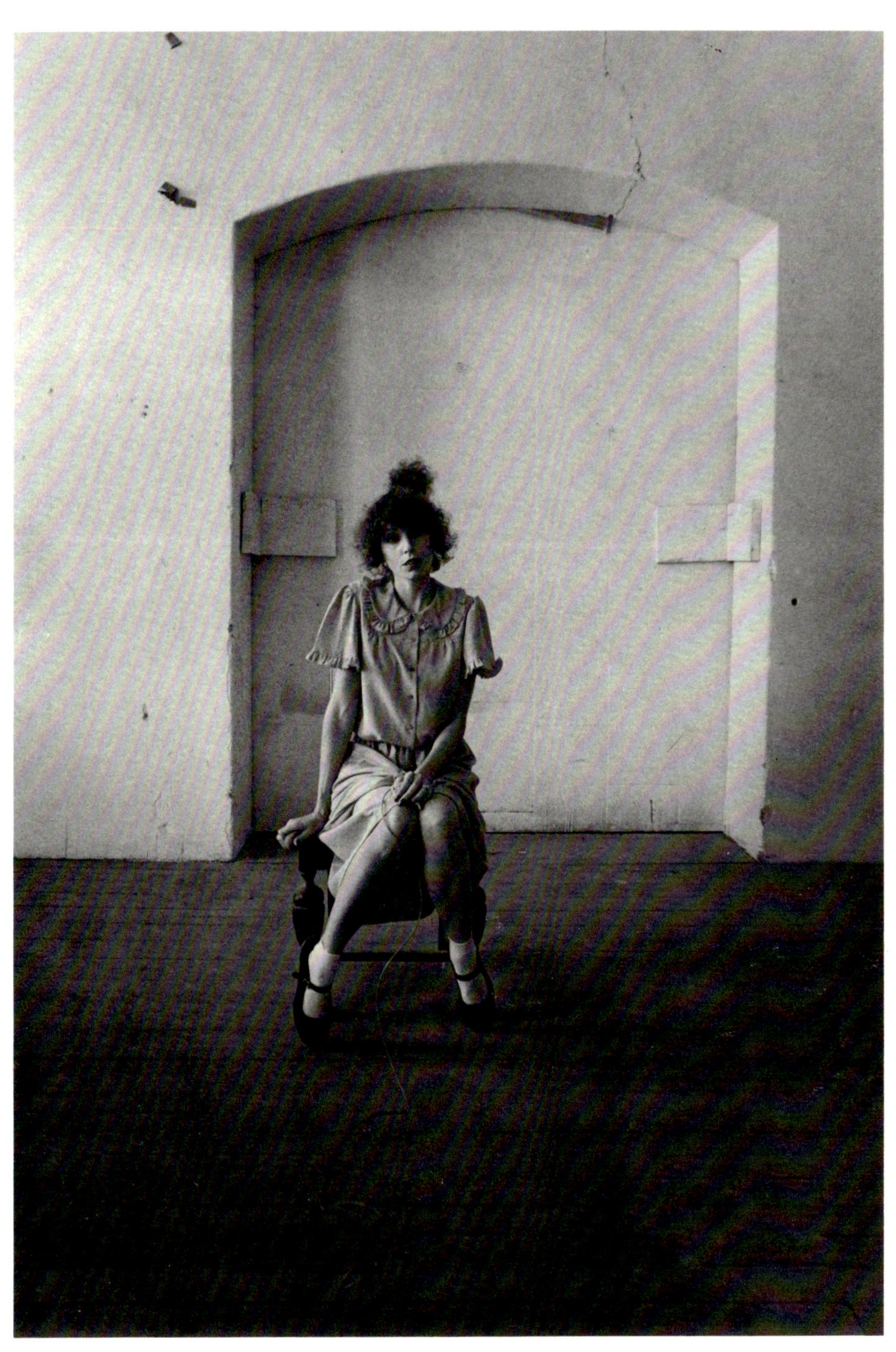

KAT MOSER
Omaha, Nebraska
Self-Portrait, 1978

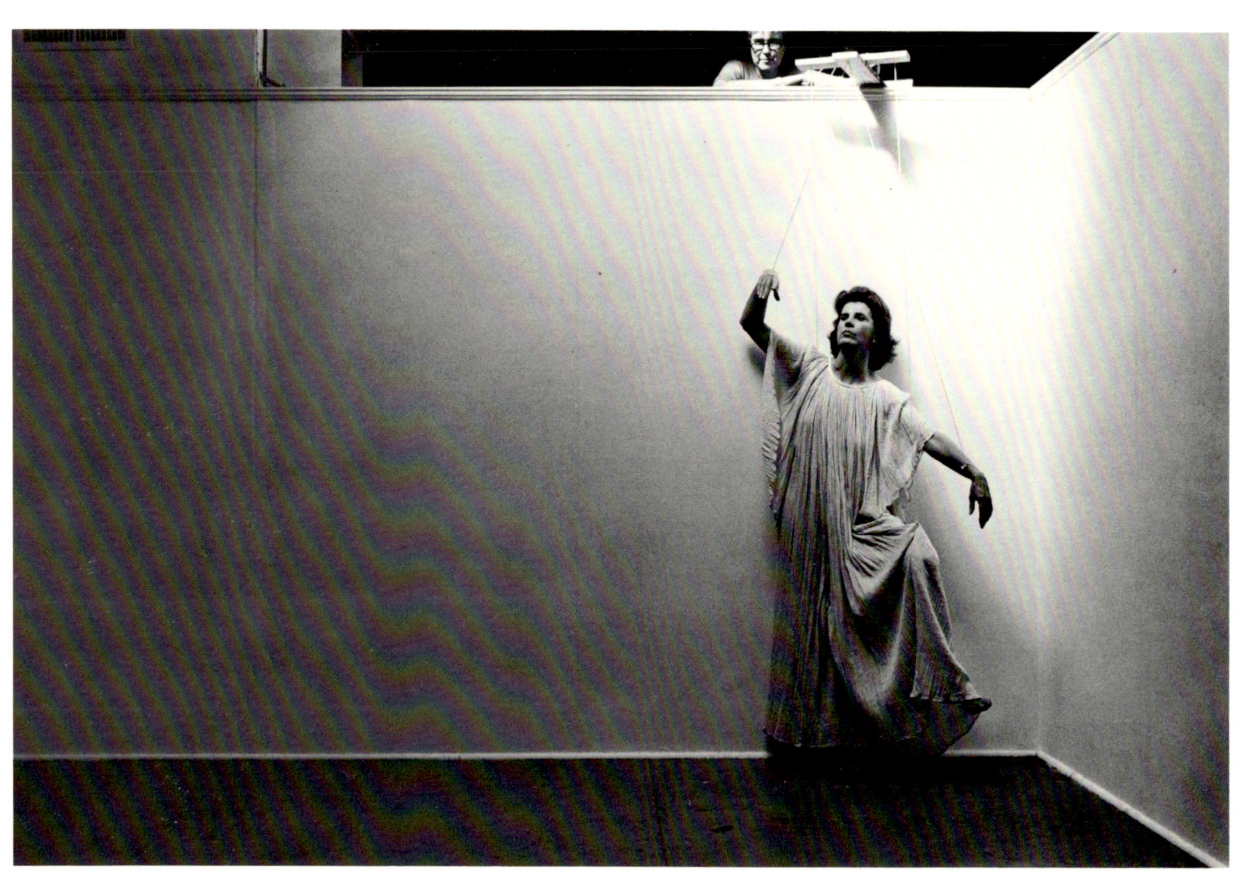

LYNN LENNON
Dallas, Texas
Marionette

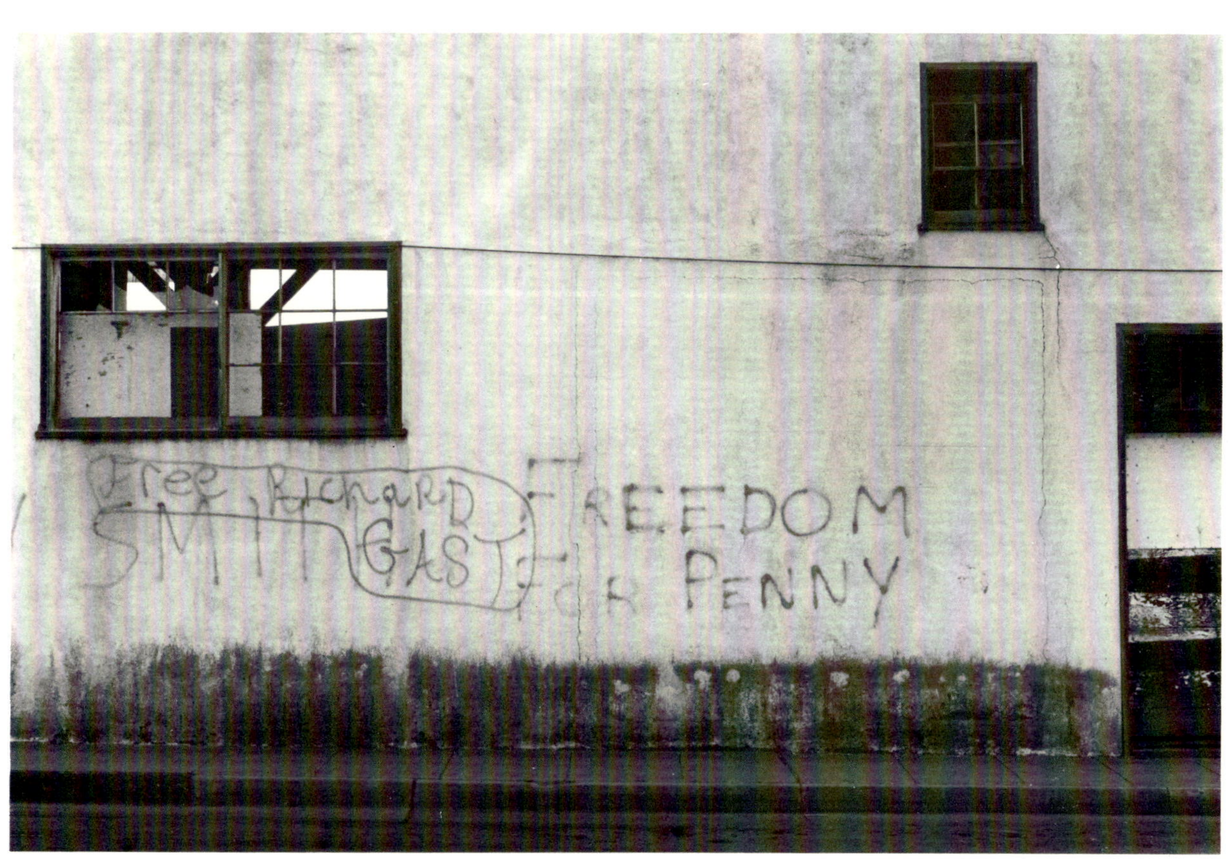

PENNY FEINBERG
Monterey, California
Untitled, 1975

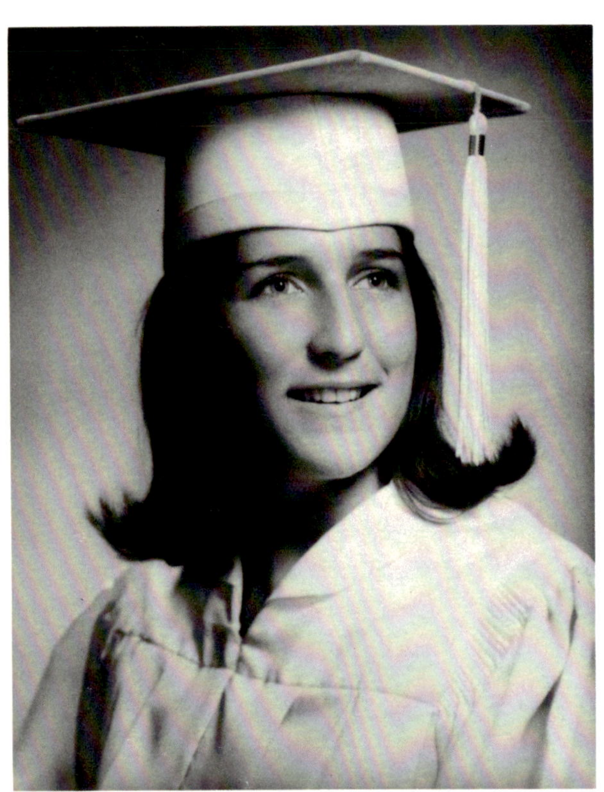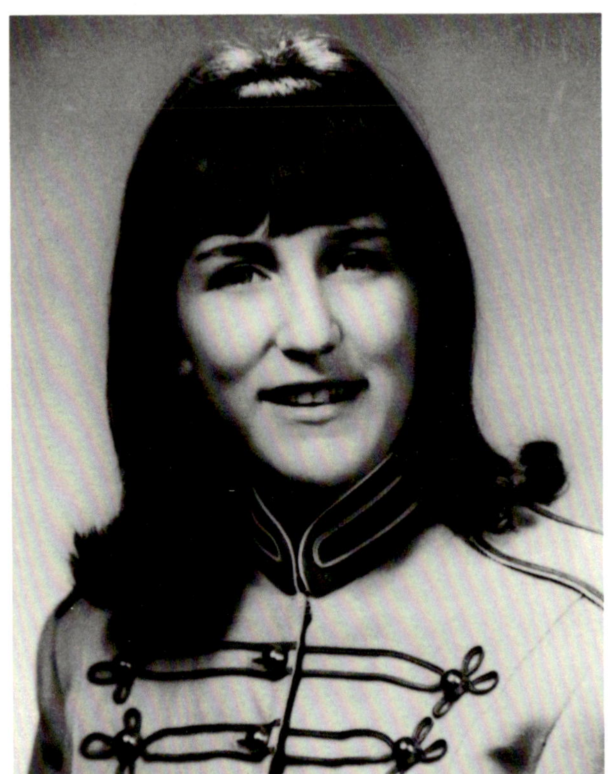

ALICE STEINHARDT
Long Beach, California
Self = Betrayal, 1978

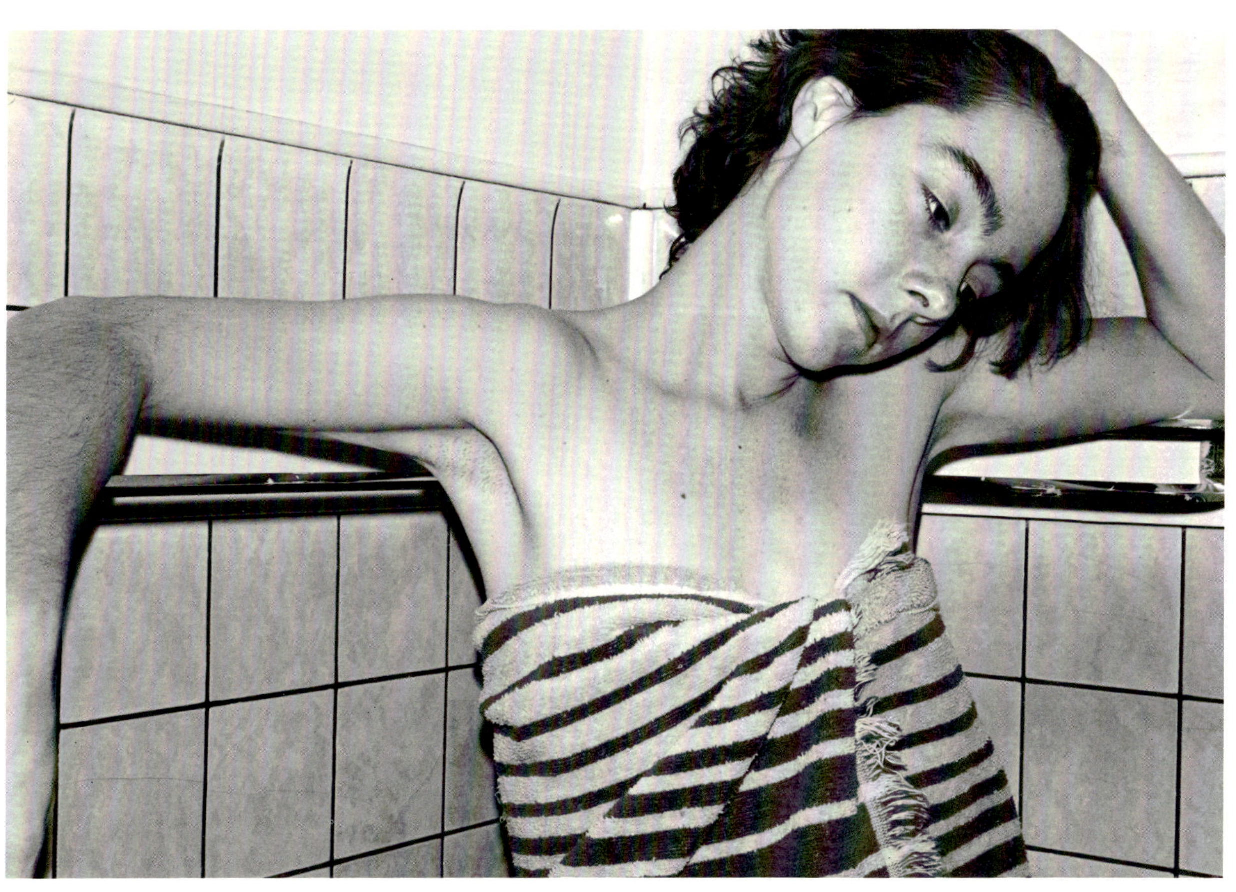

COLLEEN KENYON
Woodstock, New York
Despondent in the Christmas House, 1977

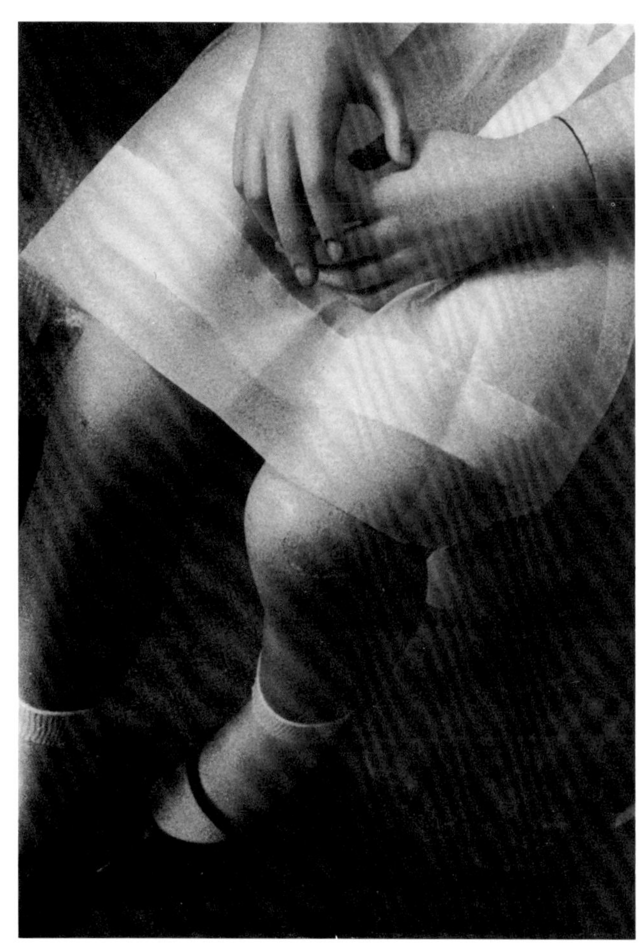

LINDA SZABO WHITE
Cambridge, Massachusetts
Untitled, 1976

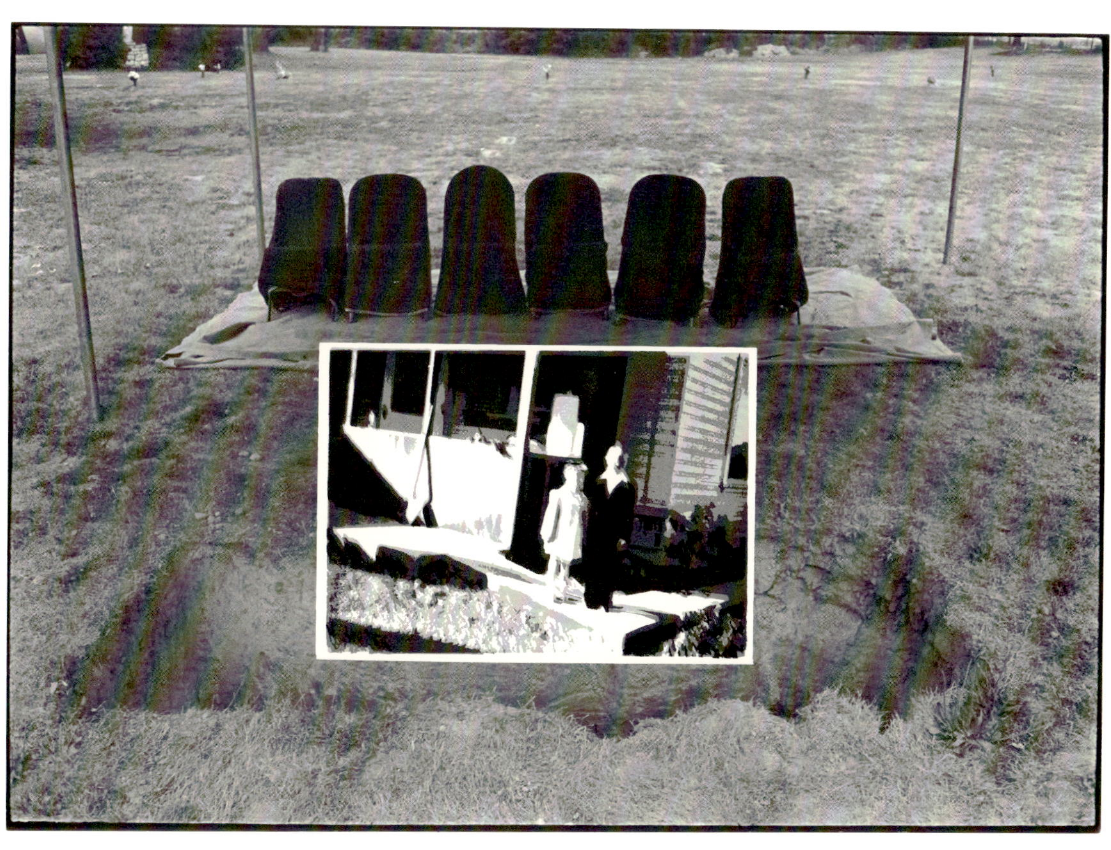

JOHN WILLIAM NAGEL
Webster Groves, Missouri
Fear of Death, 1977

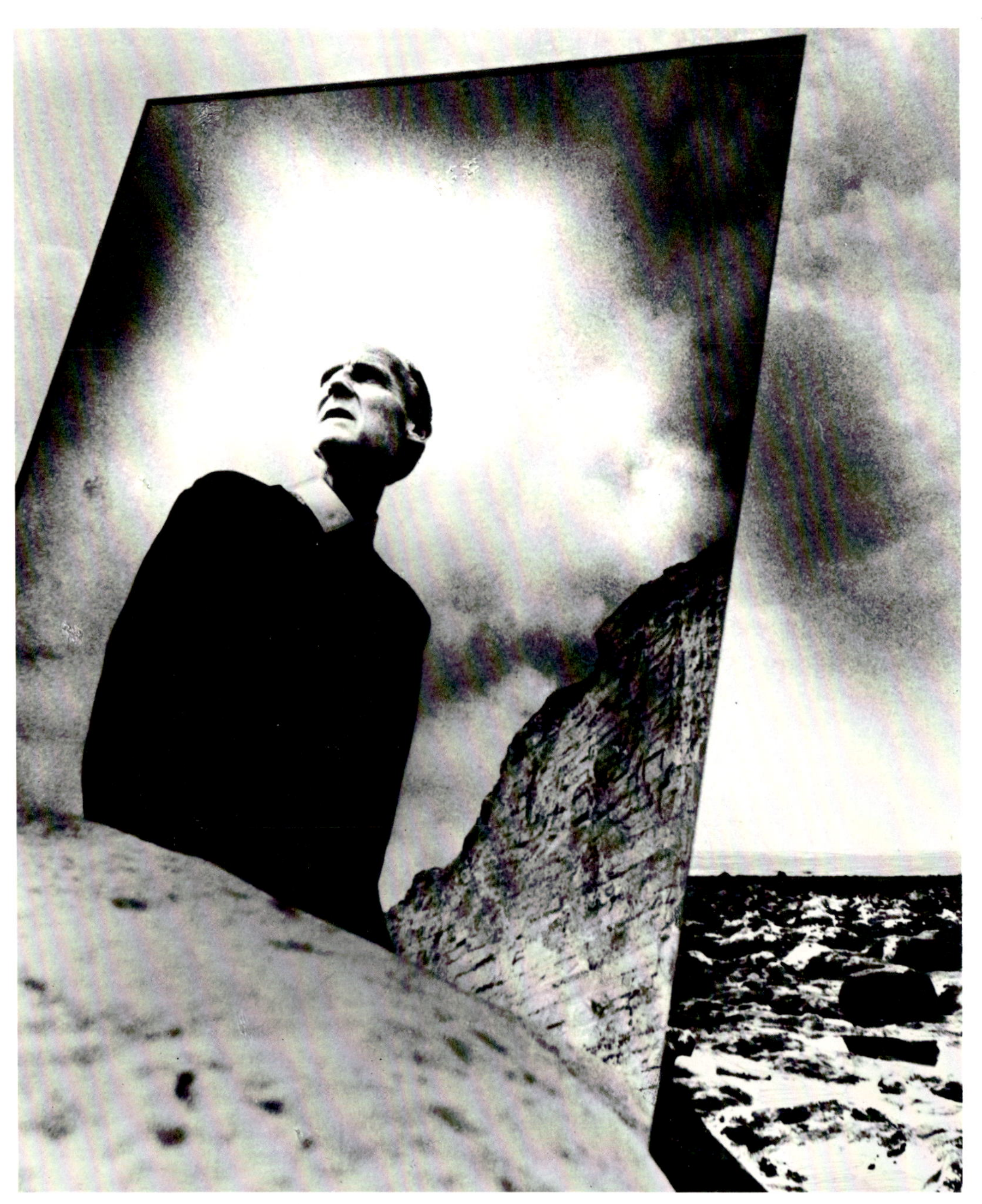

BILL BRANDT
London, England
Self-Portrait with Mirror
East Sussex Coast, England, 1966

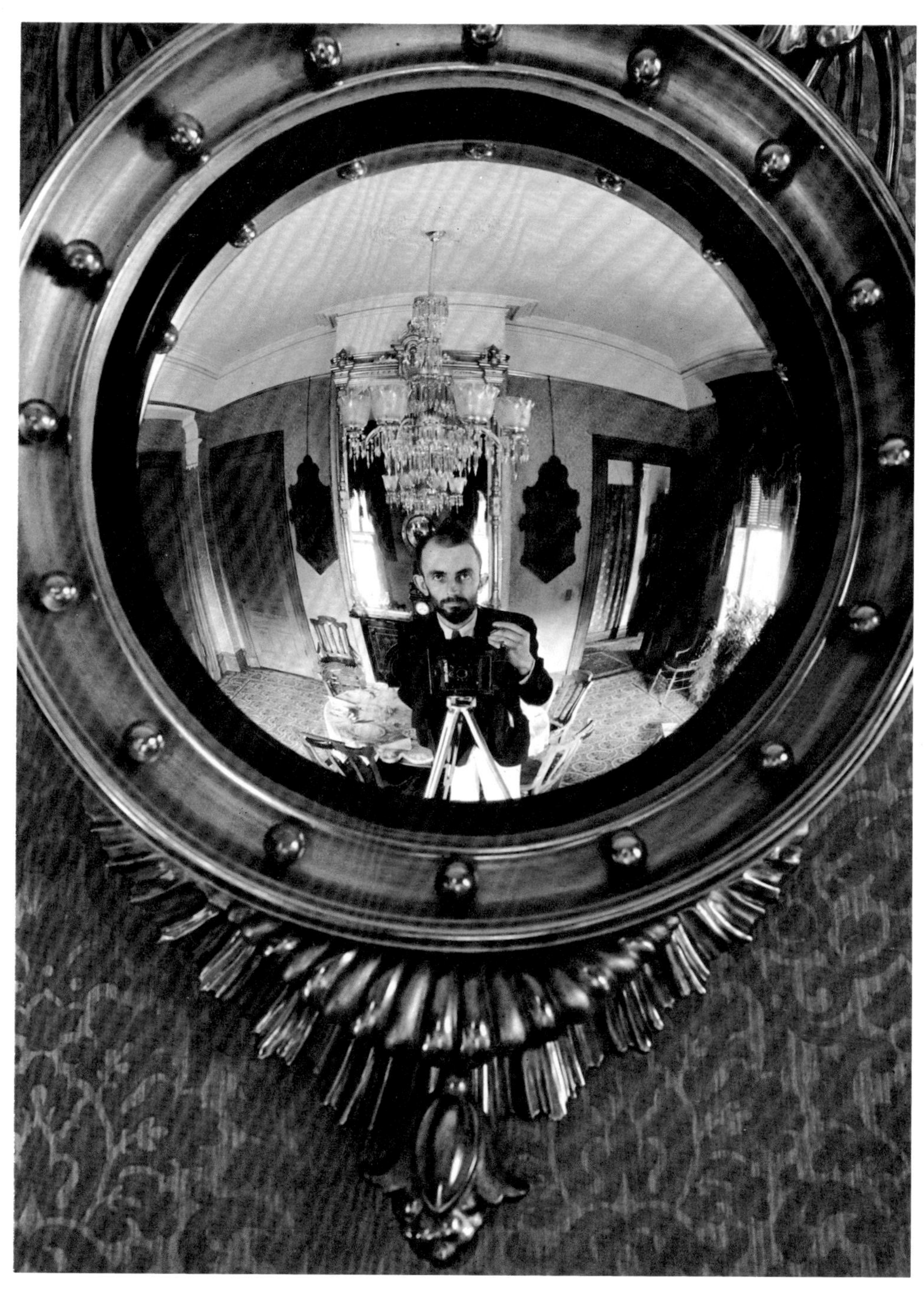

ANSEL ADAMS
Carmel, California
Self-Portrait, Atherton, California, c. 1940

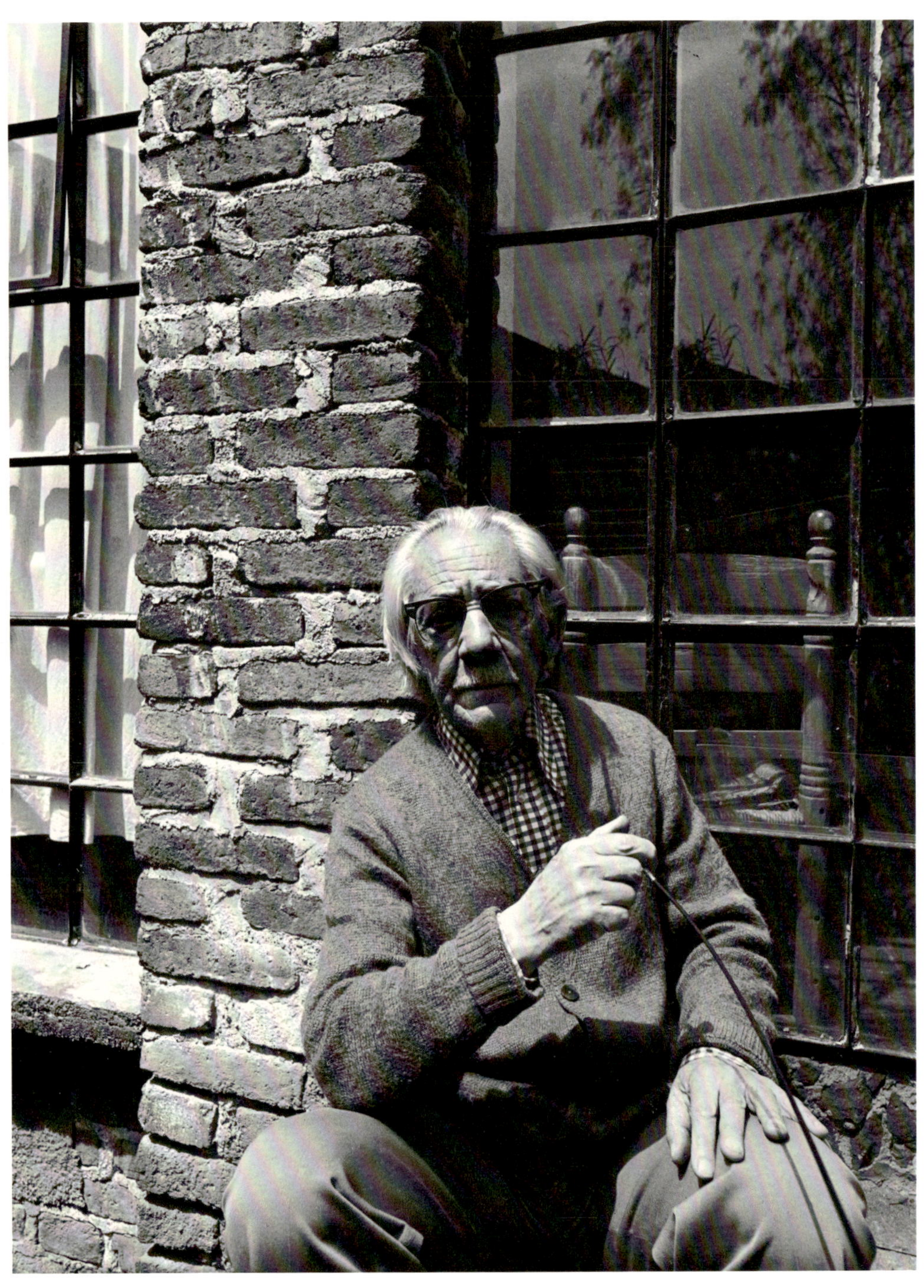

MANUEL ALVAREZ BRAVO
Coyoacan, Mexico
Por él Mismo, 1978

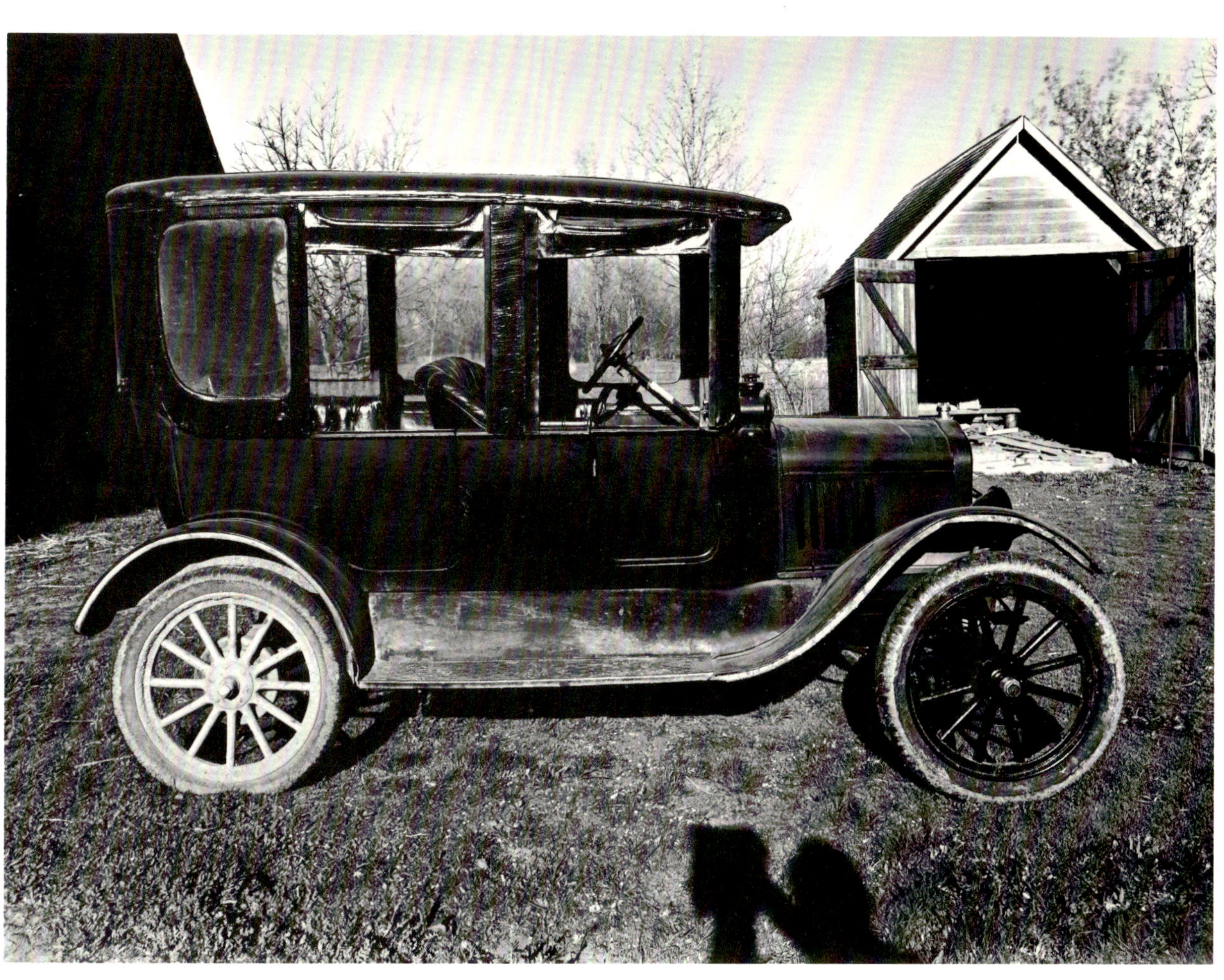

WRIGHT MORRIS
Mill Valley, California
Portrait of the Artist as a Young Man, 1947

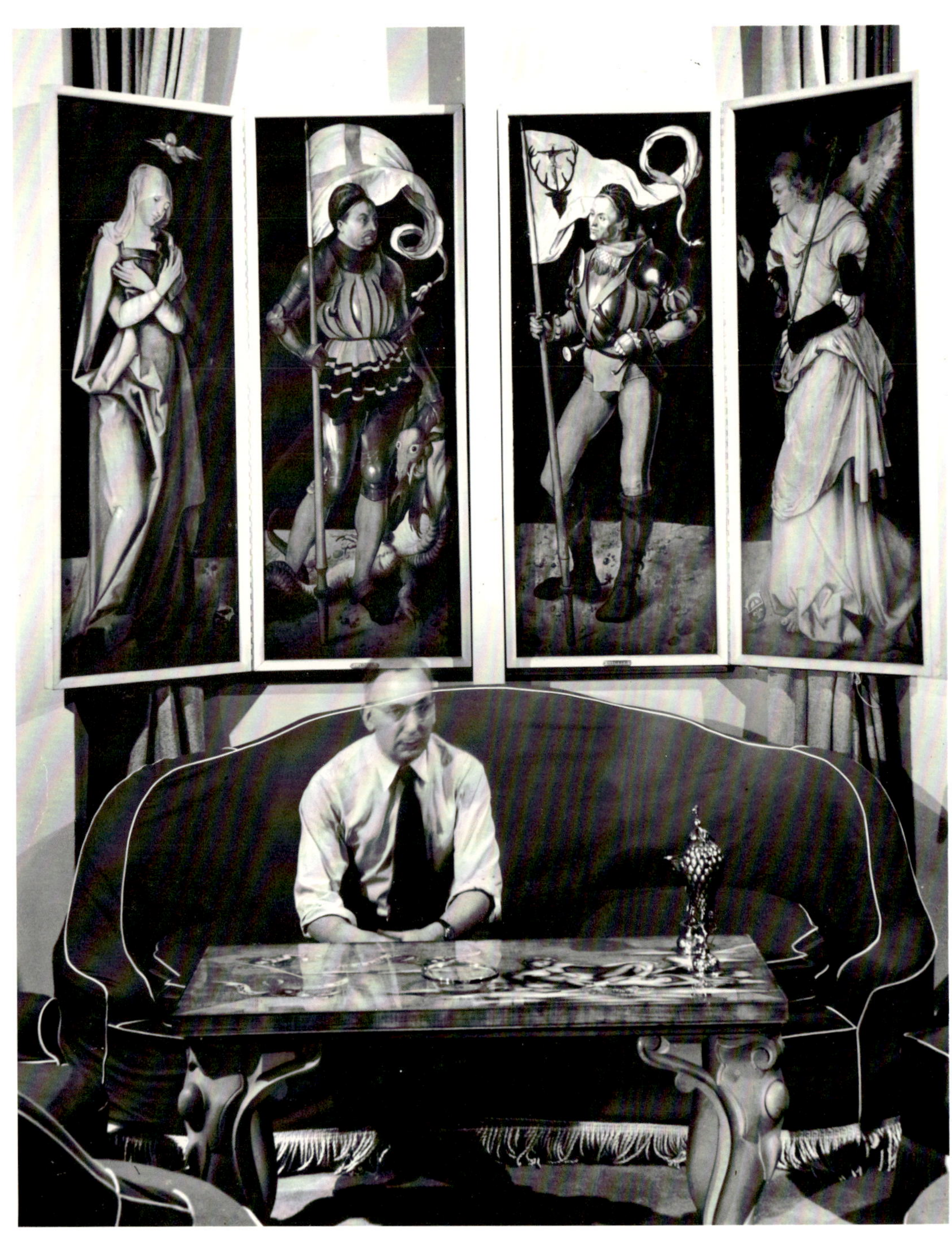

ANDRE KERTESZ
New York, New York
Self-Portrait, 1948

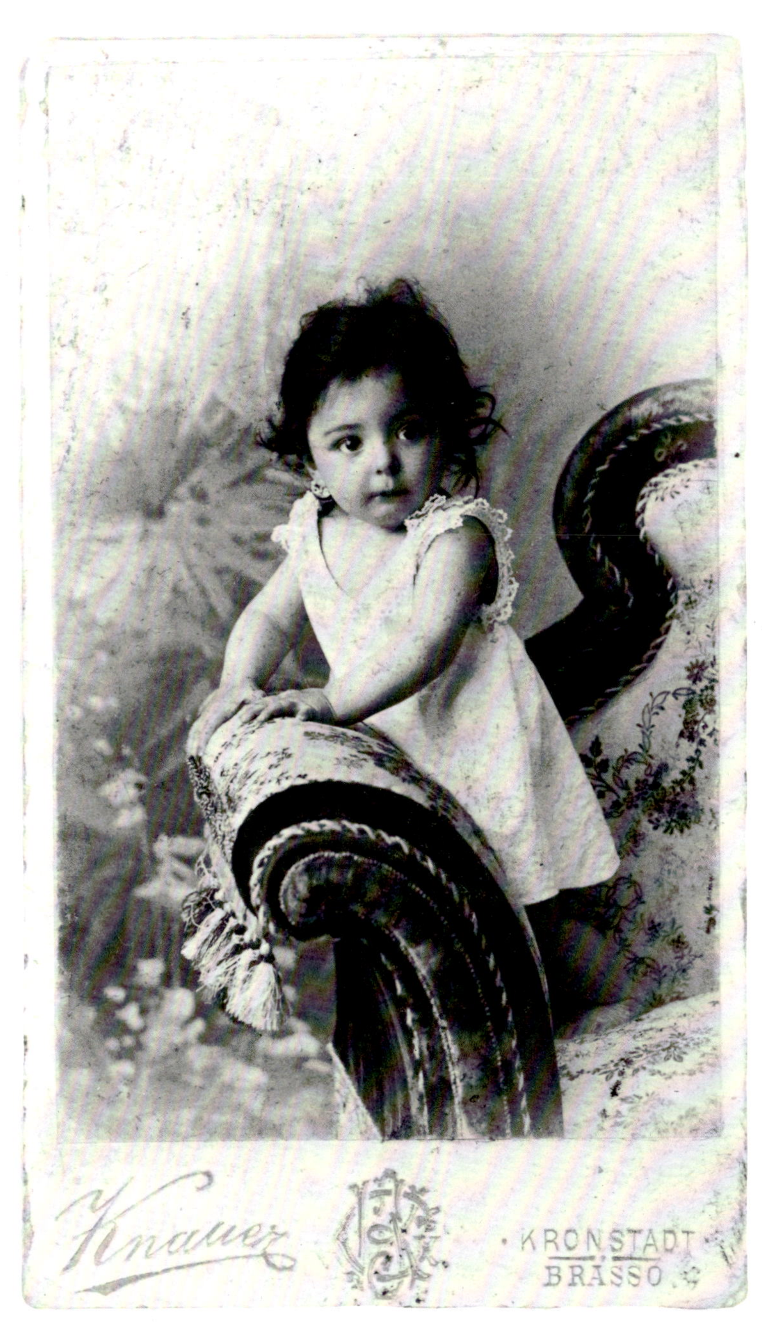

BRASSAI
Paris, France
Brassai a l'age d'un an 1900

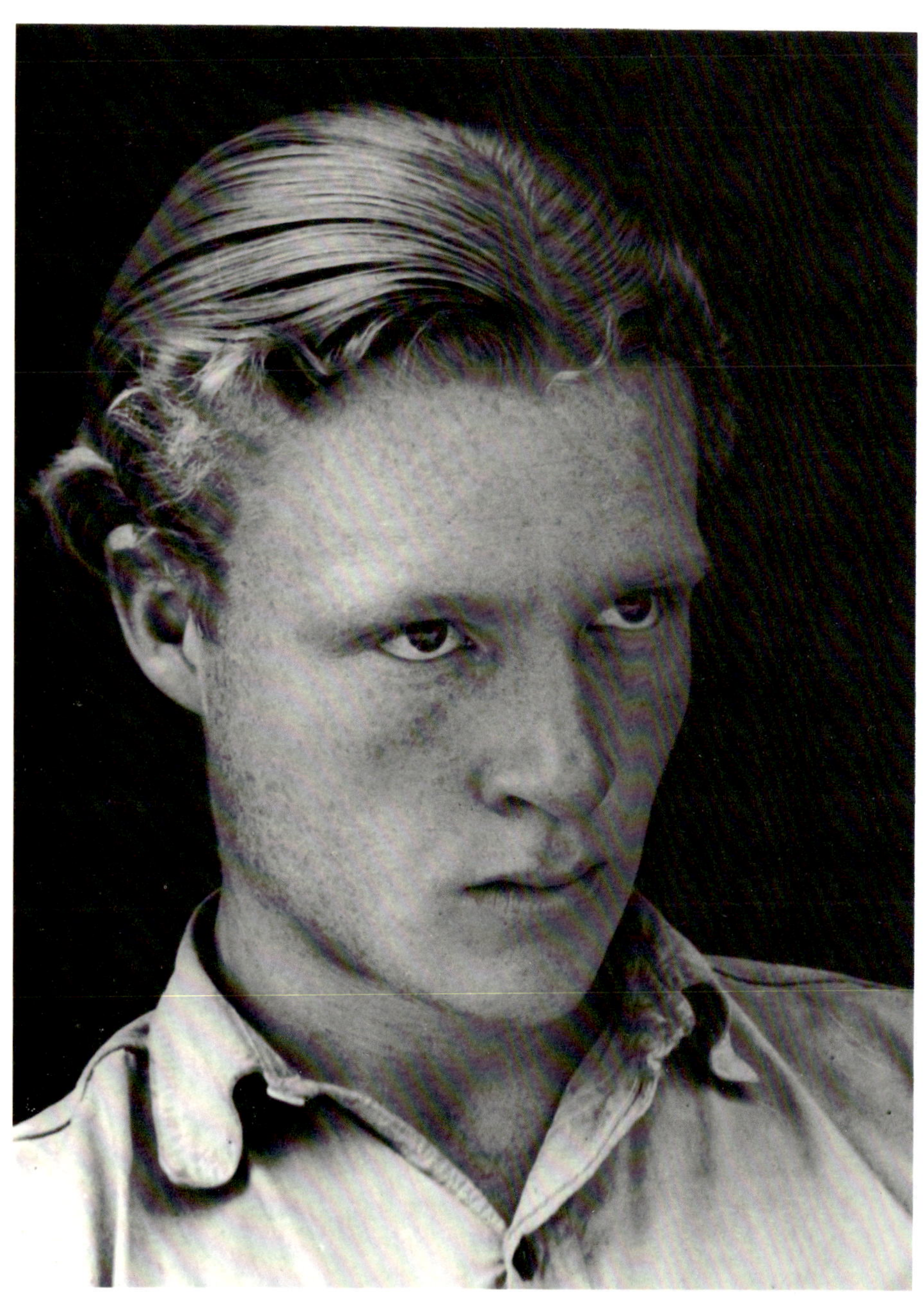

BRETT WESTON
Carmel Valley, California
Self-Portrait, 1927

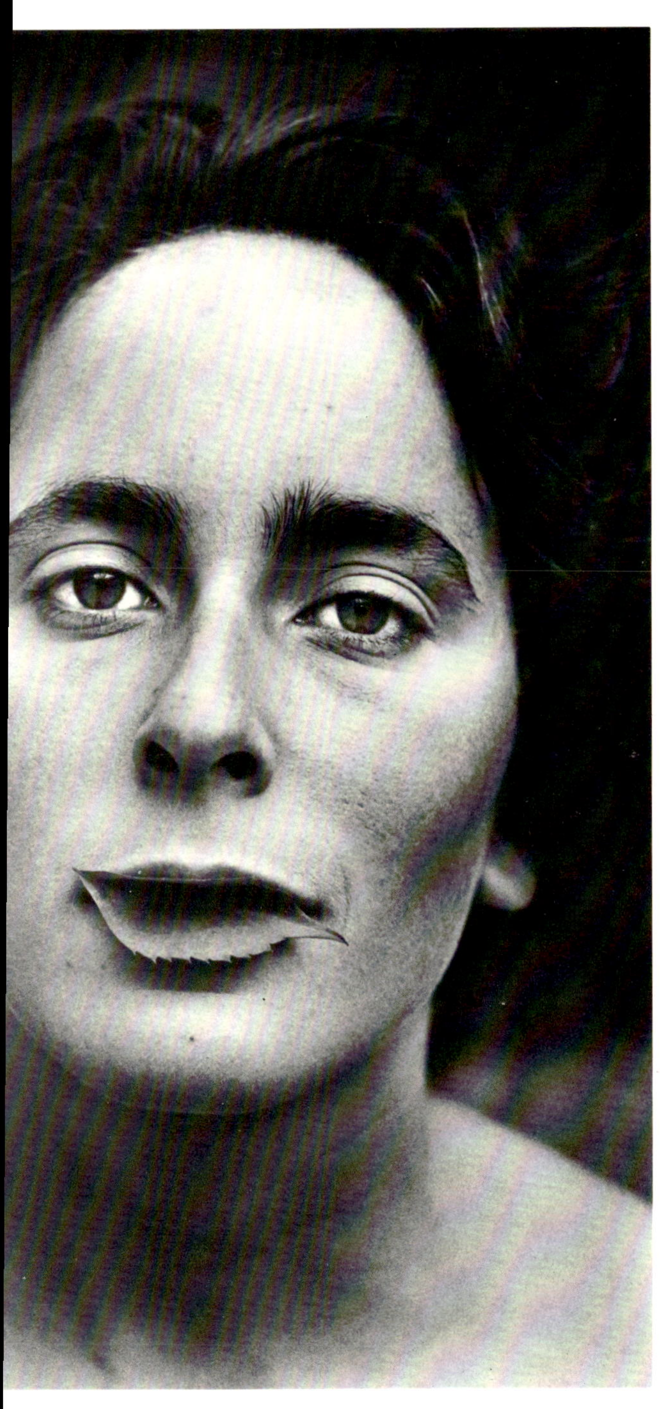

SARAH TAMOR
Santa Monica, California
Untitled, 1976

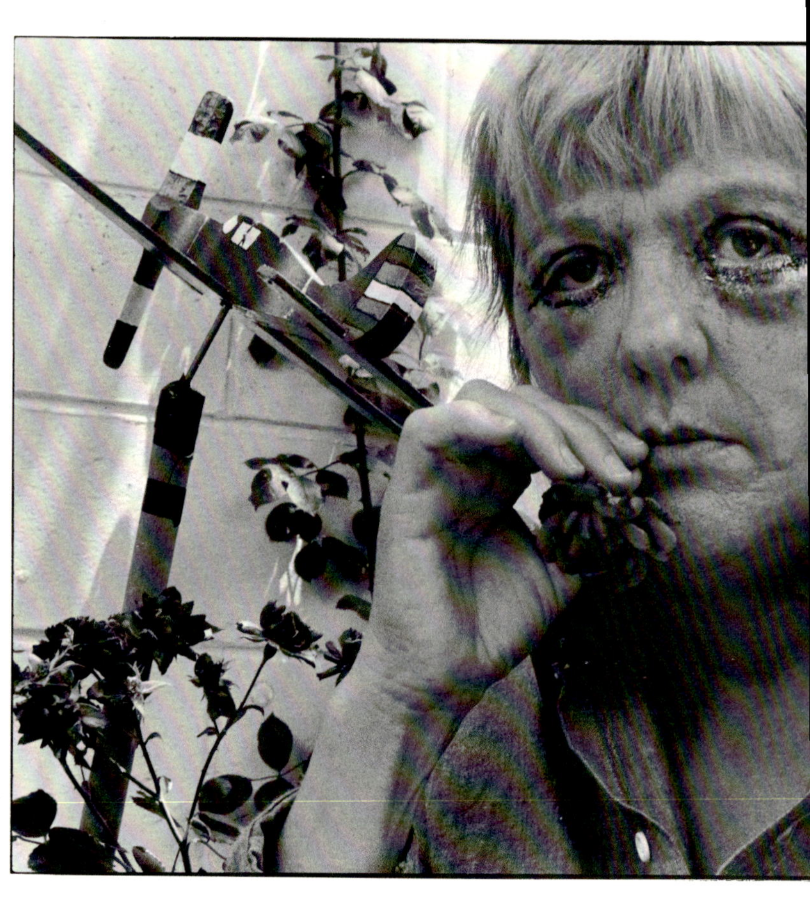

ANNE NOGGLE
Albuquerque, New Mexico
From the Series "Face Lift" #3, 1975

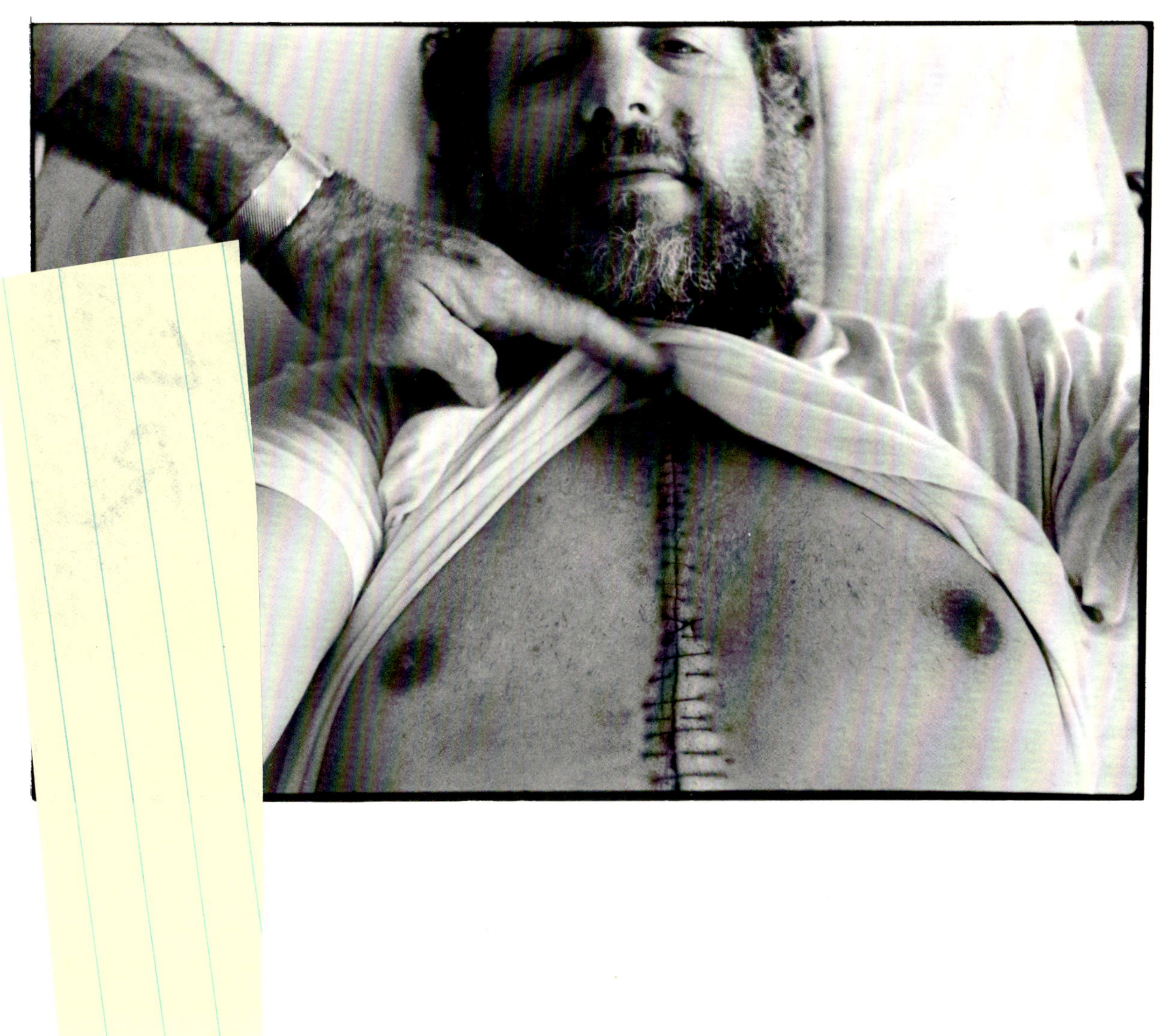

NOEL K. RUBALOFF
Los Angeles, California
Self-Portrait, 1977

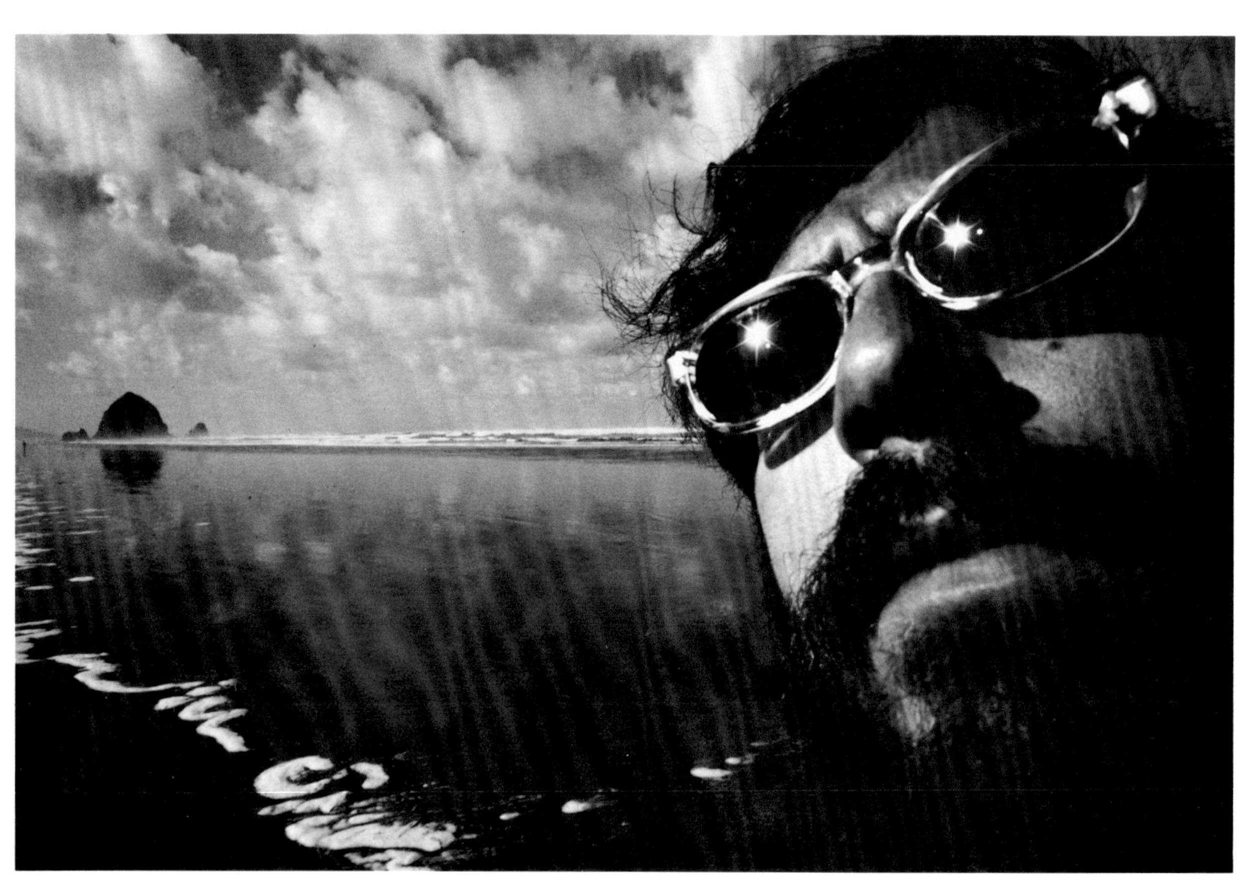

MARK KRASTOF
Chicago, Illinois
Seal Rock, 1971

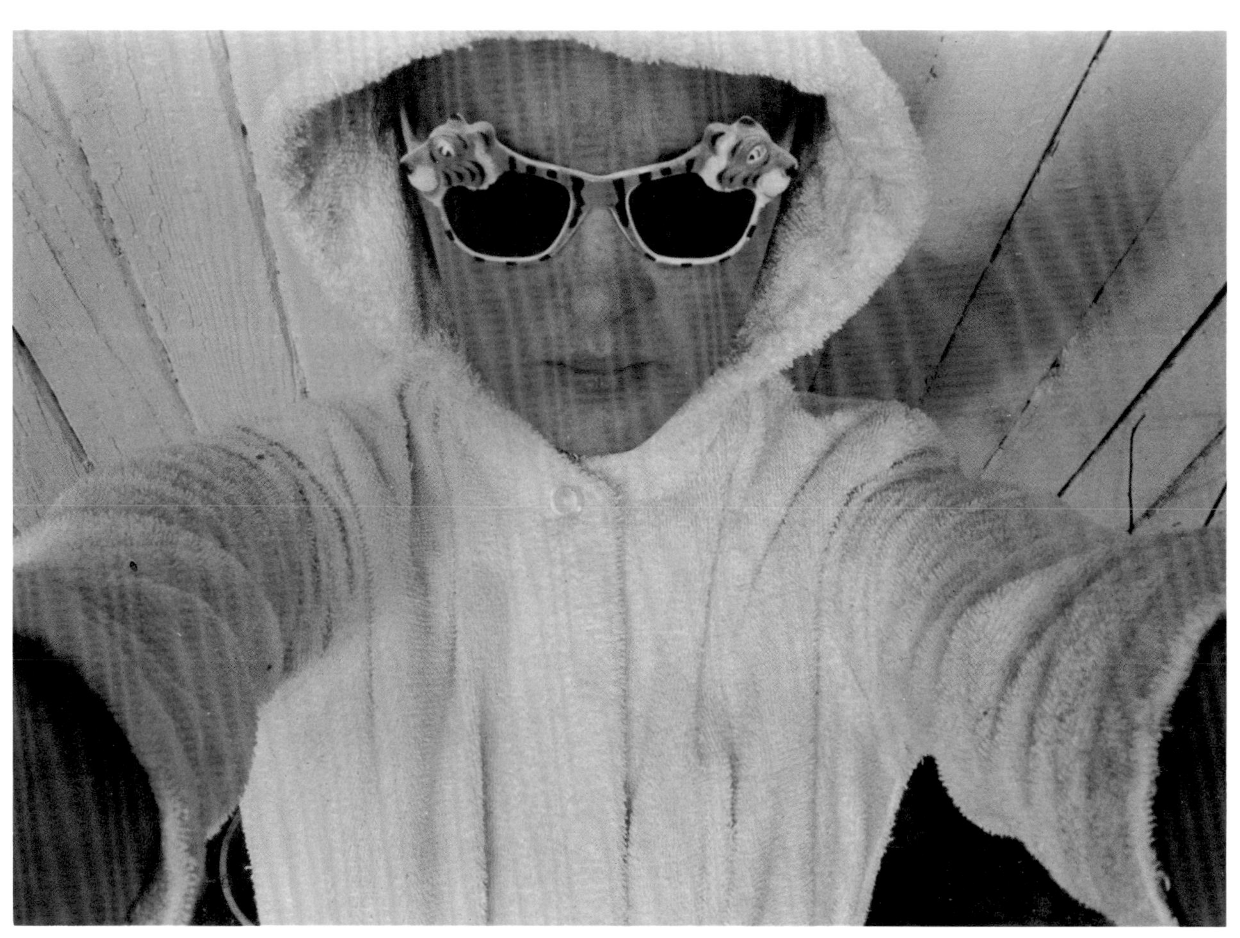

LINDA TROELLER

Pomona, New Jersey

Self-Portrait, Snowbird, 1977

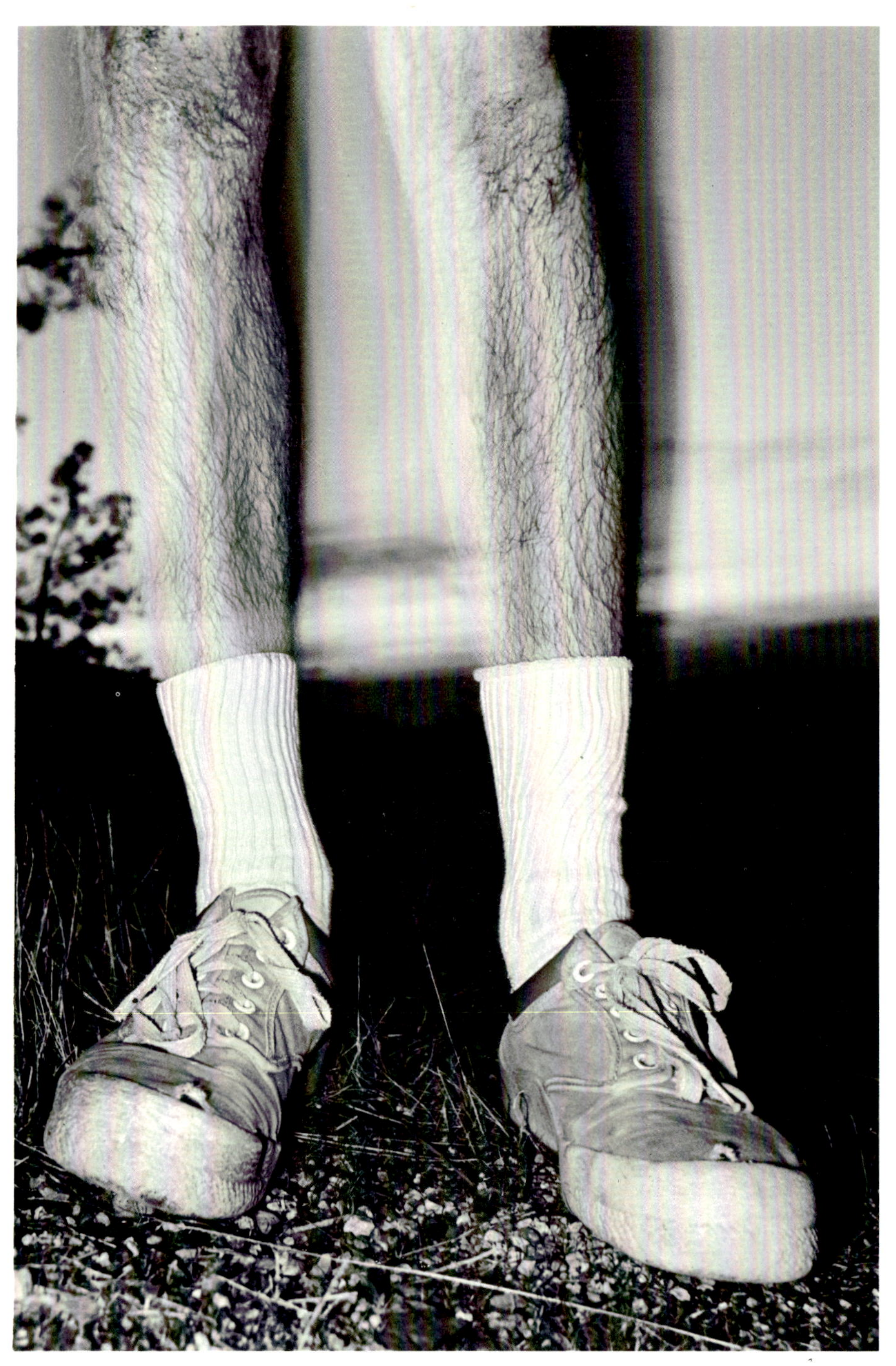

ROBERT DAWSON
Santa Cruz, California
No title, 1978

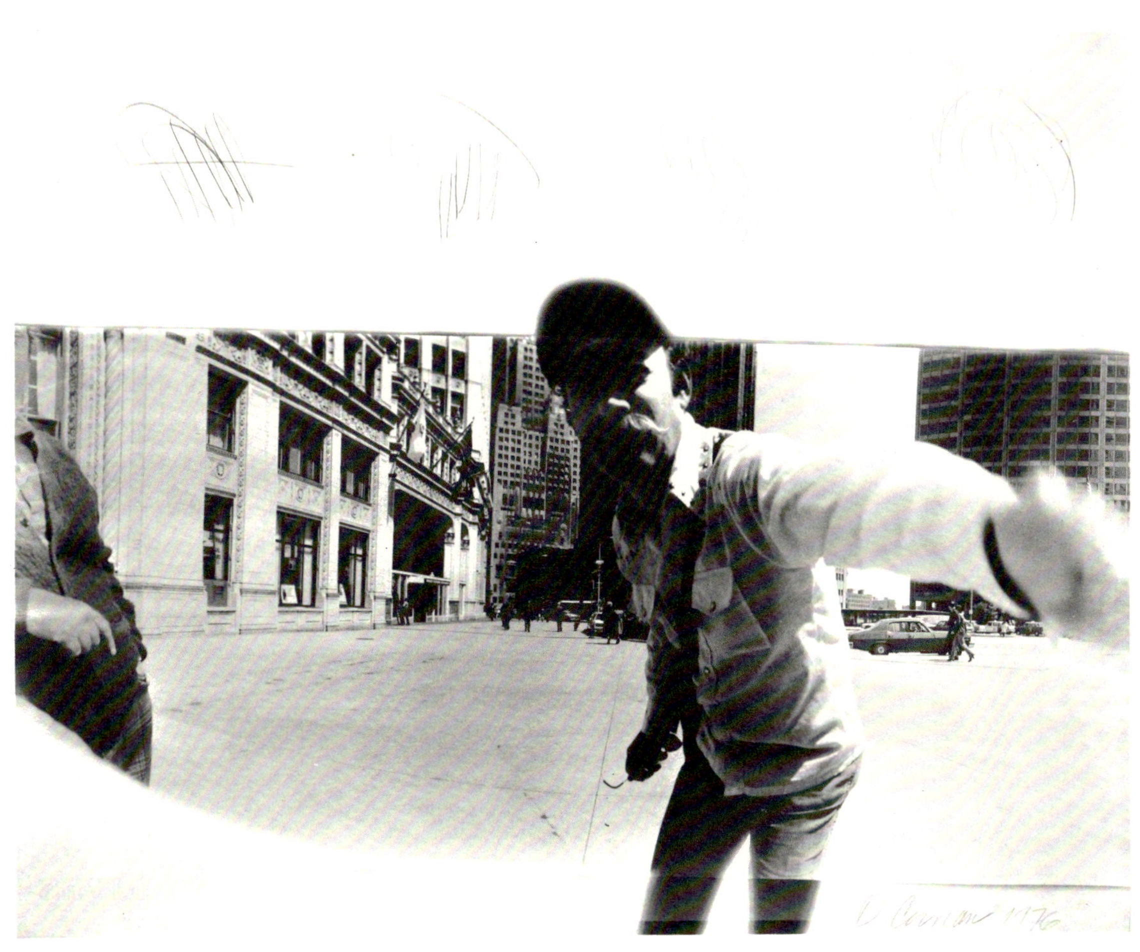

DARRYL J. CURRAN
Los Angeles, California
Lateralenigmaticalness, 1976

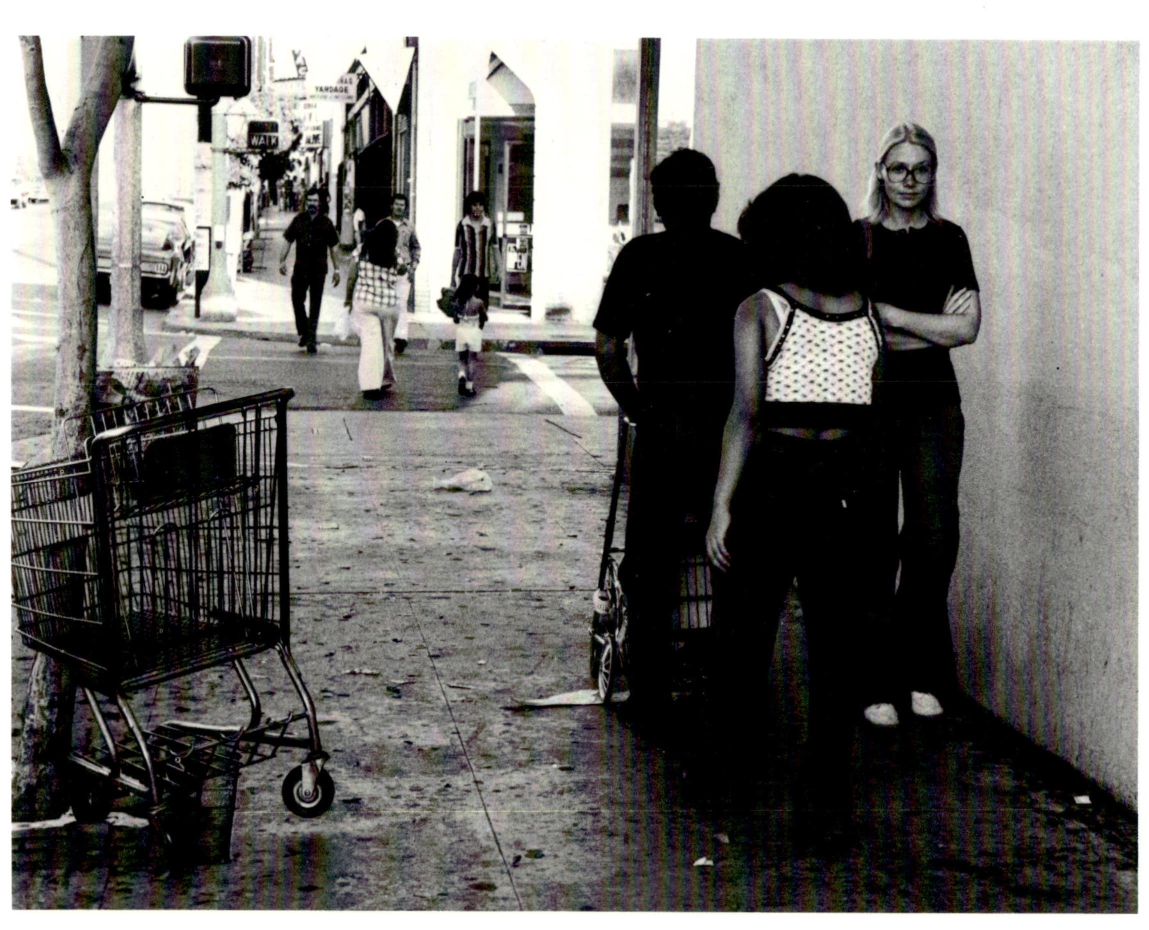

E. A. SEDILLOS
Los Angeles, California
Brooklyn Avenue, 1978

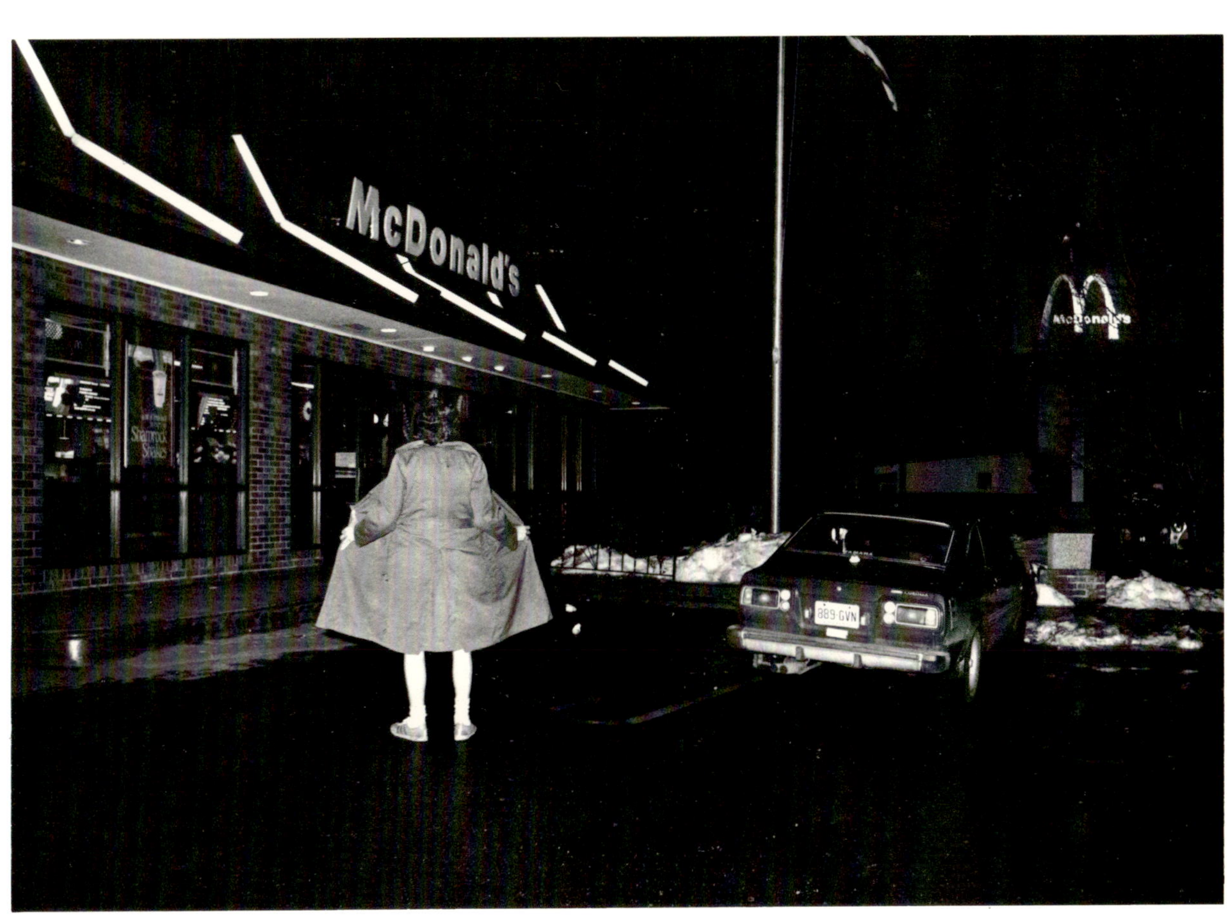

JEFFREY A. NEWMAN
Oakhurst, New Jersey
Flash Photography #4, 1977

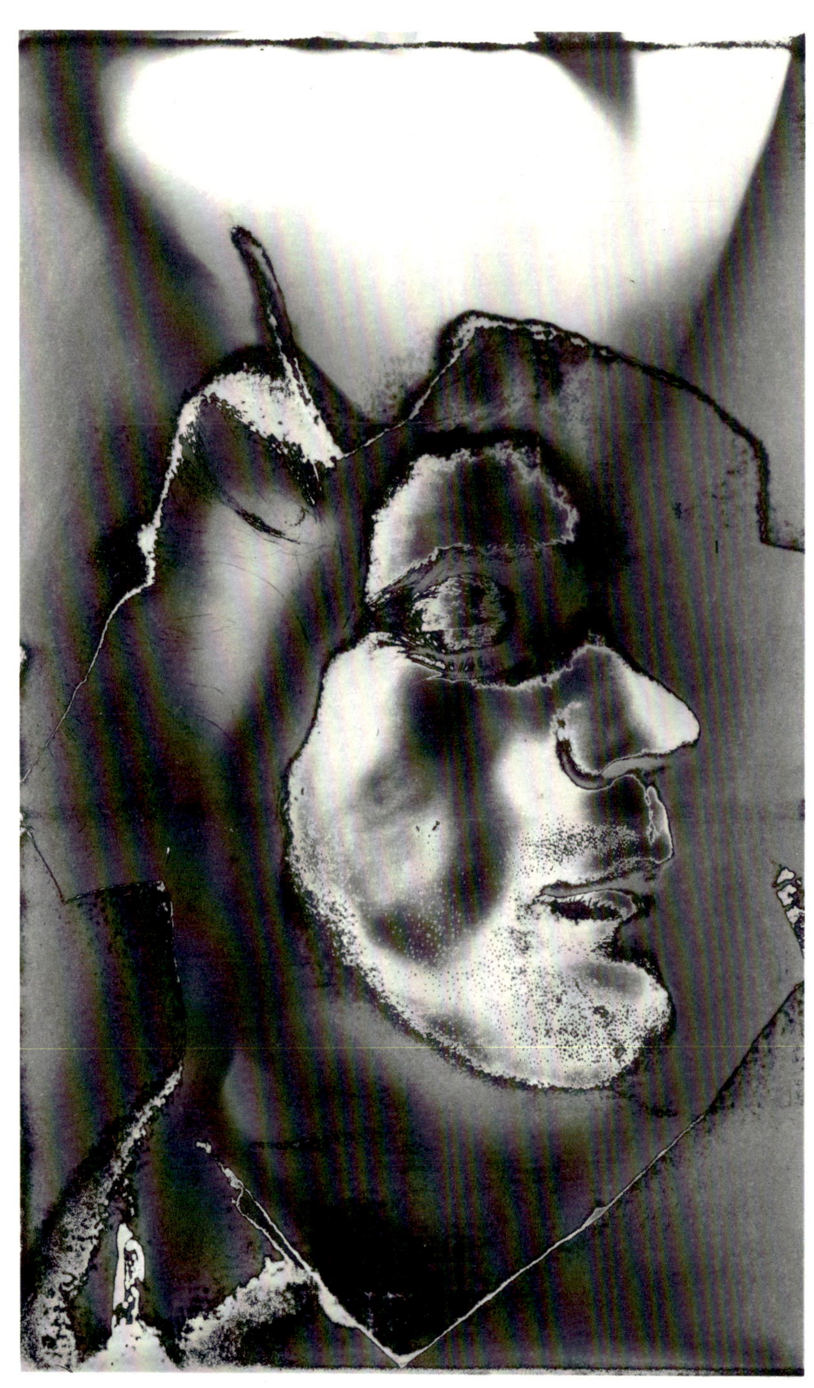

PETER HUNT THOMPSON
Chicago, Illinois
Self-Portrayal, 1977

Self-Portrayal

Peter Hunt Thompson

Self-portrayals are a kind of confession. The fascination with self-portrayal resides primarily in the viewer's appreciation of a distinctive attitude on the part of the maker: that of simply allowing others to be included in an intimacy. Unlike autobiography, visual self-portrayals are often appreciated by an audience more interested in the work as artifact than in the person or qualities portrayed. There tends to be, therefore, a leniency of judgement exercised by the viewer. The self-portrayals of most artists do not equal their best work, but the viewer is recompensed by pleasure in simply being allowed to see another person see themselves.

By definition, that self-seeing is an act which no one else can do. The act of self-portrayal is one in which every maker goes from the rank of amateur to that of professional because it is an act in which a subject treats itself as an object of its own knowledge.

The history of the genre, however, suggests that it is wise to treat that knowledge as a species of fiction. It is impossible to completely mirror a life, because that mirroring process is a part of the life itself. The history of the representation of self-consciousness shows that artists and autobiographers who believe that they can avoid their own intimate involvement in self-understanding end the endeavor in frustration. Those who think, like Rousseau, that they have succeeded, are now appreciated precisely because of the discrepancy, in the work itself, between the avowal of self-understanding and the evidence of its lack.

I think it was Sartre who, when asked for a definition of progress, replied that it was "that long road which led to Me", that is, to the sense of one's self as a unique being and of worth as such. This sense of self-consciousness and individuality is historically a recent development, and a brief look at that development can help establish the context for a consideration of visual self-portrayal.

Between the 15th and 17th Centuries the feudal order rapidly declined in favor of increasing democratization. The economic order began to change from institutionalized scarcity to sufficiency; groups of people increased from comparatively small gatherings in churches, craft guilds and universities to large armies and large cities. Upward social mobility rapidly increased and the sense of privacy — a basic requirement for introspection — was given impetus by radical Puritanism and supported by such secondary activities as the increased availability of mirrors to the common person, allowing the development of a personal self-image. The autobiography as a spiritual undertaking and as a literary form was fully developed during this period. Cross-class verbal communication progressed from orders given hierarchically to the Calvinist idea of a plain-speaking whose only justification was the sincerity of the speaker.

The most crucial event in the development of self-consciousness was the invention of sincerity. Sincerity is simply the marriage of what one professes publicly with what one feels privately. Or put another way, in spite of the fact that we are social beings with livings to make, at the base of the idea of sincerity is the belief that one has a self which is separate from one's social role, to which one owes primary allegiance.

Such an understanding of selfhood seems obvious, and it is surprising to learn that historians are generally agreed that sincerity as a moral ideal came into being in the 15th Century. Concurrent with the emergence of sincerity was the invention of the self-portrait — the self-portrayal in a non-religious context of an individual as an individual. The term self-portrayal refers to a representation of a particular body of information: one's concepts of self and one's interpretive relationships to those conceptions. The term also makes explicit that self-consciousness is basic to the organizing principle of the work, that it is the interplay between time and a subjective consciousness of that time. The act of self-portrayal is, therefore, a projection of a being, in relation to its own identity, upon the unifying screen of a formal work or action. Because self-portrayal takes this consciousness of self as its theme and organizing principle, it is one of the most vital formulations and formalizations of the modern Western mind.

Both visual and verbal self-portrayals are distinctly Western cultural forms. There are, to be sure, verbal recountings in other cultures of personal histories, but those histories are generally truncated pieces written for such pragmatic social goals as political asylum or judicial redress. The authors never quite come to see the totality of their lives as worthy of the telling and fleshed with the integration of their public and private selves.

Like the autobiographies of poets and novelists, the self-portrayals of artists have always been dominated by the representation of themselves as artists. The history of visual self-portrayal is a casebook of the ways in which artists have seen themselves as both artists and as role-players within society. Between the 15th and 17th Centuries, Western artists gradually became aware of their activities as not only the exercise of an honorable craft but as an intellectual pursuit as well. The self-portraits of the time mirror that double awareness in their tendency to show the artist either at work or as a contemplative being, at home with either emblems belonging to intellect or to those of the aristocratic milieu to which artists were becoming accustomed.

The idea of the villain — a person who, like Shakespeare's Iago, lied and manipulated to achieve a social end — arose in the popular imagination of the 16th Century as an emblematic response to the lack of professions which would allow a person to achieve a place in society commensurate with ability. As an extension of that idea, role-playing and disguise became an increasingly common artistic artifice in the 16th and 17th Centuries. Rembrandt is an example of an artist whose love of personal artifice coincided with his love for the artistic technical feats which were demanded of him by exotic costumes.

Some artists reflected the tension between artifice and sincerity in their acceptance of artistic patronage and in their editorializing against aristocracy within commissioned works. Velasquez and Goya are examples of artists who used art both as a means of upward social mobility and, in their portraits and self-portraits with royalty, as a recording medium for their ethical and political concerns.

When artists became aware of their activity as something more than craft, the intellectual burden produced an awareness of the mission of being an artist. The tradition of the artist as spiritual advisor, and as sufferer because of that vision, developed from the combination of the religious tradition of art and the artist's need to witness to the vague spiritual values inherent in the process of artistic creation. Dürer portrayed himself as Christ, Michelangelo portrayed himself as a torn skin, Caravaggio as the decapitated Holofernes — the examples are numerous.

By the 19th Century, artists' social mobility diminished because of decreasing upper-class patronage coupled with reduced understanding and appreciation by the general populace of their work. By mid-century, photography, newly invented, carried the burden of the artistic search for the depiction of reality, leaving artists the freedom to begin exploring the nature of their media without the necessity of hooking it into the objective world. At this point, artists — that is, non-photographers — began to lose their audience, and the tradition of the artist as spiritual seer and sufferer became ever more strongly entrenched.

Prior to the development of photography, the introspection of self-portrayal was divorced from the action of responding to events as they arose. With photography came a kind of active introspection, a self-reflection at a moment in which the self finds itself. Inherent to photography is the balance between subjective awareness and the concrete evidence of being in the world. As a diary of perceptions, actions and environments, photographic self-portrayal is a more or less objective record which requires later subjective interpretation.

Today, the use of relatively non-self-expressive modes of representation, such as the snapshot, is an outgrowth of the search for authenticity. A significant number of artists from other media, such as John Baldessari, Douglas Heubler and William Wegman, have taken up the medium of photography because the myth surrounding its use proclaims it anonymous and objective. It is worth noting that photography is now also being chosen for its use in artifice, for the exploration of roles which are marked by obvious artificiality and perhaps historical nostalgia, by artists such as Eleanor Antin, Judith Golden, Lynda Benglis and Lucas Samaras.

The 20th Century artist's relationship to technology has had a marked effect on the continuation of the tradition of artist as sufferer. New technologies allow an artist to alter or to begin again without annulling what formerly might have been the fruit of a year's labor. At that point, the artist begins to question the whereabouts of the art work — and finally comes to see that the controller of that process, and the one crucial factor in it, is the artist. From there it is an easy step to the position that the art resides within the artist, that the artist is, finally, the work of art. When that concept is married to the tradition of the artist as both sufferer and role-player, one gets, to take but two examples, Chris Burden lying on a highway or nailing himself to the back of a VW, or Vito Acconce telling personally compromising information to strangers who approach him on a New York dock at night. The tradition reaches finality in Rudolph Schwartzkogler who, in a variation on Rauschenberg's action to a de Kooning drawing, "erased" himself as an artistic artifact by dying of self-amputation.

The self-portrayal of the artist as sufferer seems to have run out of nourishing things to say. There is the feeling, materially aided by the women's movement, that artists and their activities might somehow be a little more humble in their aims — even that both might be models for a new kind of health. That health is connected with sheer awareness of subtle reaction to the everyday, of self-transformation, of an affirmation of both play and of social interaction — even to an affirmation of what Heidegger saw as the basic characteristic of human beings: care. We can perhaps look forward to a fuller and presently unforseen translation of those qualities into the tradition of self-portrayal.

One question to ask now is this: which future men and women, standing before the works and examples of prior artists, will carry forward this tradition in a manner which does not betray them? They are those who, realizing the barrenness of their meal, as William Burroughs says, in the "frozen moment when everyone sees what is on the end of every fork," nevertheless can affirm that meal, saying, with Cage, "Here we are, let us say *Yes* to our presence together in Chaos."

Peter Hunt Thompson is Director of the Generative Systems Program at Columbia College in Chicago. He was Curator of The Friends of Photography between 1971 and 1974 and has taught photography at the University of California, Santa Cruz.

WALLACE WONG
Pacifica, California
Rainbow, 1975

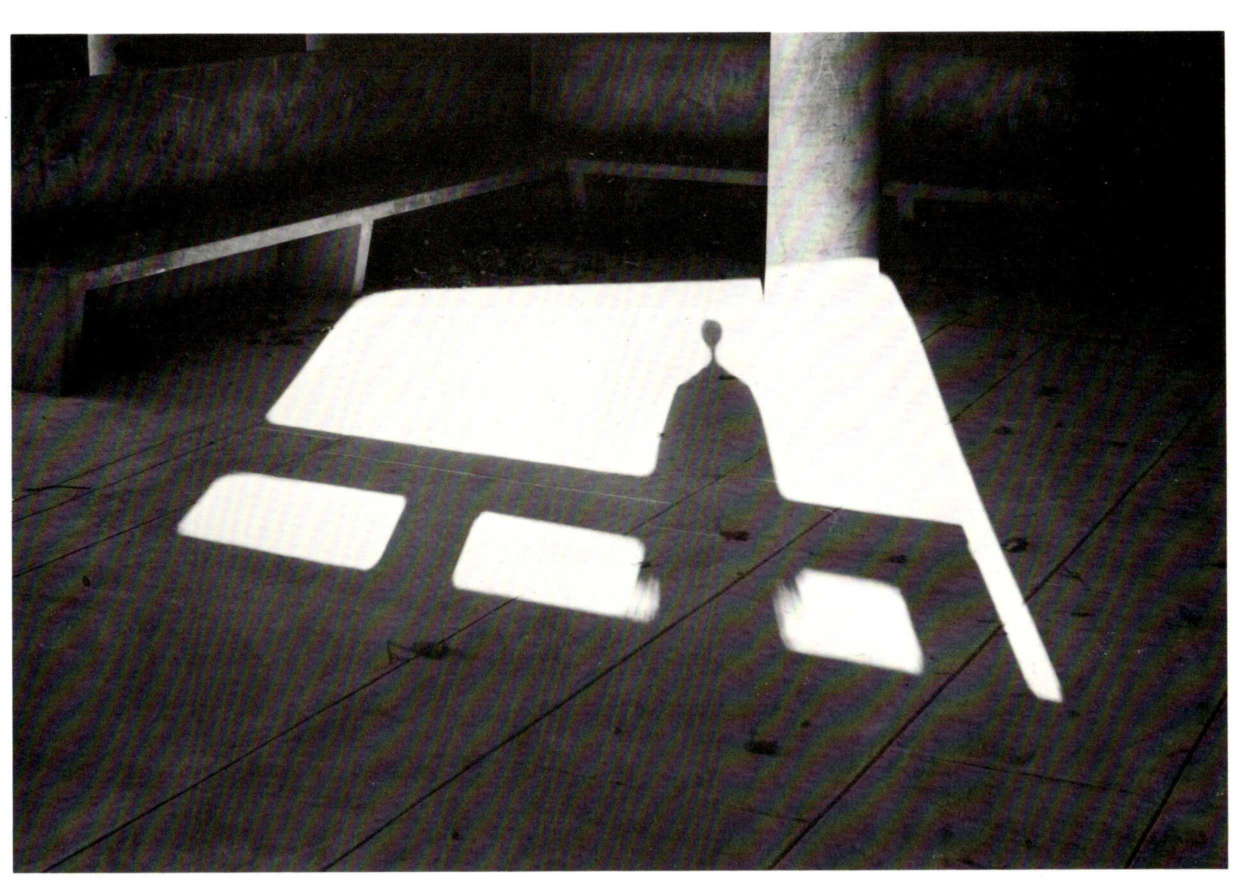

ELAINE FISHER
Cambridge, Massachusetts
Untitled

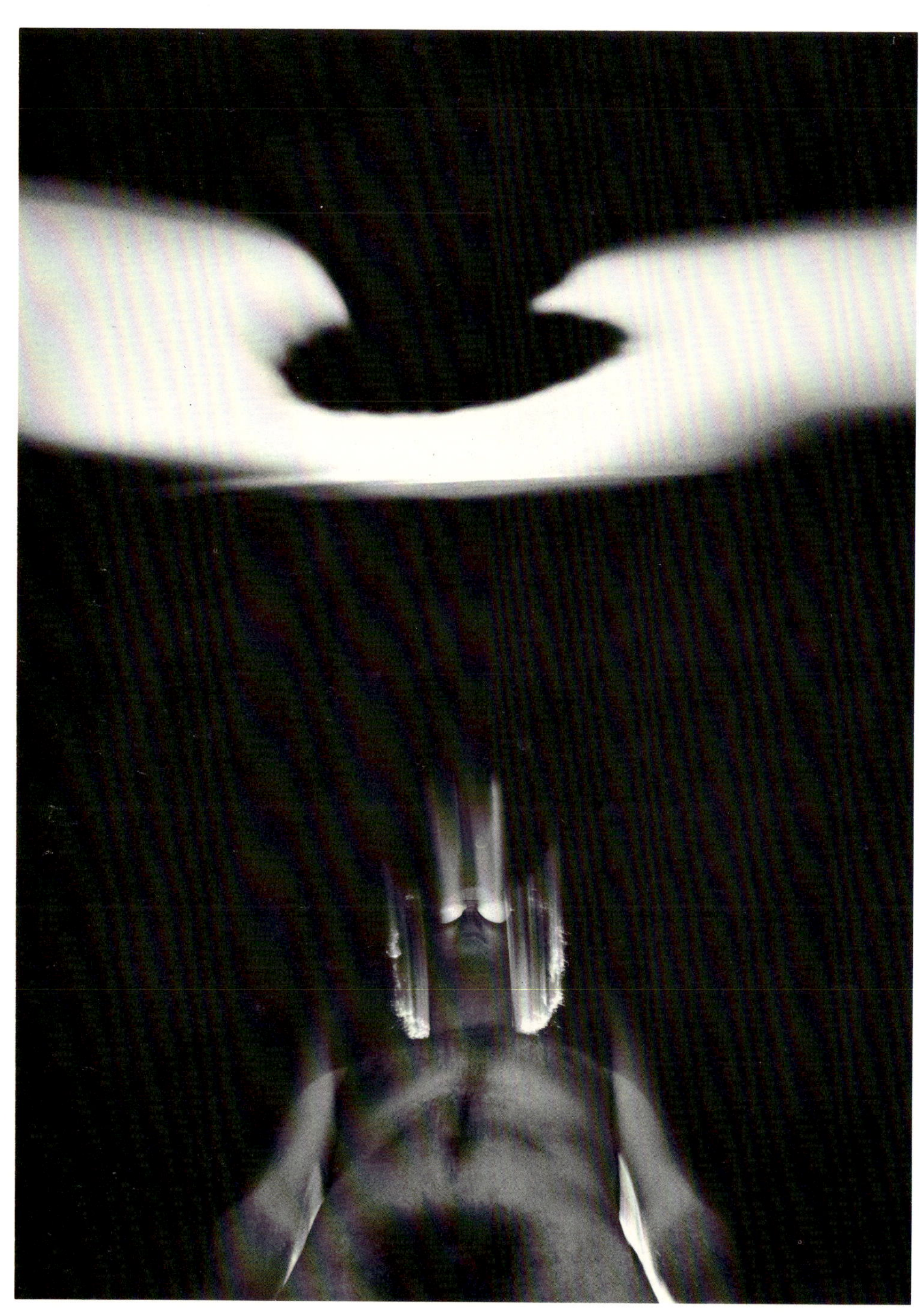

MARK TUTTLE
Columbus, Ohio
Self-Portrait, 1975

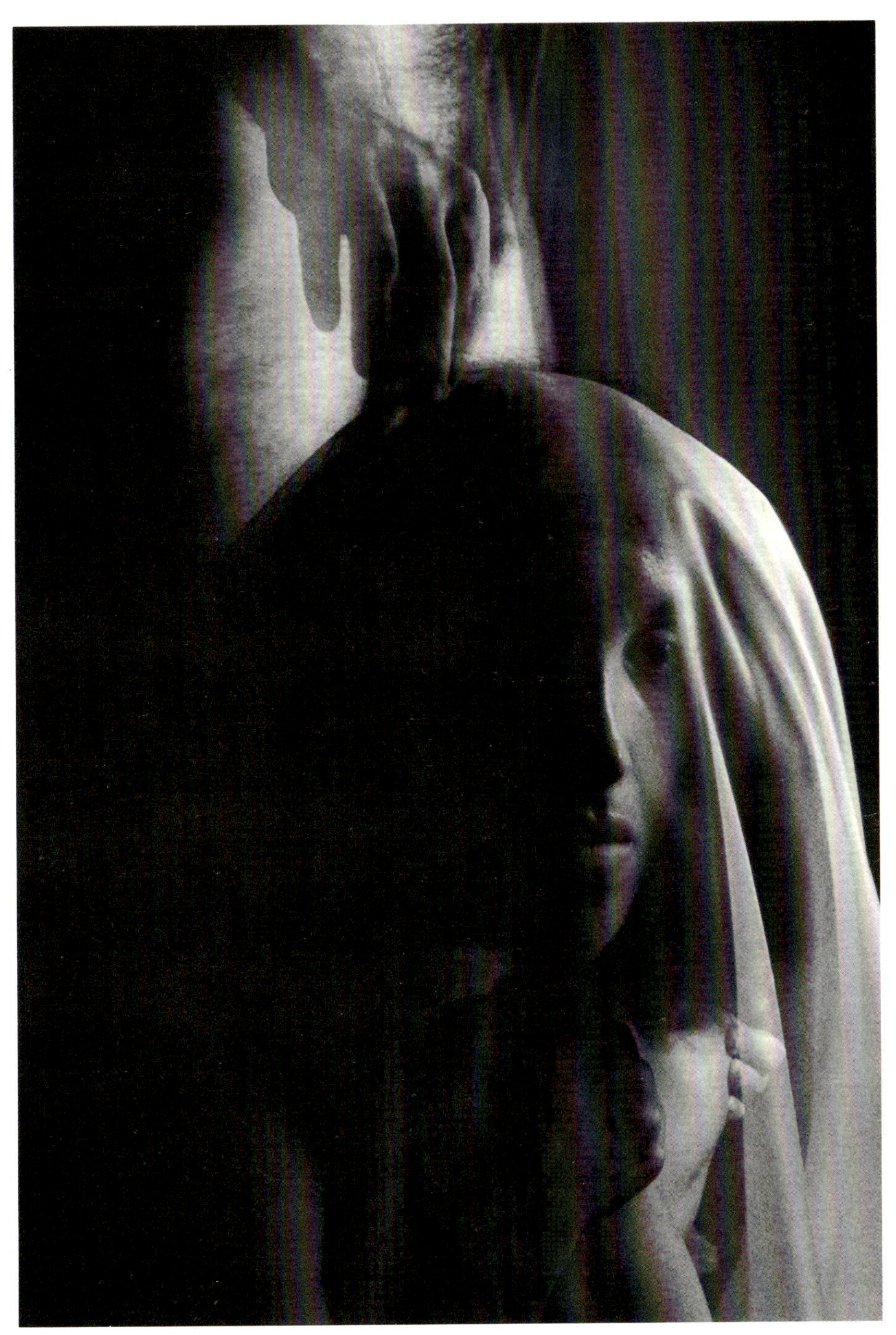

JEFF GATES
Los Angeles, California
Anima #2, 1976

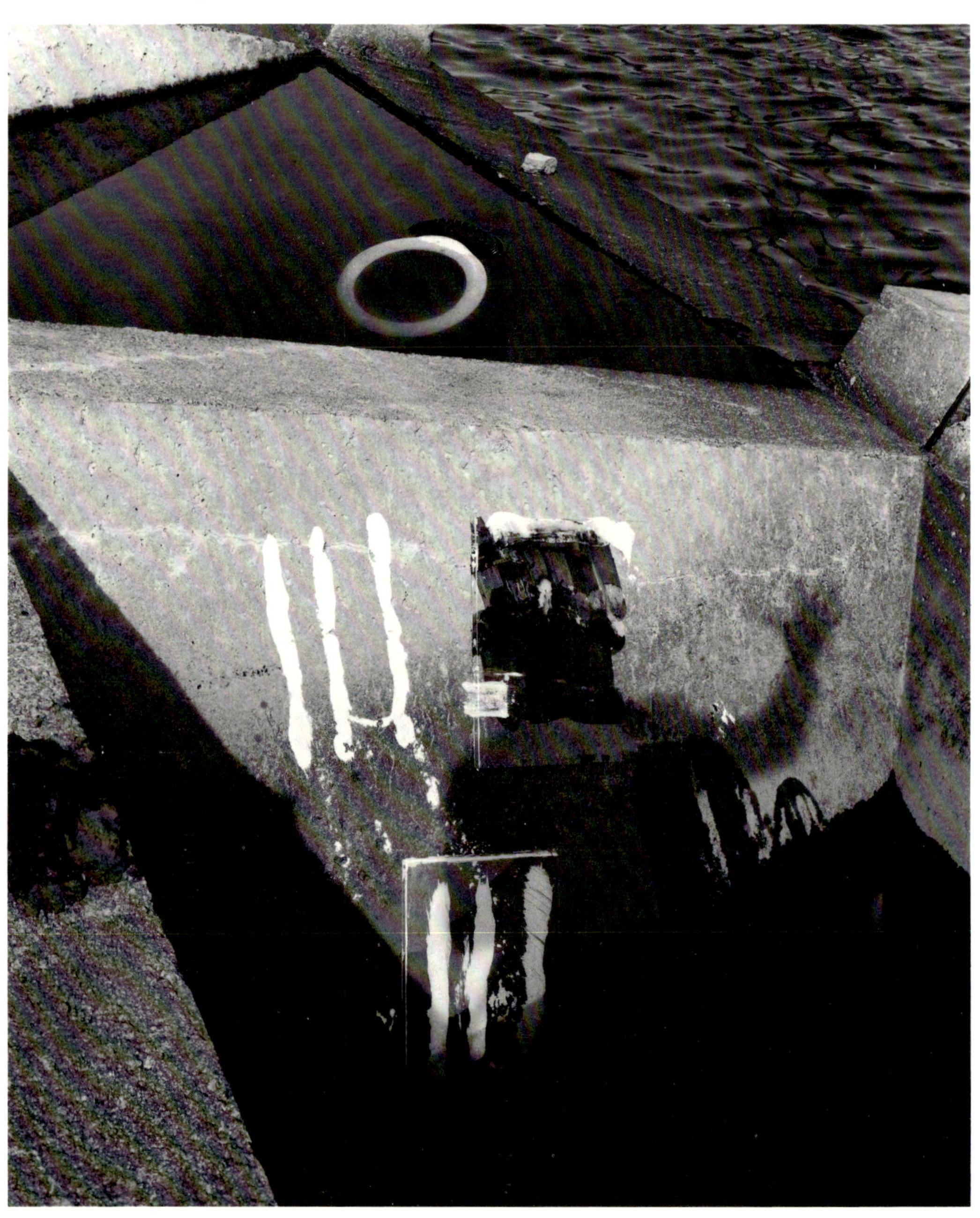

DAVID S. MACLAY
San Francisco, California
Concrete Tubs, 1975-1976

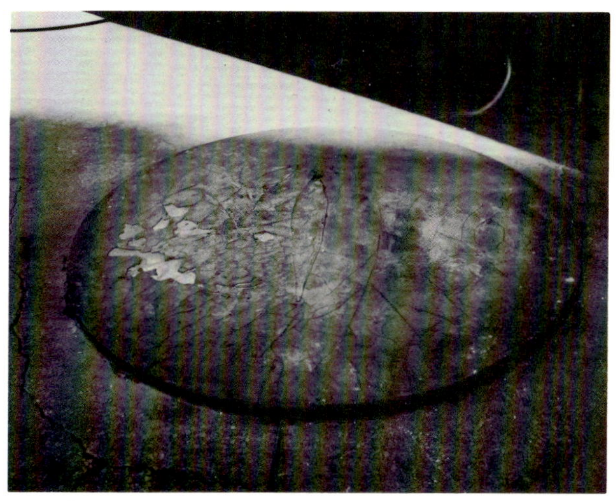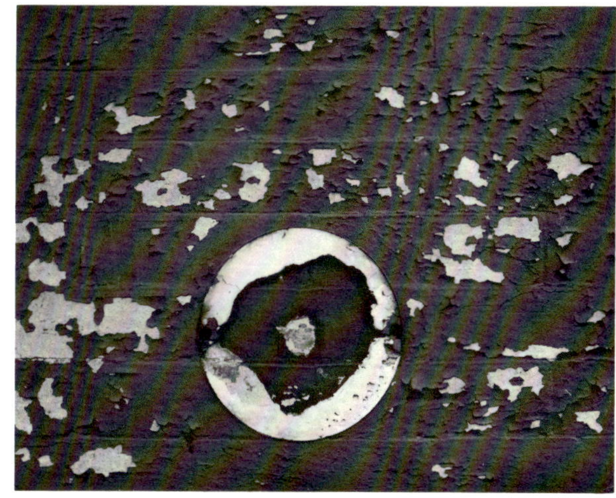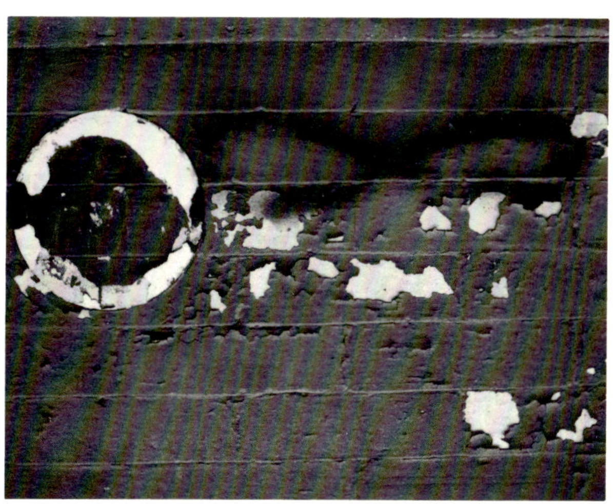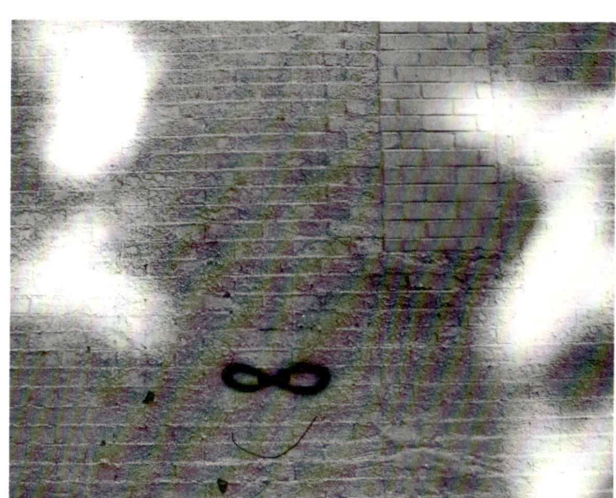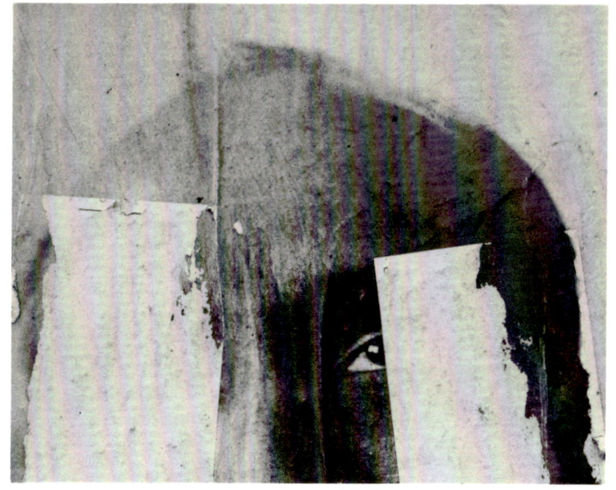

MICHAEL DI BIASE
Brooklyn, New York
Ekagrata, 1977

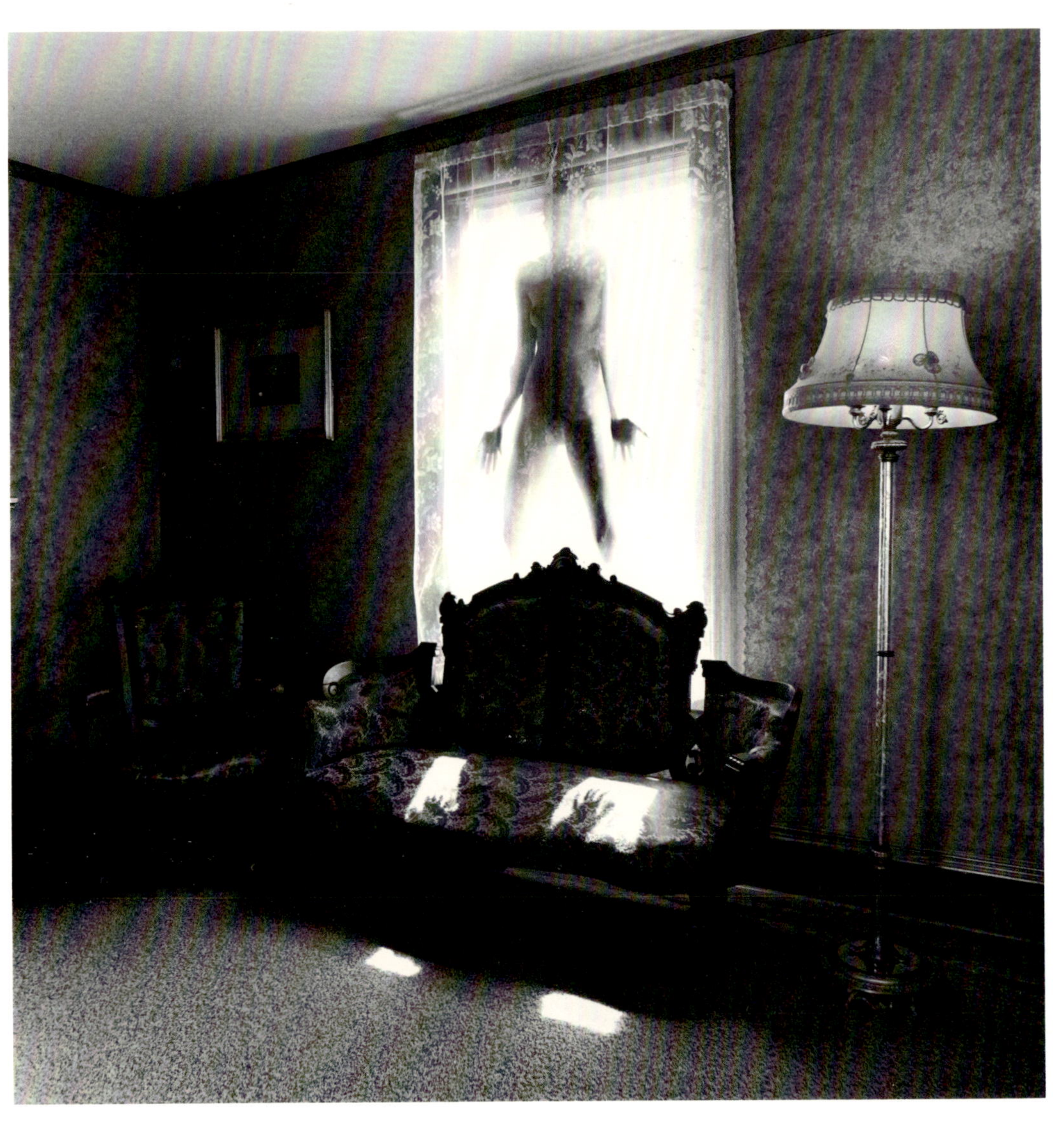

JENNIFER TUCKER
Lemont, Pennsylvania
Victorian Lace Window — Self, Canada, 1977

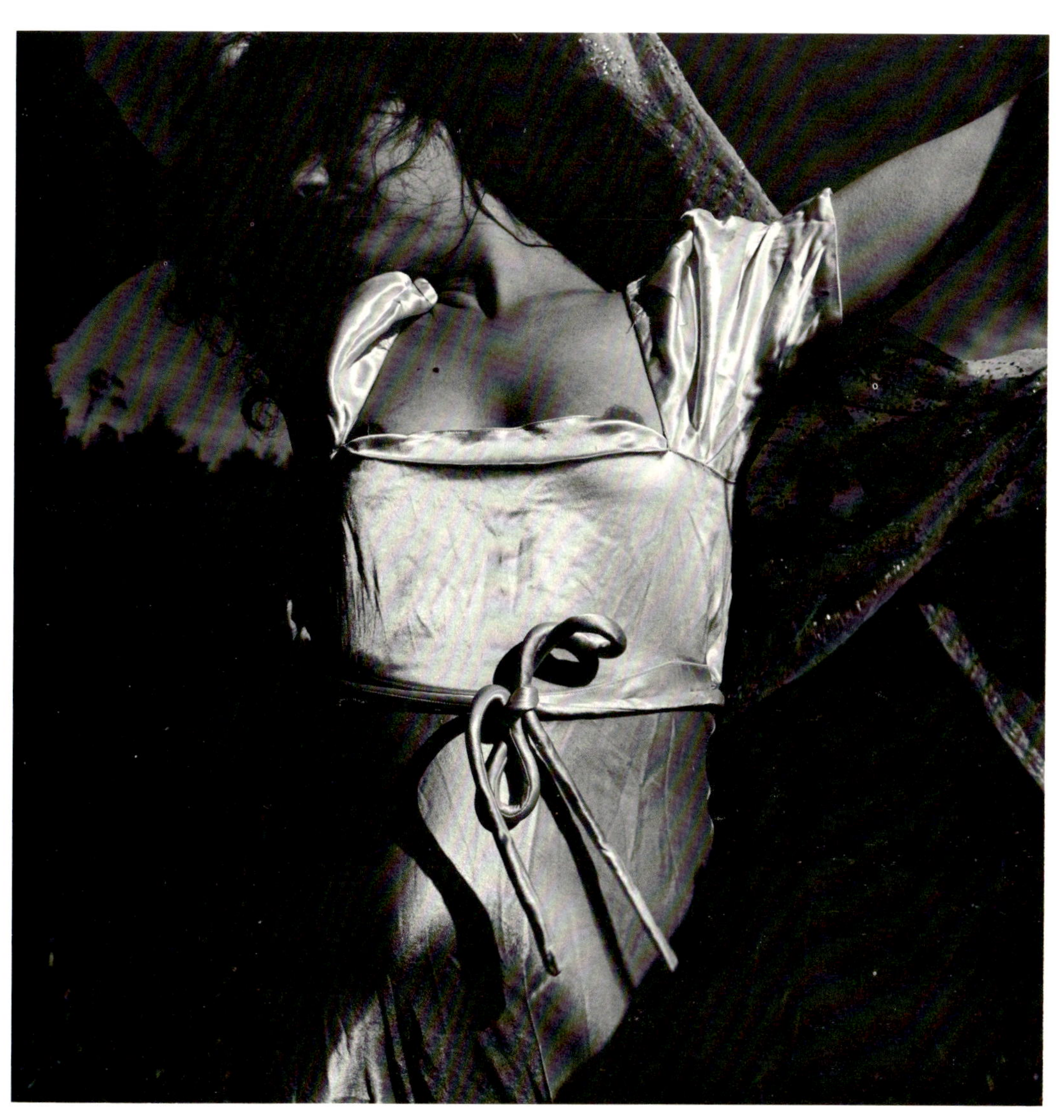

SUSAN FRIEDMAN
Pescadero, California
Untitled, 1971

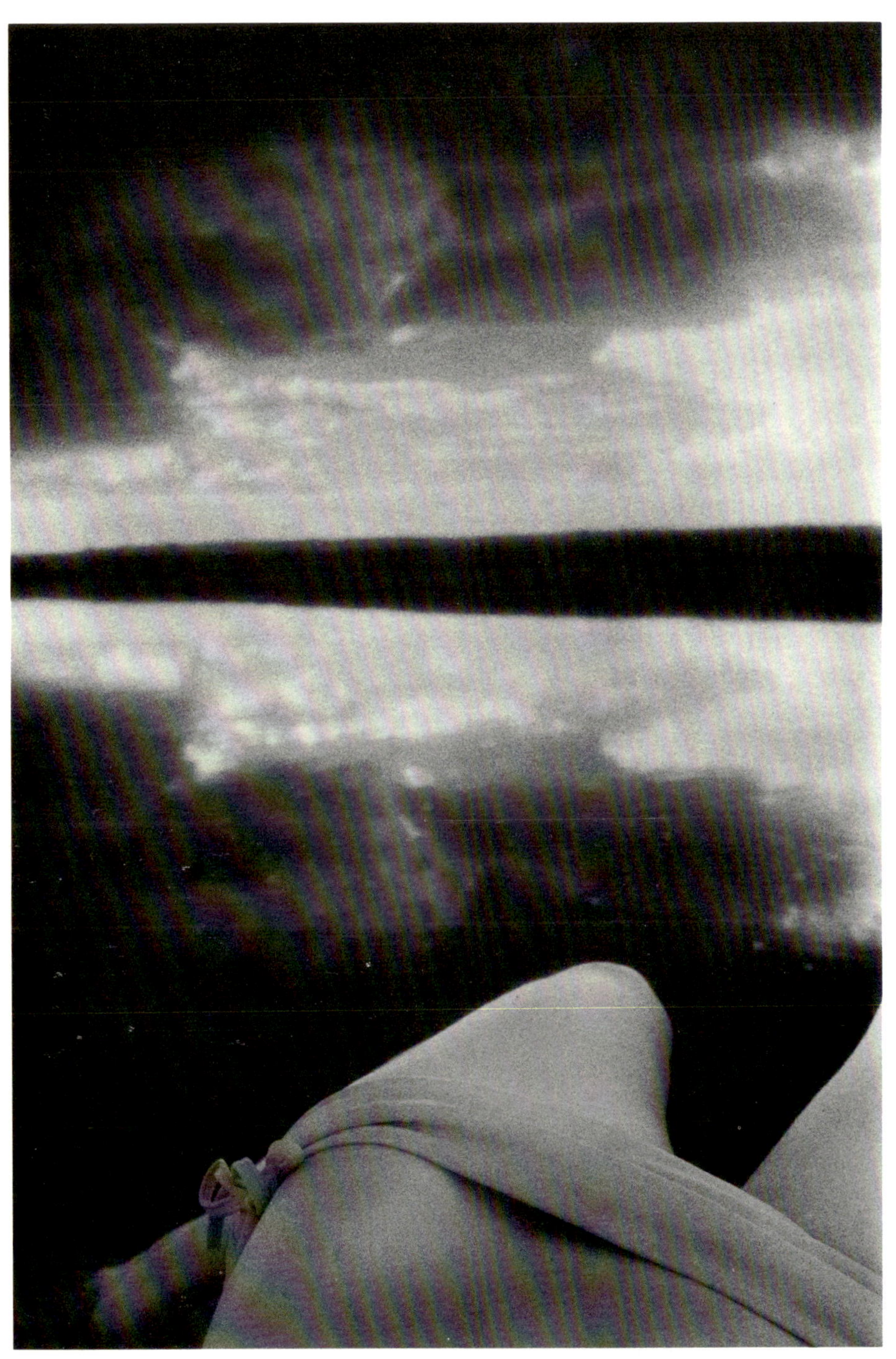

JANE TUCKERMAN FOLEY
Boston, Massachusetts
Untitled, 1976

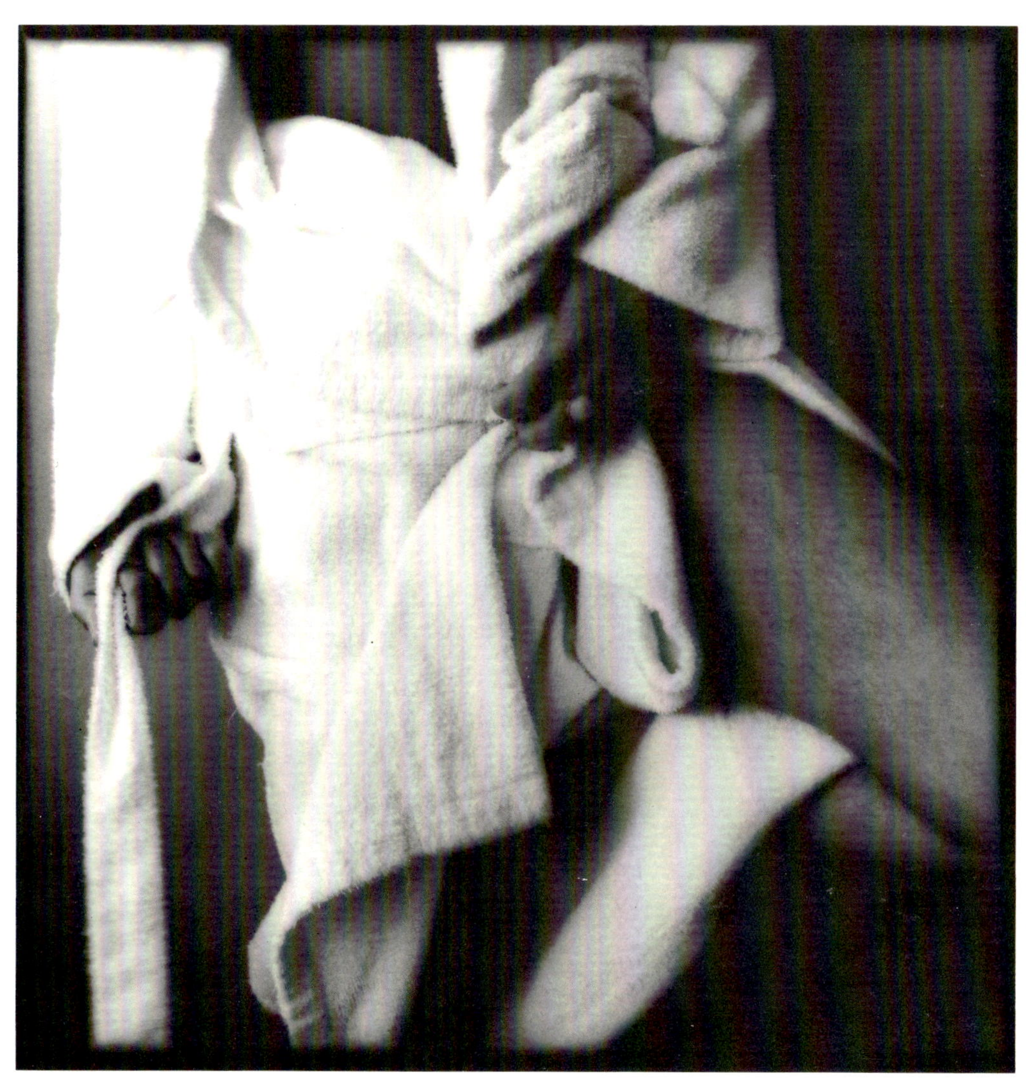

CRAIG MOREY
San Francisco, California
No title, 1977

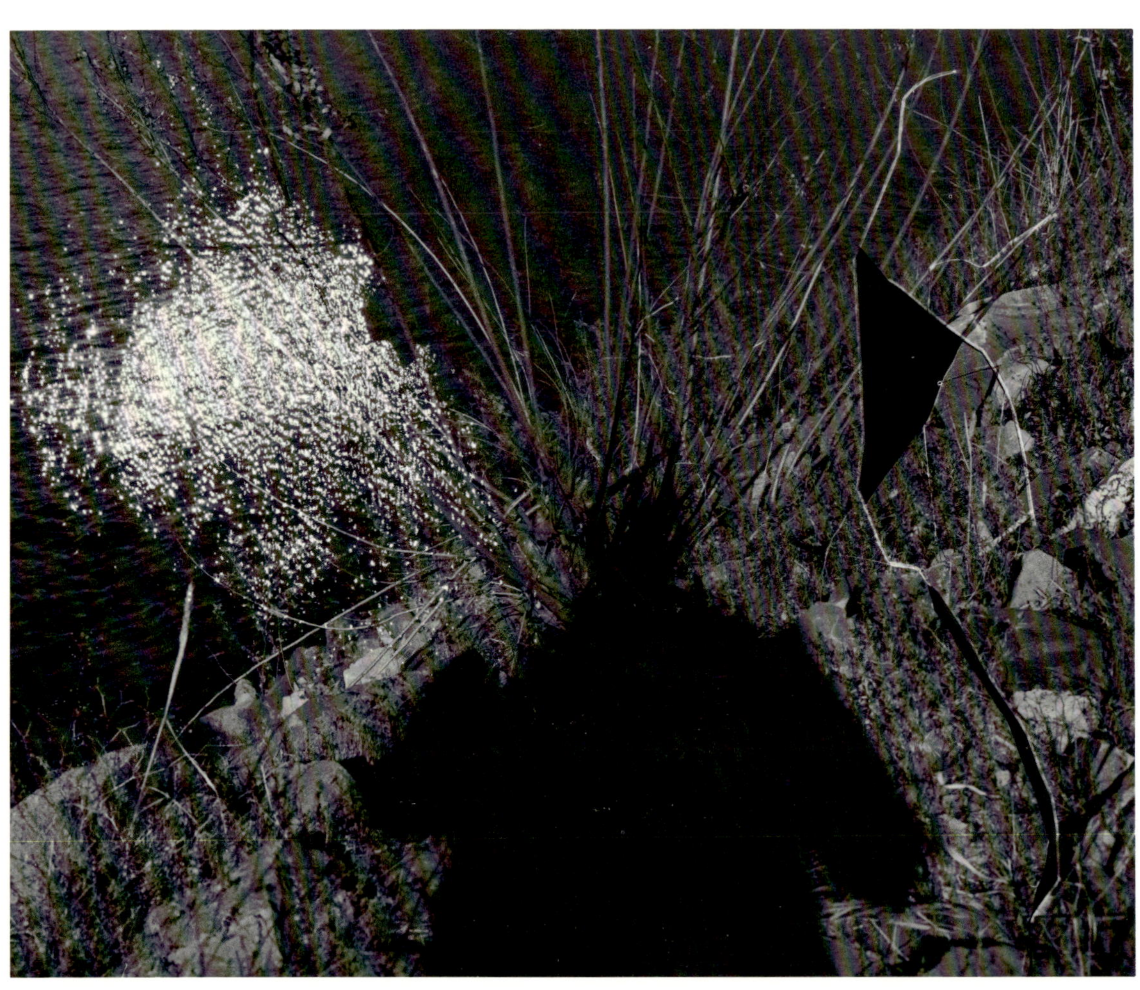

JOE PHILLIPS
Conway, Arkansas
Untitled, 1977

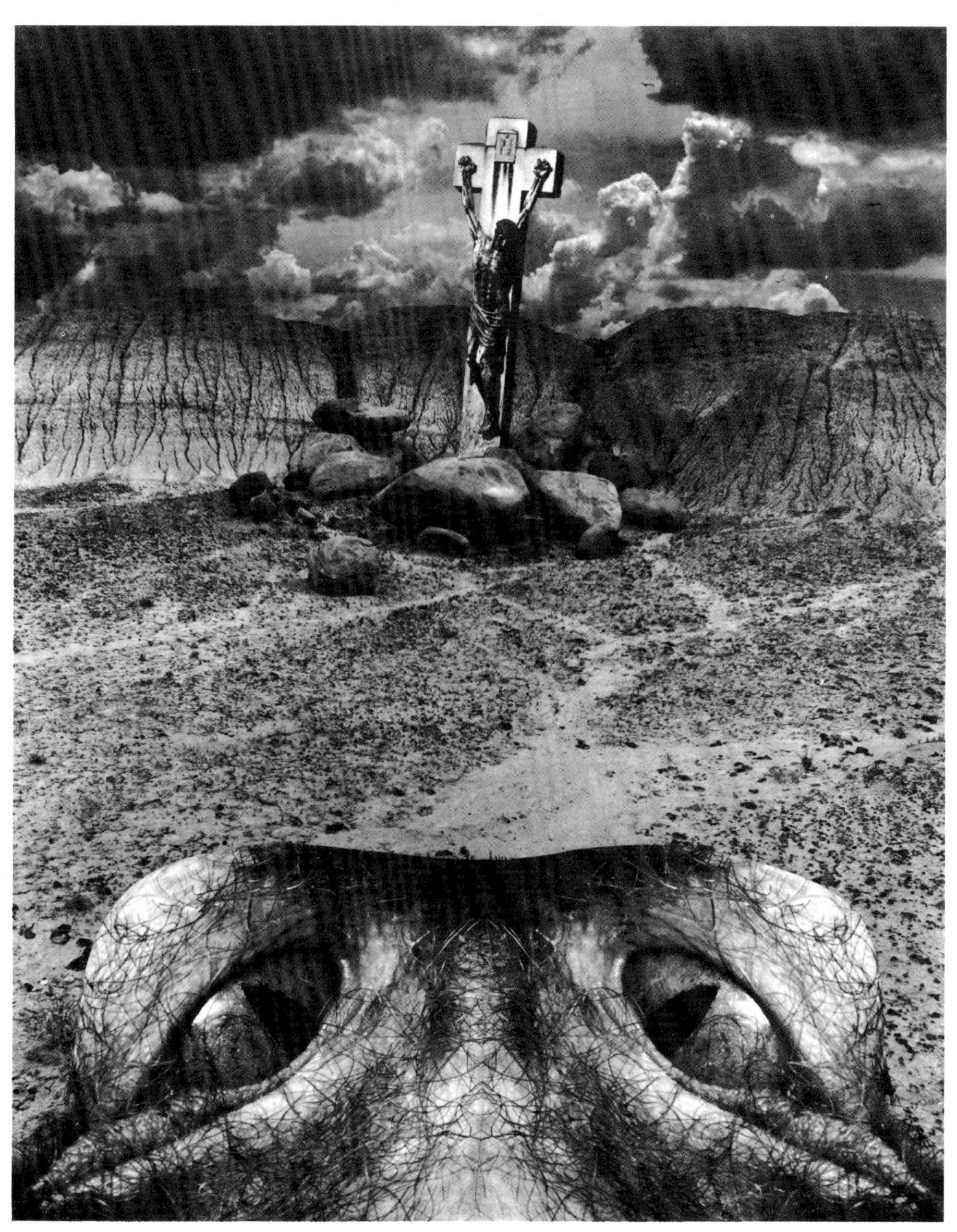

ALLEN A. DUTTON
Glendale, Arizona
Nike Or Niobe, 1977

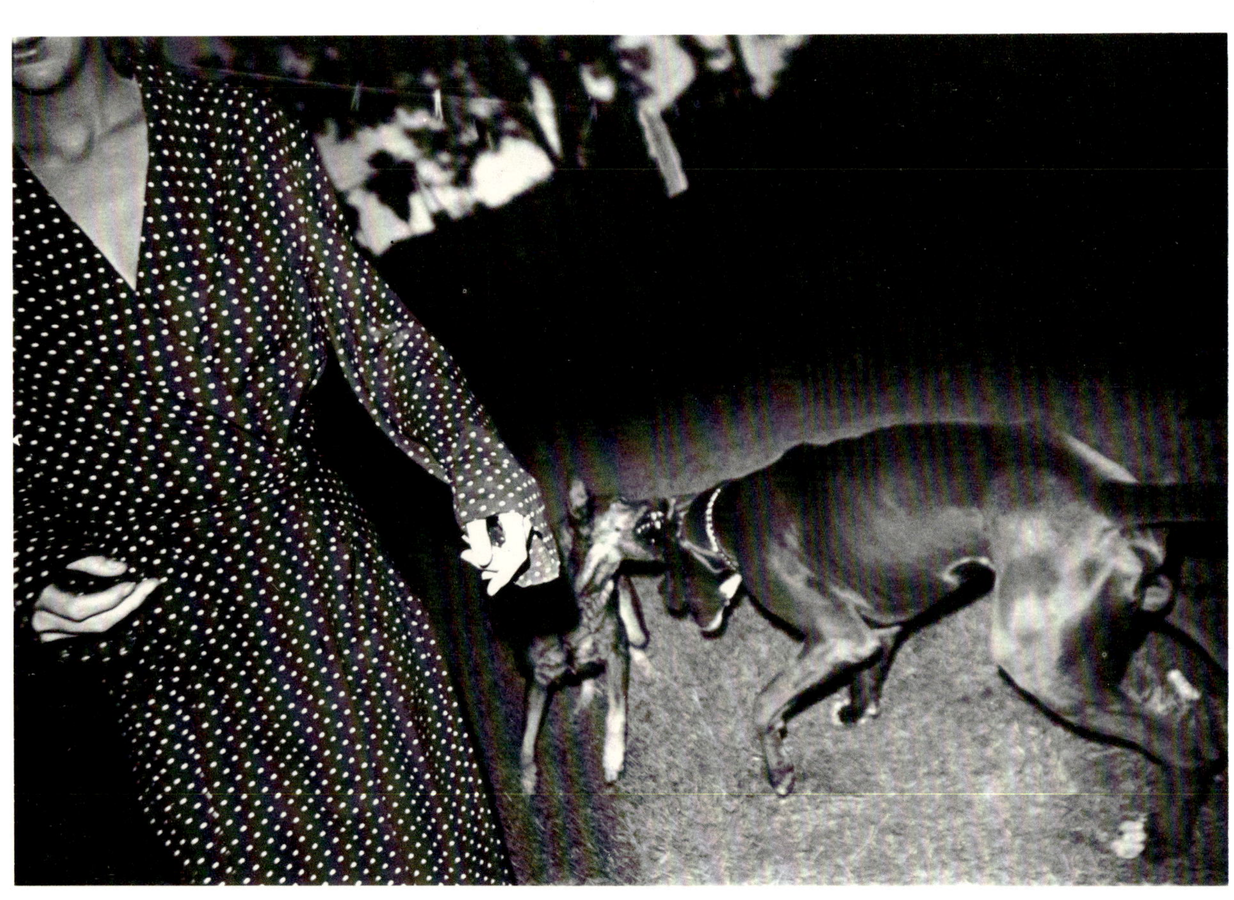

KENNETH SHORR
Culver City, California
Untitled

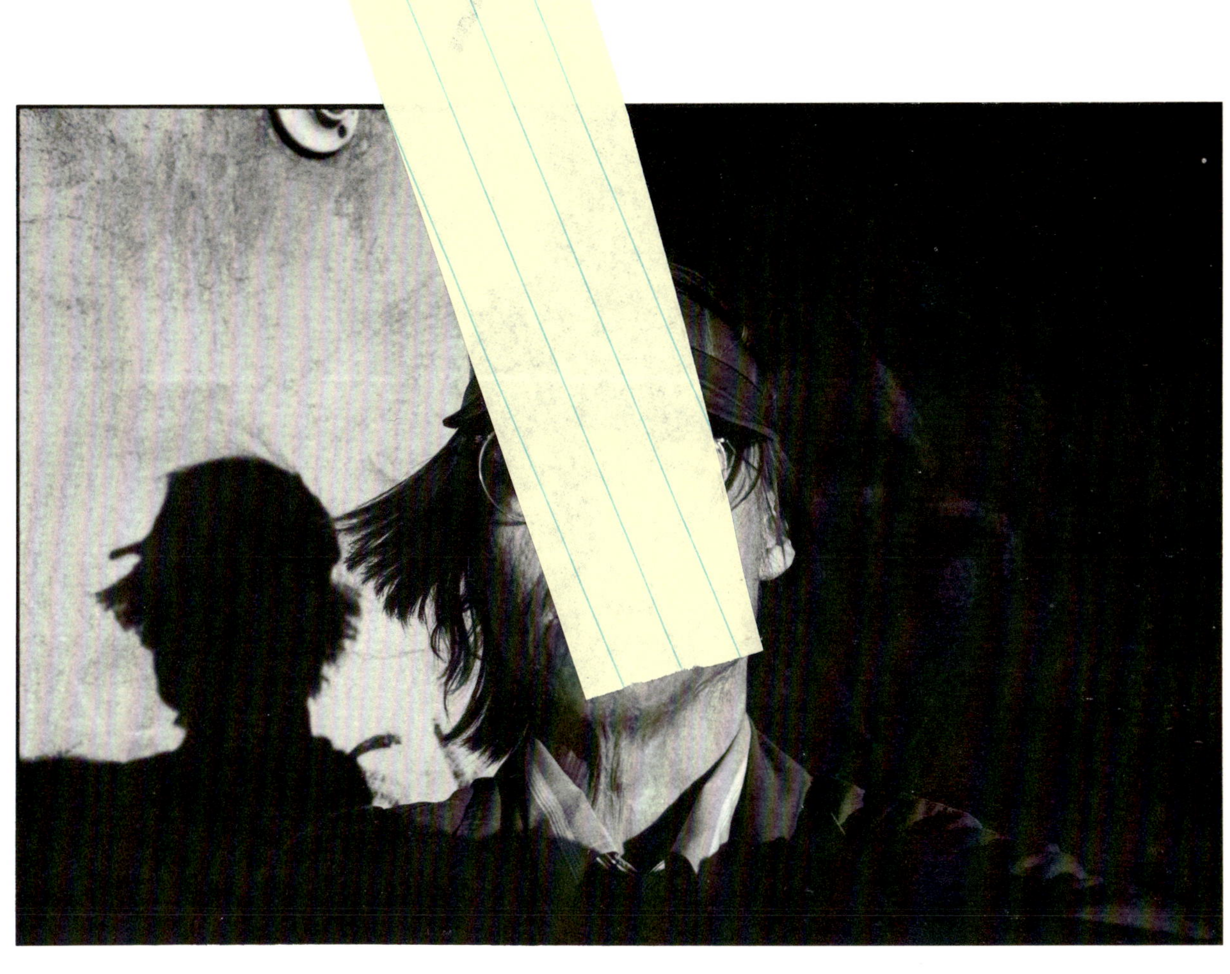

RICHARD R. HUTTER
San Francisco, California
Untitled Self-Portrait, San Francisco, 1973

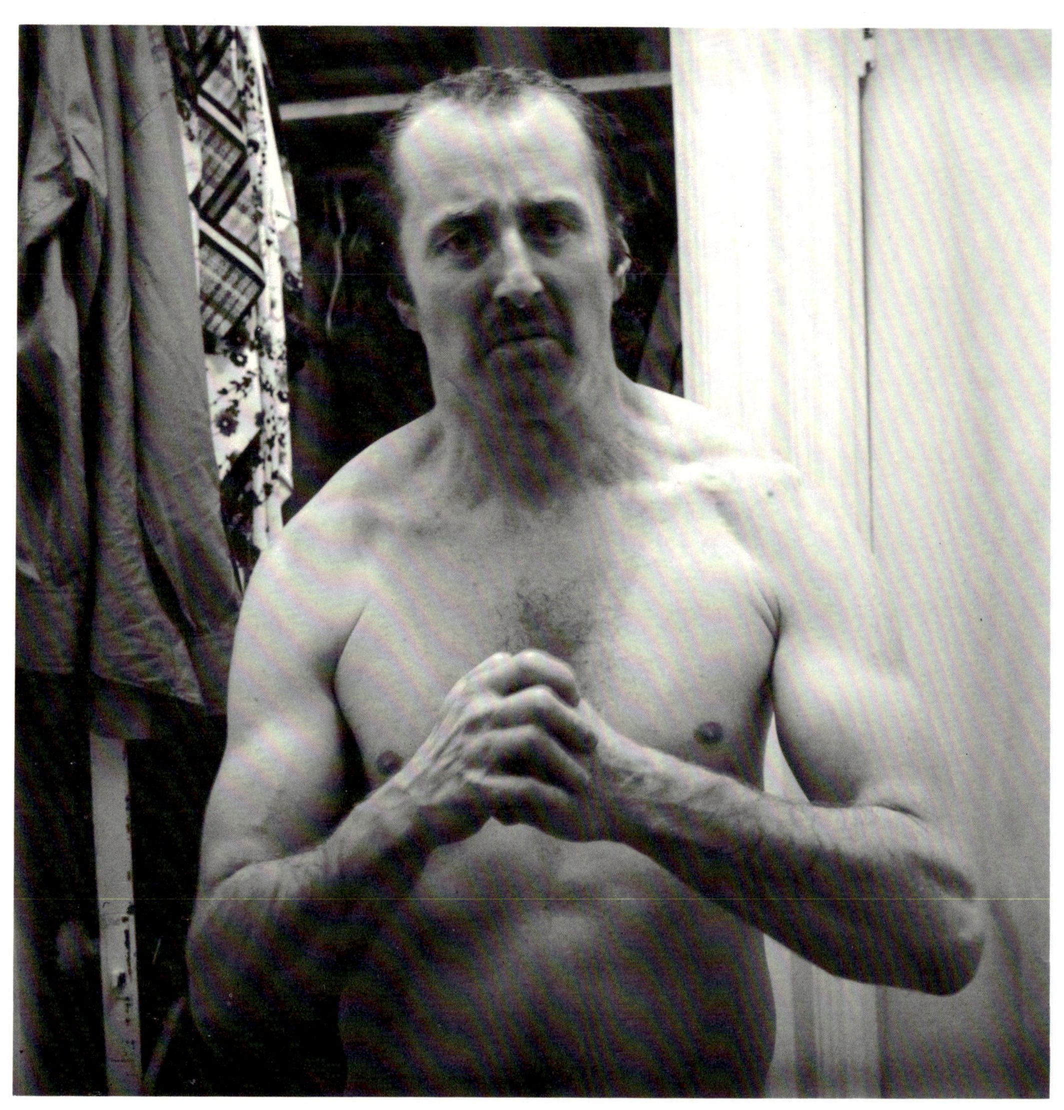

TOM DUGAN
Bayonne, New Jersey
From series "Self-Death Ritual (Fantasy)," 1975

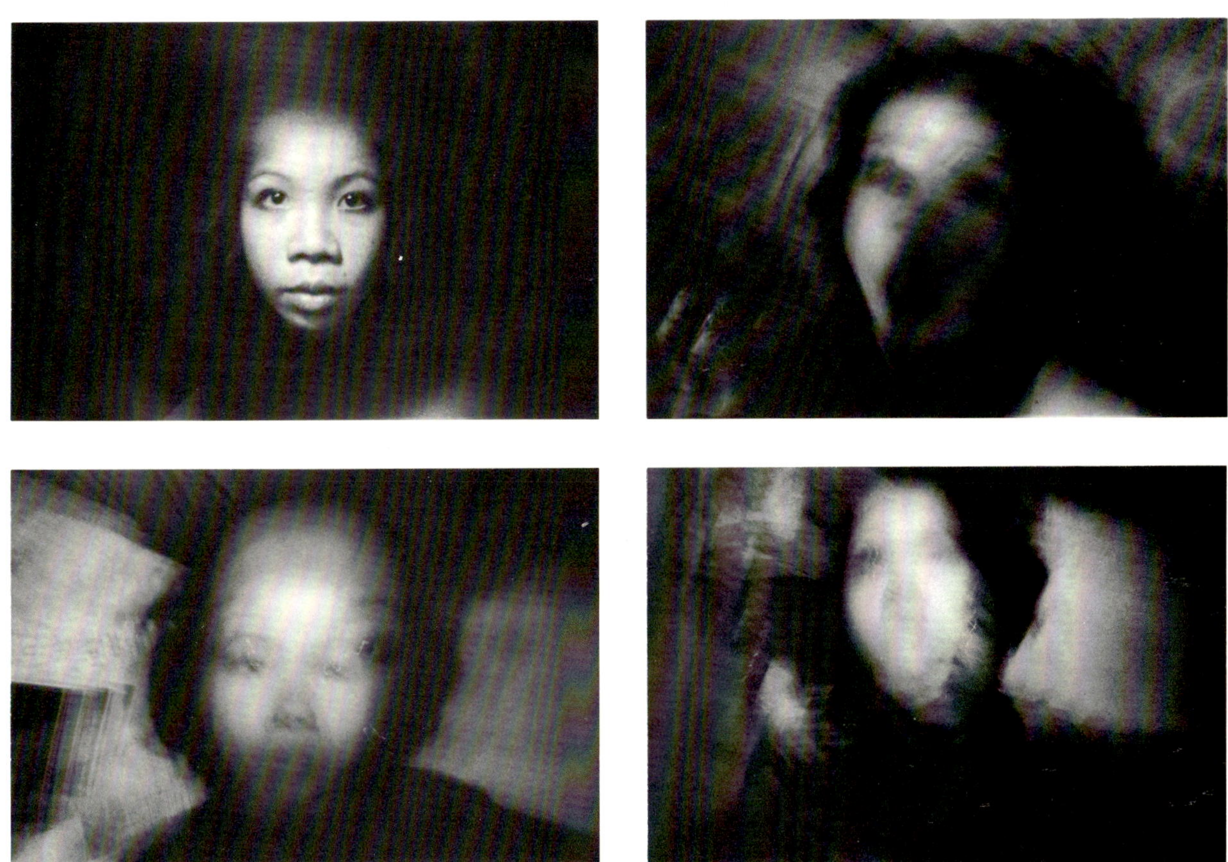

EVA SEID
New York, New York
The Awakening, 1975

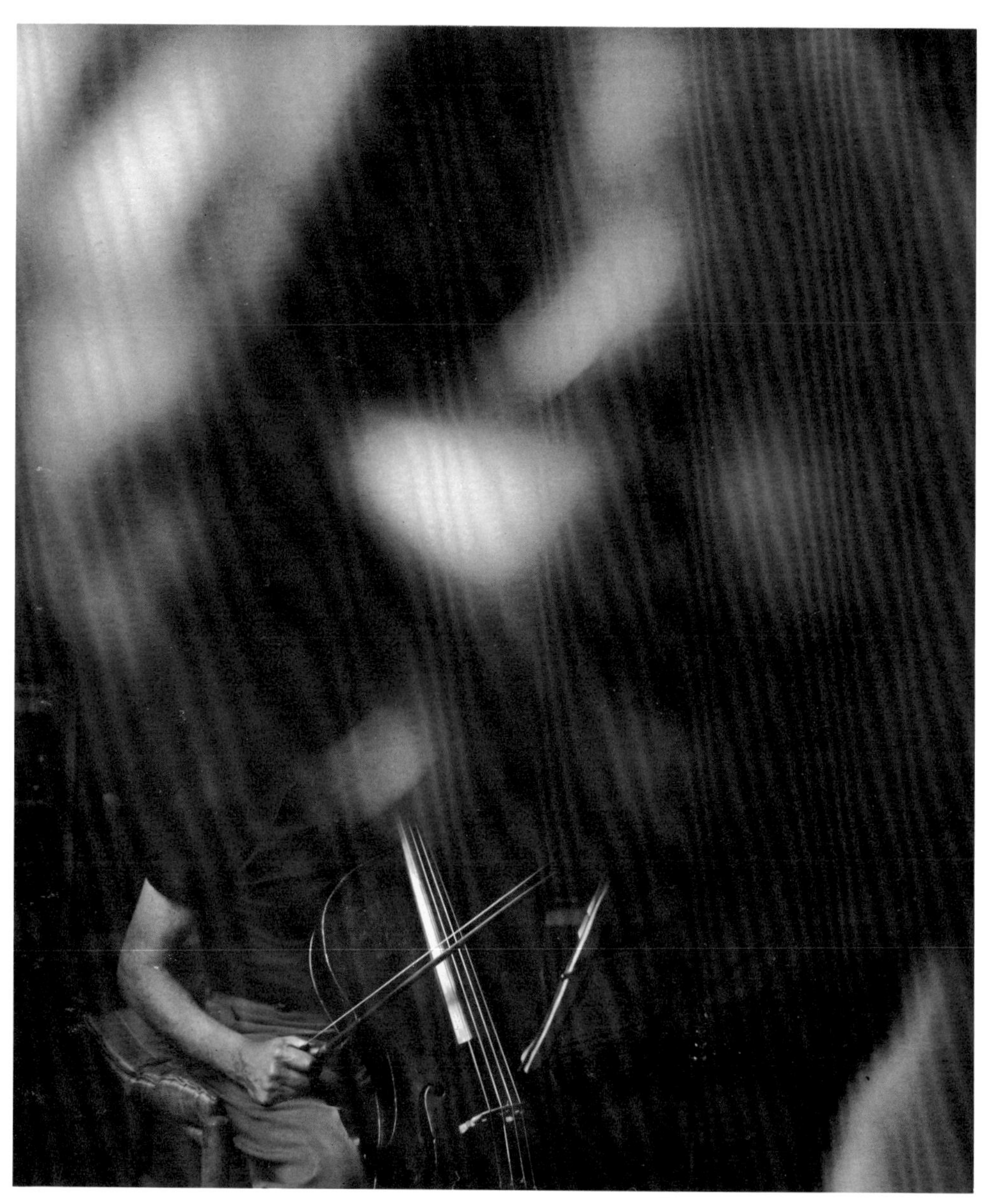

W. EUGENE SMITH
Tucson, Arizona
Self-Portrait

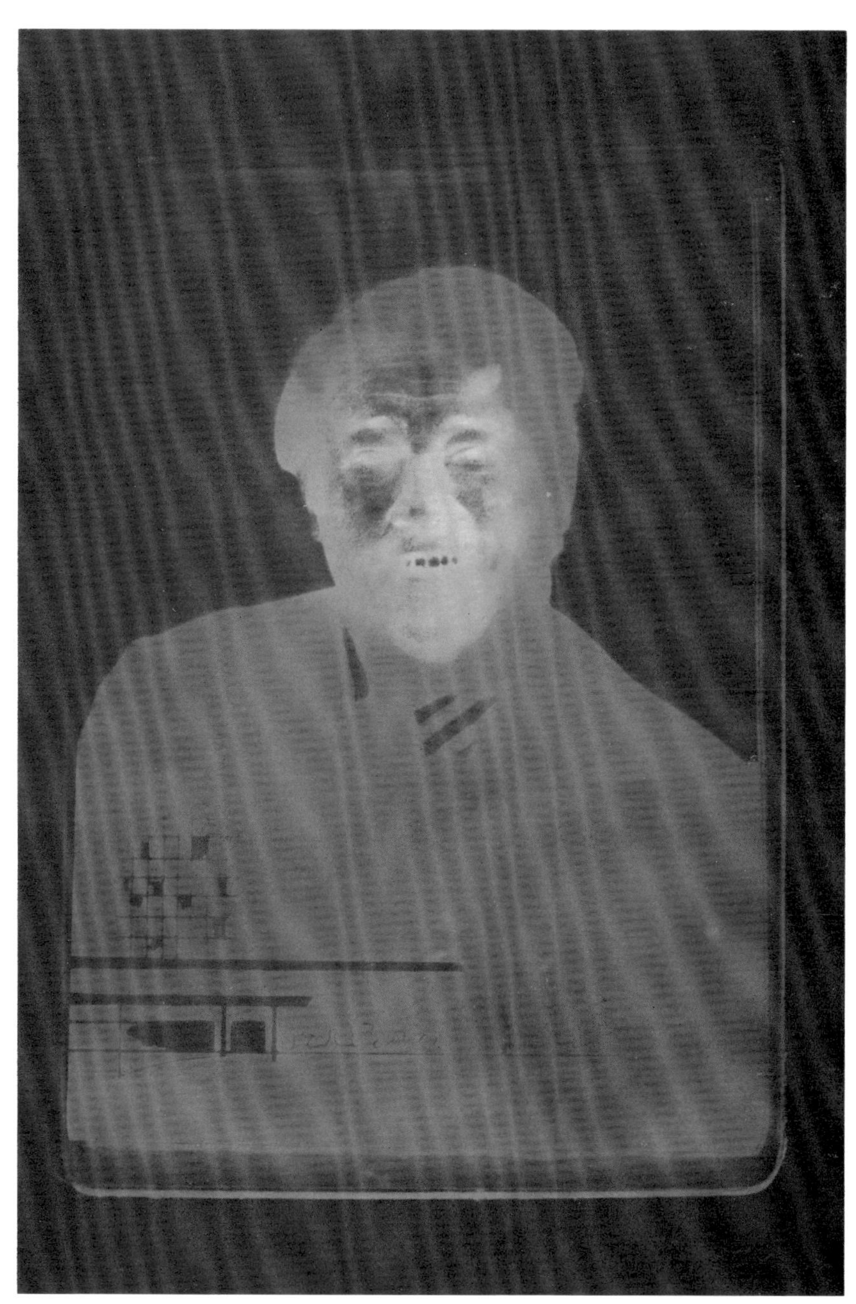

VAN DEREN COKE
San Francisco, California
Me As Mao, 1970

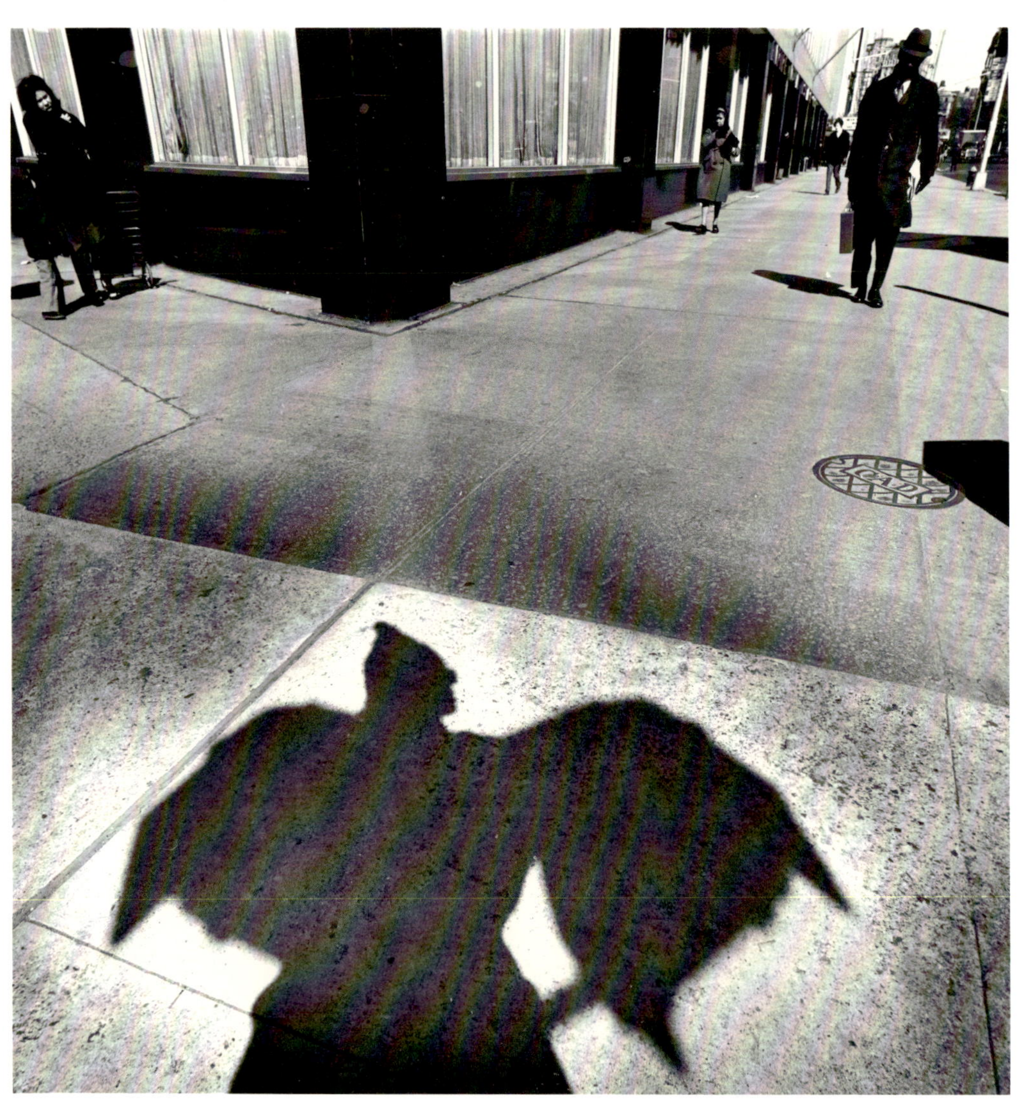

ARTHUR TRESS
New York, New York
Shadow as Bird of Prey, 1973

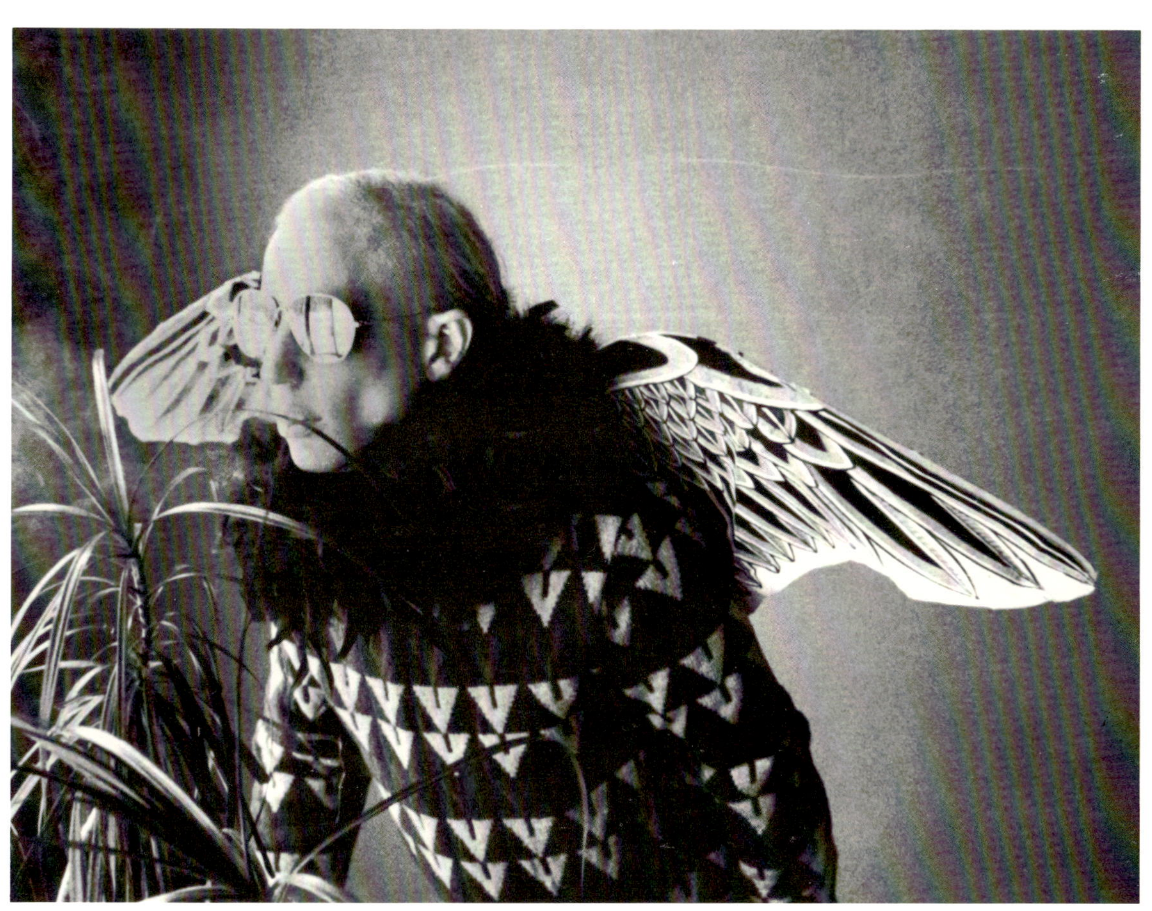

BARRY SAVENOR
Cambridge, Massachusetts
Self-Portrait with Wings
(In Memory of Dora Kagan Savenor)

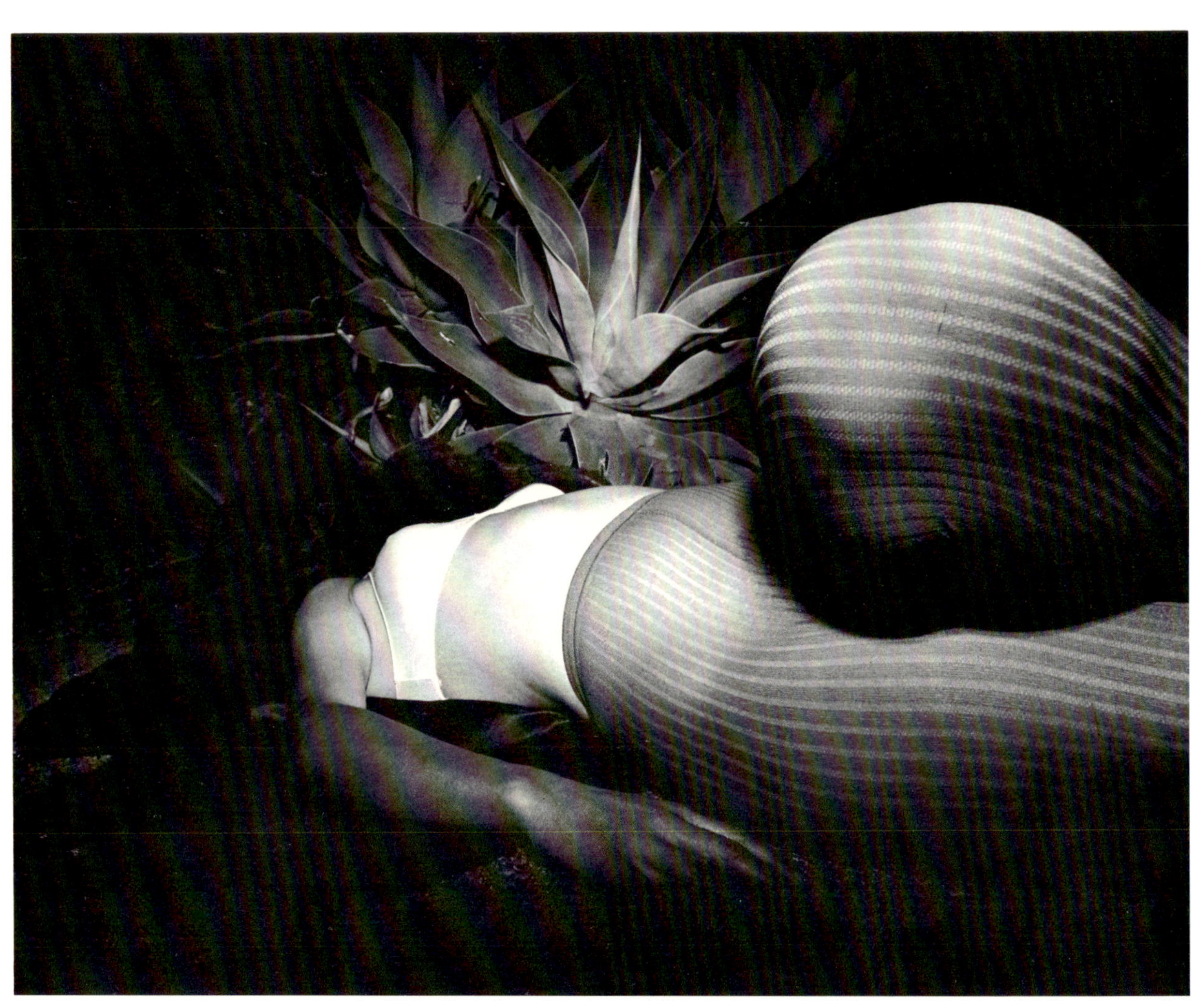

DE ANN JENNINGS
Los Angeles, California
From the series "Fears and Phobias," 1976

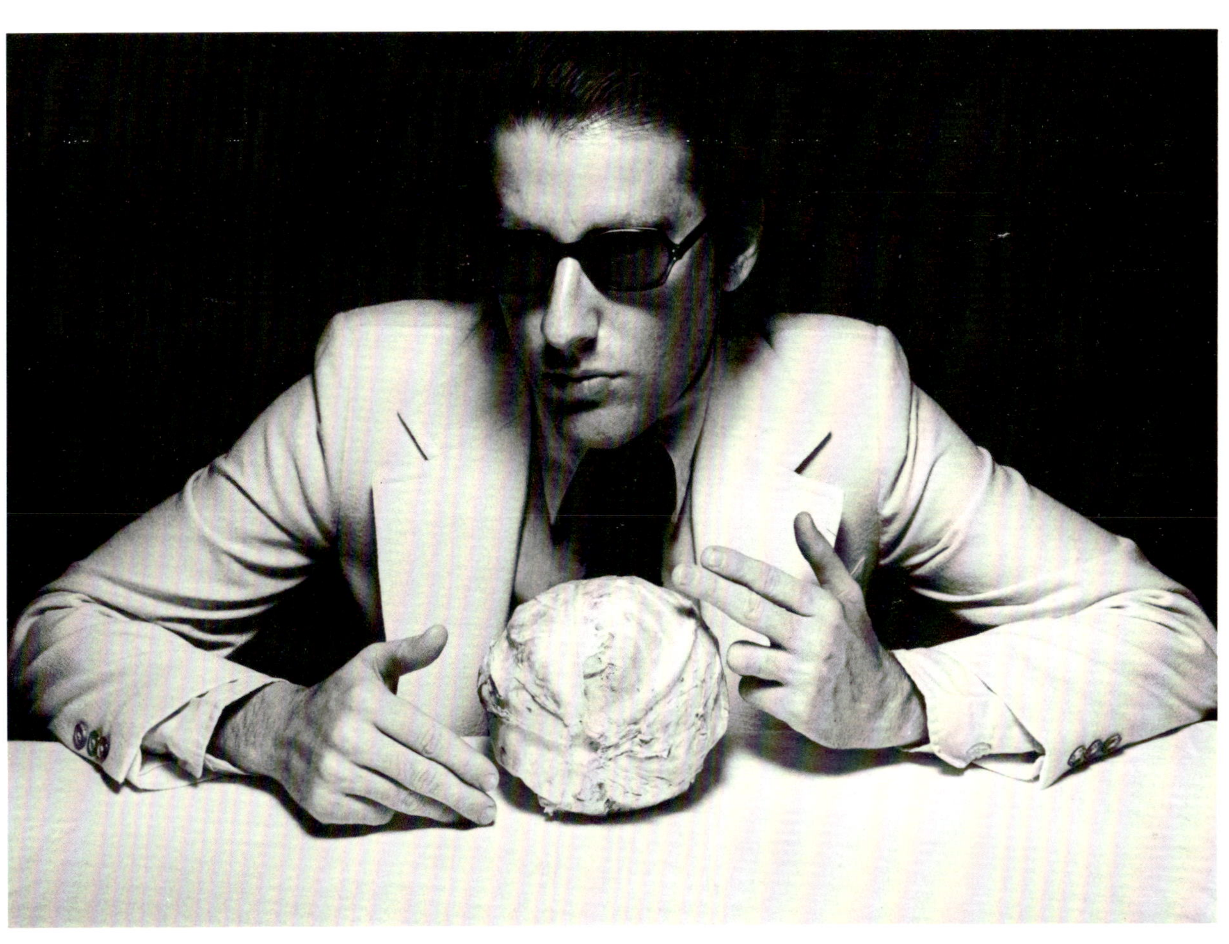

KERRY T. CAMPBELL
Lubbock, Texas
A Dull Friday Night, 1978

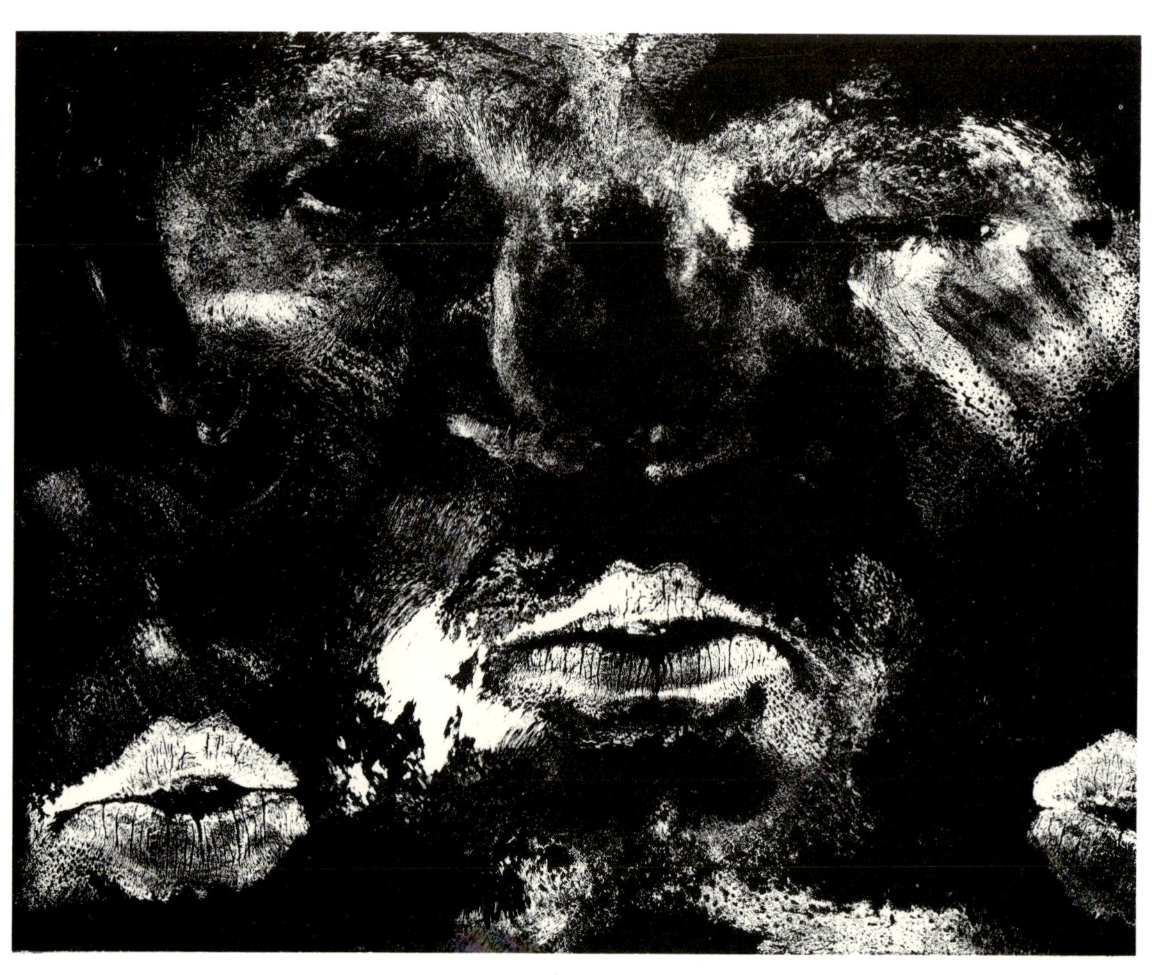

JIM HILL
Half Moon Bay, California
Untitled, 1978

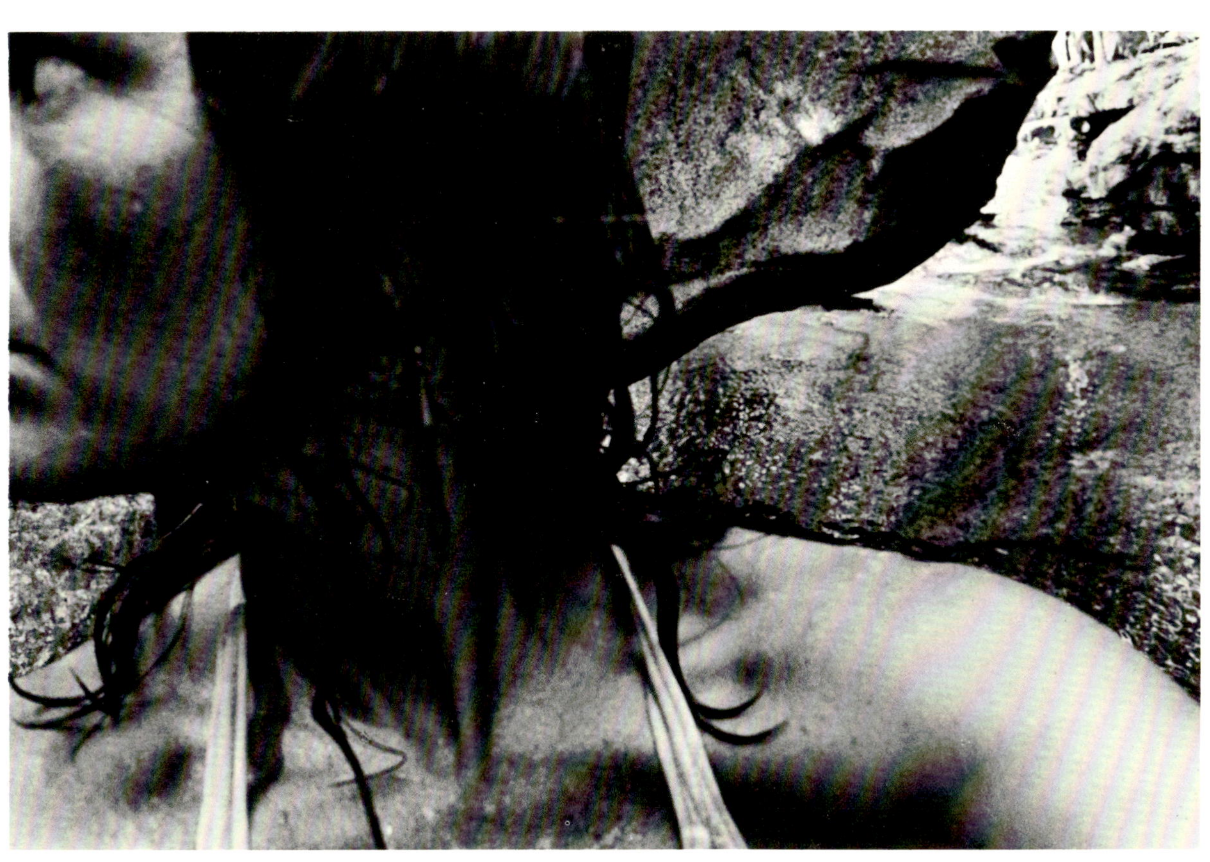

CHRIS ENOS
Boston, Massachusetts
Self-Portrait, 1975

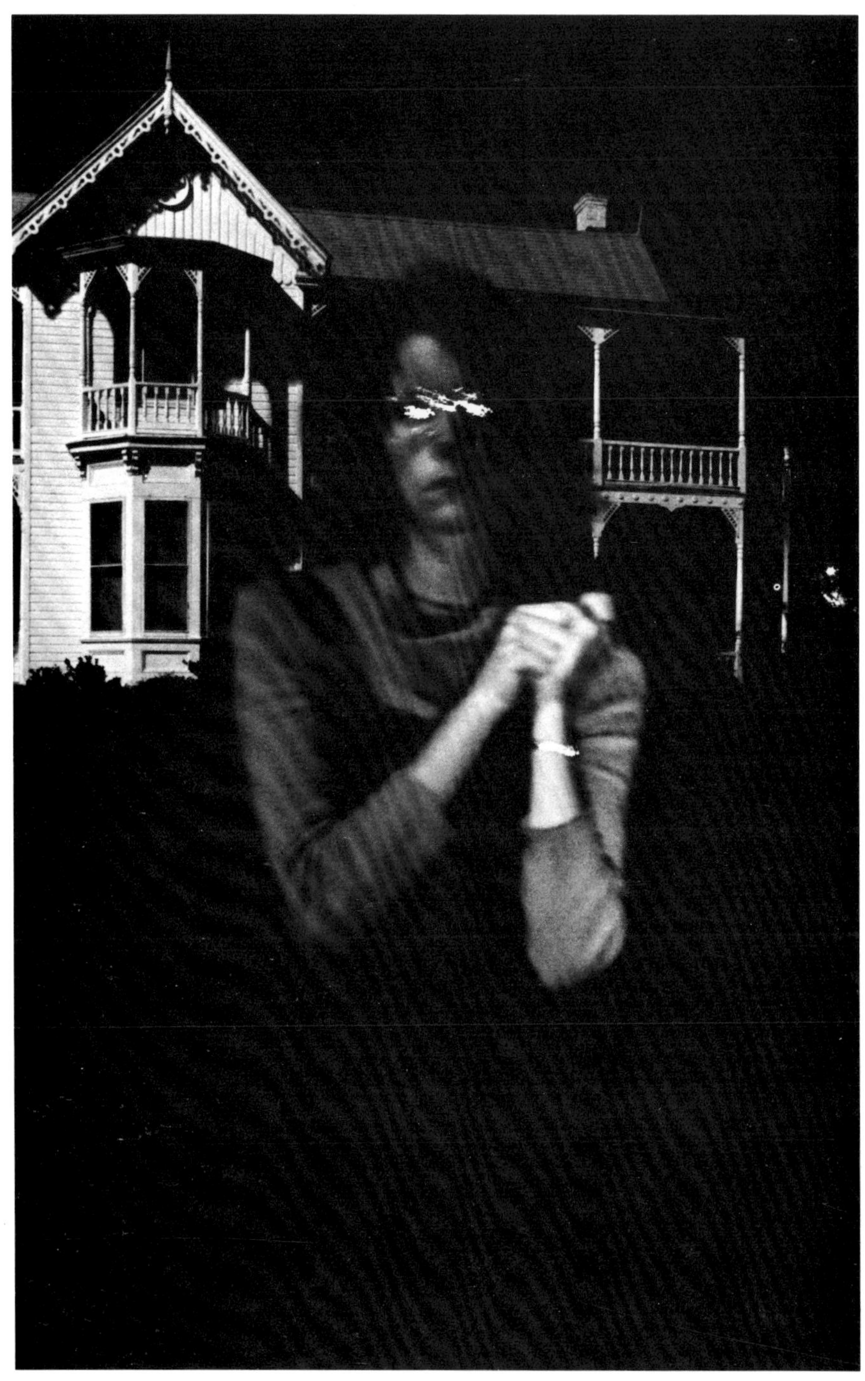

DANA ASBURY
Albuquerque, New Mexico
Untitled, 1977

Photographing the Interior
The Self-Portrait as Introspection

Dana Asbury

One reason I so deeply care for the camera is just this. So far as it goes . . . and handled cleanly and literally in its own terms, as an ice-cold, some ways limited, some ways more capable eye, it is, like the phonograph record and like scientific instruments and unlike any other leverage of art, incapable of recording anything but absolute, dry truth.

James Agee
Let Us Now Praise Famous Men

When Agee wrote that statement sometime around 1937, the photographer with whom he was most intimately involved, Walker Evans, was affecting the course of photography with his then unusual recording of bare-faced fact. Although he may have turned an ice-cold lens toward his subject (as opposed to, say, Edward Weston's sensuous one), his photographs are remarkable now not so much for their *absolute, dry truth,* but for the poetry and humaness they depict with the sparest artifacts in the simplest surroundings. Contemporary photographers, having finally caught up with Twentieth Century scientific and philosophical thinking, recognize that not only is absolute, dry truth no longer the sole provenance of the camera, but also that it no longer exists at all.

If, as has been thought in the past, the camera never lies, the reason is simply that it is not smart enough. Except perhaps for NASA landings on the moon or the automatic surveillance cameras of banks and stores, there is usually a human being behind the lens capable of distorting, mis-representing and altering, through the filter of his perceptions, that awesomely authoritative model called photographic truth. But if the camera were indeed incapable of recording anything but what is out there in front of the lens, then the medium, despite its relative youth, would long ago have grown bored with that facile occupation and would never have been a viable means of creative expression. The camera may not be smart, but photographers are getting smarter and becoming more aware all the time. With this awareness, what is out there is no longer in itself particularly unique or amusing. As Garry Winogrand has suggested, there is no news; it is no longer possible for the camera to *reveal* with bare-faced information. Winogrand's solution is to play the game by certain rules, by relinquishing total control and thereby making it possible to surprise himself with how the *there out there,* as Gertrude Stein called it, looks on film. Winogrand is but one photographer who has made his own rules to evolve a personal style. The point is that as photographic consciousness evolves in the seventies, the investigation is shifting away from quantifiable fact to an intensely personal exploration of less tangible realities, and in some cases, of one's inner feelings.

Henri Cartier-Bresson once said, "We photographers deal in things which are continually vanishing." Nothing is more continually vanishing, more ephemeral, than the expression on the human face; yet to capture it on film, to freeze the split second for eternity seems to imply *revelation.* Questioning the nature of truth as reflected through photographs has been especially vital in the area of portraiture. As one of the most revered and popular categories of photography, portraiture has traditionally been valued for that revelation, a glimpse into the subject's soul as well as the record of his likeness. Julia

Margaret Cameron, for one, believed she was recording the image of an immortal soul in her portraits of famous men. (Consistent with the age of Queen Victoria, however, it was the superficial aspect of a woman's immortal beauty that made her a worthy subject.) August Sander believed that his systematic documentation of German types and occupations would define a national character; the English translation of the title of his book *Men Without Masks* implies that the camera can pare away the layers of daily habit to show us as we really are. Although his pictures are sensitive, quiet studies, whatever revelations they contain depend upon the advantages of historical hindsight. These myths live on. A photographer as contemporary as Richard Avedon has said that the series of portraits of his dying father show "what it is to be any one of us."

Ultimately, for anyone involved in any form of creative expression, the blockbusting question will arise: What am I doing and does it really mean anything? Do we really learn anything about people through their portrait? Does the soul really give up onto film its intimate secrets? Or is it not as Cartier-Bresson said, that to make a portrait is to put a question mark on someone? Consider, for instance, the unabashedly straightforward portraits of our cultural and literary superstars by Arnold Newman and Richard Avedon. We search the photographs for the answers, the secrets of success, but Newman's pictures, by exploiting the camera's unique ability to juxtapose information, show us simply the person with some artifact of his career. Avedon's portraits are intriguing but even more difficult; his emotionless, unblinking lens presents his subjects so uniformly that they become permutations on his formal, empty set. The aura of importance he gives them does not vary from one to the next. The staff of radio station WBAI carries the same authority as the Saigon Mission Council; the camera is a completely democratic instrument and cannot make hierarchical distinctions. Avedon's portraits all have the indelible mark of Avedon, but rather than any universal insight into the nature of superstardom, all we really learn is more than we care to know about the look of rumpled trousers and aging skin. There is no absolute, dry truth here, but neither is there any intimate, personal fiction.

Consider also, the work of Diane Arbus. Her pictures were at first hailed as an unsentimental but not insensitive view of people at whom we are taught not to stare. Her work is, without a doubt, revealing, but it is not about the freaks and *normal* people who are facing the *angst* of modern life with horror, alienation, loneliness or whatever else we see in their faces. What remains after all those parades, drag balls and ordinary Sunday outings is a disturbing, reverberating portrait of Arbus herself. There are, of course, other photographers who have made images of people in search of their own place in an alien world. The recently discovered work of Mike Disfarmer, for instance, reflects, in so many of his subject's faces, a look of such intense anxiety that we can read it also as his own.

In her recently published book *The Life of the Mind,* Hannah Arendt discusses the disparity between appearances and reality. Although her ostensible subject is Western philosophy, the language she uses invokes photography in general, and specifically portraiture. She makes the distinction between how we appear and how, on the inside, we really are. Photographers like Arbus and Disfarmer draped their personal interpretation over others' appearance in the world; thus there is to their portraits that tension between fact and interpretation that renders their work so affecting. Their pictures unveiled a new approach to portraiture. Photographing people became introspective. Despite the otherness of their subjects, Arbus' and Disfarmer's portraits are inquiries into their interior self-images. I believe they both saw in appearances some private reality of their own. It seems that the truest examples we have of the nebulous notion of psychological portraiture come from those photographers who most actively impose their world view upon their pictures. The psychological insights are introspective; the people they photograph are no more than the vehicles for this confrontation with self.

One other photographer who succeeds not only in illuminating the notion of psychological portraiture but who also fuses her portrayal of others to a sense of personal revelation is Anne Noggle. Her images of aging women, who all seem vital but just a bit mad, become infinitely more meaningful when seen in the context of her self-portraits. The haunting series documenting her face-lift operation, which is brutally direct but laced with macabre humor, lays Noggle's fears, anxieties and vanities so bare that all her work reads as a self-portrait. Her photographs further indicate a trend in contemporary photography toward introspection, or to use a term the Boston Museum of Fine Arts applied to a group exhibition there, *Private Realities*. Noggle's images reveal the possibility of approaching the portrait not strictly from a standpoint of likeness-as-information, but from a more idiosyncratic attitude of likeness-as-emotional-interpretation. Just as Arbus saw in the doubt-ridden faces of her subjects a visual equivalent of her world view, Noggle finds in other women echoes of her own state of mind. If photographing people is a charged activity because of the tensions inherent in it, self-portraits are logically even more charged.

In my own work, the route to self-portraiture was circuitous but perhaps inevitable. Photographing people was always, though at first subconsciously, a search for commonality of experience. It was a logical step from a shy beginner's first tentative attempts at that awkwardly-phrased genre of people pictures to the more self aware use of portraiture, although the distinction between them was often foggy. As a document of an autonomous and in some way physically interesting individual, portraiture retains a certain specificity, however, that for me left little room for personal interpretation, my own or the viewer's. Because of the camera's equal recording of significant and irrelevant detail, my intentions were unclear. My first experience with self-portraiture came, as often happens in photography, by accident. One hapless evening, with neither a model nor daylight, but a strong urge to photograph, I made my first self-portrait by moonlight and street-lights for lack of any alternative. The result was a revelation.

Previously it had not been evident to me that I photographed others for what I saw in them of myself. My search continued for Cartier-Bresson's *continually vanishing* quality of expression that will, perhaps, reveal something ineffable. By using myself as the subject, I was freed from the search for that specific and peculiarly interesting trait in another person that catches the eye; by using available night light, I was freed from the ice-cold, split-second, diamond-hard resolution of modern photographic equipment. Chance was allowed a role as it seldom is in more formal portraiture. After making self-portraits, I have been able to return to photographing other people, to express a generalized way of feeling, but without the binds of portraiture. These recent photographs portray deeply personal feelings, but ones which I recognize in others.

As the recording of the human visage turns toward introspection, portraits, and especially self-portraits, become diaristic. Whereas the work of a photographer such as Darryl Curran is explicitly diaristic in its use of personal events for imagery, the photographs of Arbus, Disfarmer, Noggle and others are similarly so. Rather than from the facts and events of daily life, the images draw on the emotions. This quasi-diaristic way of working from a personal repertory of feeling is indebted, in part, to the feminist art movement. It is unclear, however, whether the rise of feminism is a cause or a result of the recent trend toward introspection in the visual arts. As critic Lucy Lippard writes in *From the Center,* "It is time that the word *intuitive* regain its dignity and rejoin the word *conceptual* as a necessary esthetic ingredient". In the hard-edge sixties it seemed that certain taboos had emerged against sentiment, emotionalism and lyricism; the use of personal experience in one's work moved counter to the reductive and formalistic styles through which both painting and photography had once reached the rarefied stratospheres of High Art. In recent years we have returned to a healthy respect for the intimate, decorative and figurative elements which were so maligned by formalist critics. Whatever sociological reasons can be disinterred, the effect of this kind of work is a heightened sense of personal involvement which carries an emotional impact that cannot be avoided.

Perhaps it could be argued that this emotional commitment produces work which is related, from one photographer to the next, by its visualization of nightmare. Certainly it is true that one of my own concerns has been with the possibility that, despite the camera's fundamental reliance on external reality, photographs need not be bound by mimesis. Perhaps when they depart from Agee's absolute, dry truth, they depart also from our notions of real and enter a shadowy, sometimes eerie world between night and day that is often associated with nightmare.

The making of the self-image is the kind of activity that dwells necessarily in a subjective, non-quantifiable world of dreams. Who has any objective idea of what he looks like? Appearances, we know, can conceal as much as they reveal. The kind of self-portrait most common in this collection uses a specific event or setting through which to convey some essential feature of self. No longer present is the mystical but passive belief in the power of appearances to reveal themselves; the artist has made it his job to transcribe his personal reality into a more accessible form of appearance.

Western thinkers since Don Quixote have understood this disparity between appearance and reality. The camera, with its unique relationship to reality, seems particularly well suited to the exploration of that notion. No longer the handmaiden of outward appearance, photography is capable of defining a more subjective, and therefore possibly truer, representation of things-as-they-are than absolute, dry truth ever could.

Photography in this decade also owes a debt to conceptual art for its expanded horizons. The lesson of conceptual art was that the act of photographing need not necessarily be the end in itself. To use the photographic document as a vehicle not only for visual ideas but for conceptual ones as well is a new phenomenon for artistic photographers. Thomas Barrow, for example, whose self-portrait is one of the few in this book without a human figure, has assimilated this kind of conceptual approach. Aware of the uncertainty of what, if anything, the camera can tell us about a given person, Barrow made a self-portrait from a document of his library shelf. While the photograph does have an immediate visual interest in the arrangement of the books, how they line up against each other and against the other objects on the shelves, the photograph is, like all the other work mentioned here, more than the sum of its parts. It represents his involvement with literary ideas, and Barrow's use of the library shelf is at once appropriate and punningly clever.

The remarkable interest in the self-portrait that this book evidences is part of a significant conceptual leap for the medium. The photographs are not just about what they depict; they repre-sent a heightened commitment to both emotional and literary ideas. These photographs are what they are — portraits of the artist — but they are also interpretations of self from the broader scope of personal reality. Photography, we should be gratified to learn, has entered at last the mainstream of Twentieth Century ideas. The progress is due, in part, to the imploding of tendentious photographic myths, to the camera's release from its role as guardian of common sense. There has also been a relinquishing of absolute, dry truth for a more gripping visualization of the interior. If photographs are still of the world, they have become, more importantly, about ideas and feelings. The camera no longer merely duplicates reality; it creates it.

Dana Asbury received a Master's Degree in the History of Photography from the University of New Mexico in Albuquerque. She graduated with a Bachelor of Arts Degree from Wesleyan University in Middletown, Connecticut and is currently completing work on a Master of Fine Arts Degree at the University of New Mexico.

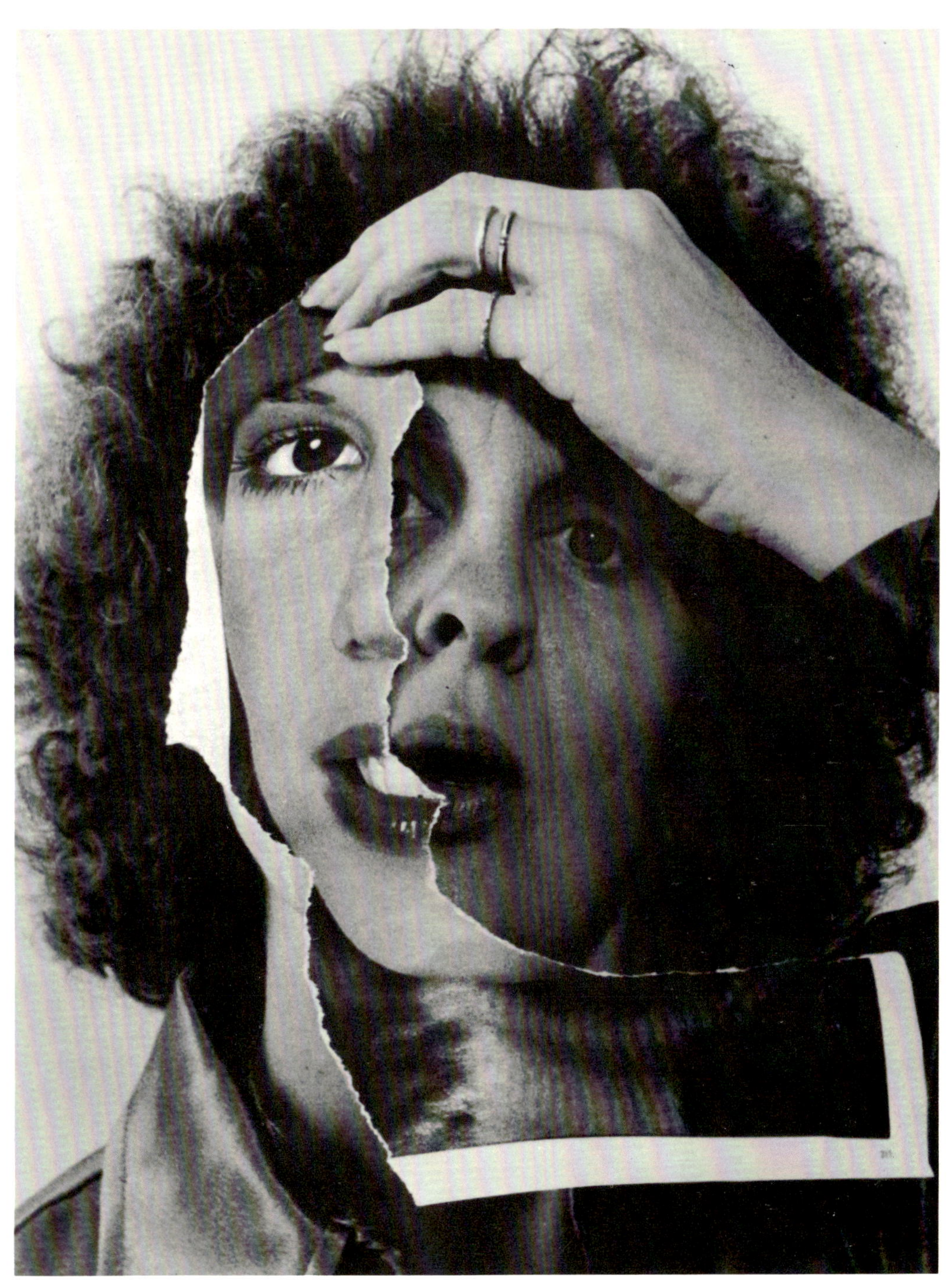

JUDITH GOLDEN
Inglewood, California
from ''Magazine Series,'' 1975

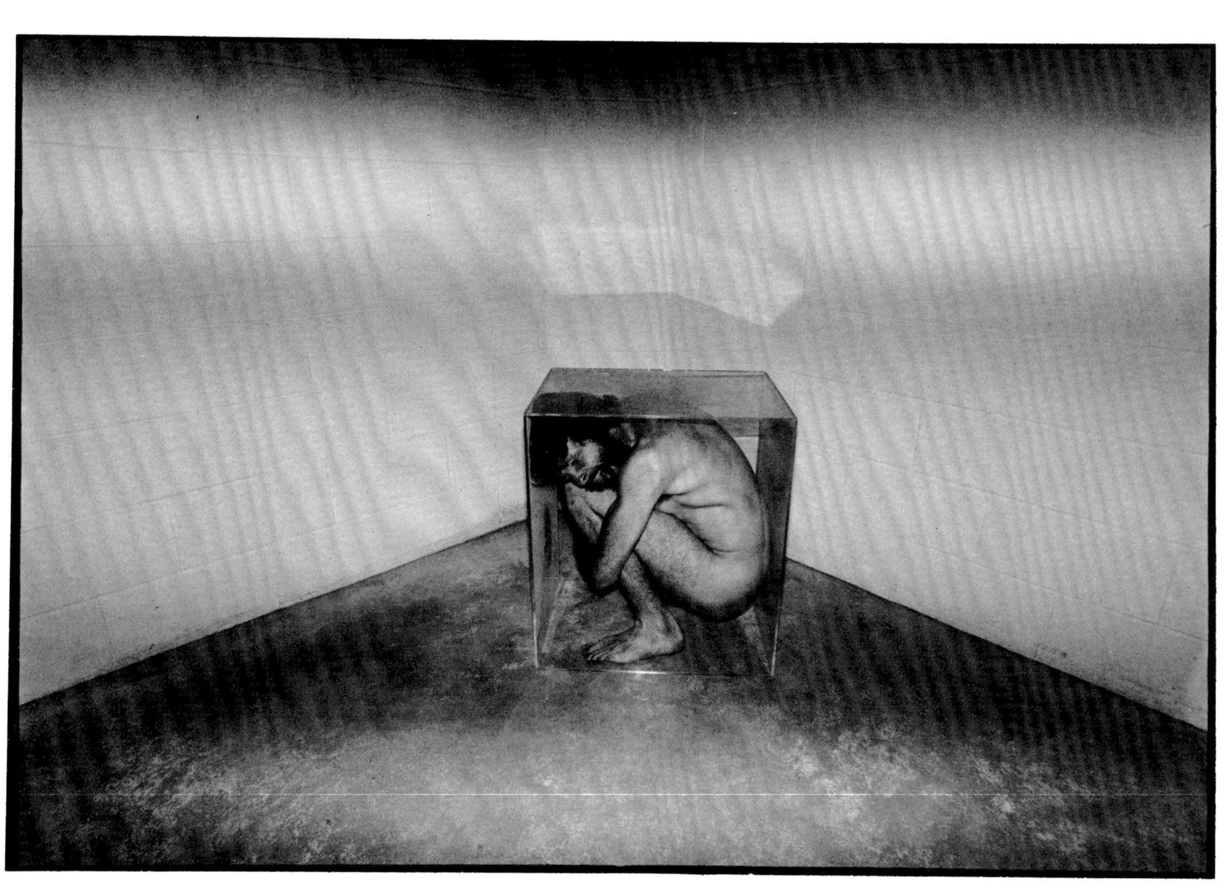

MICHAEL K. PUIG
Houston, Texas
No title, 1975

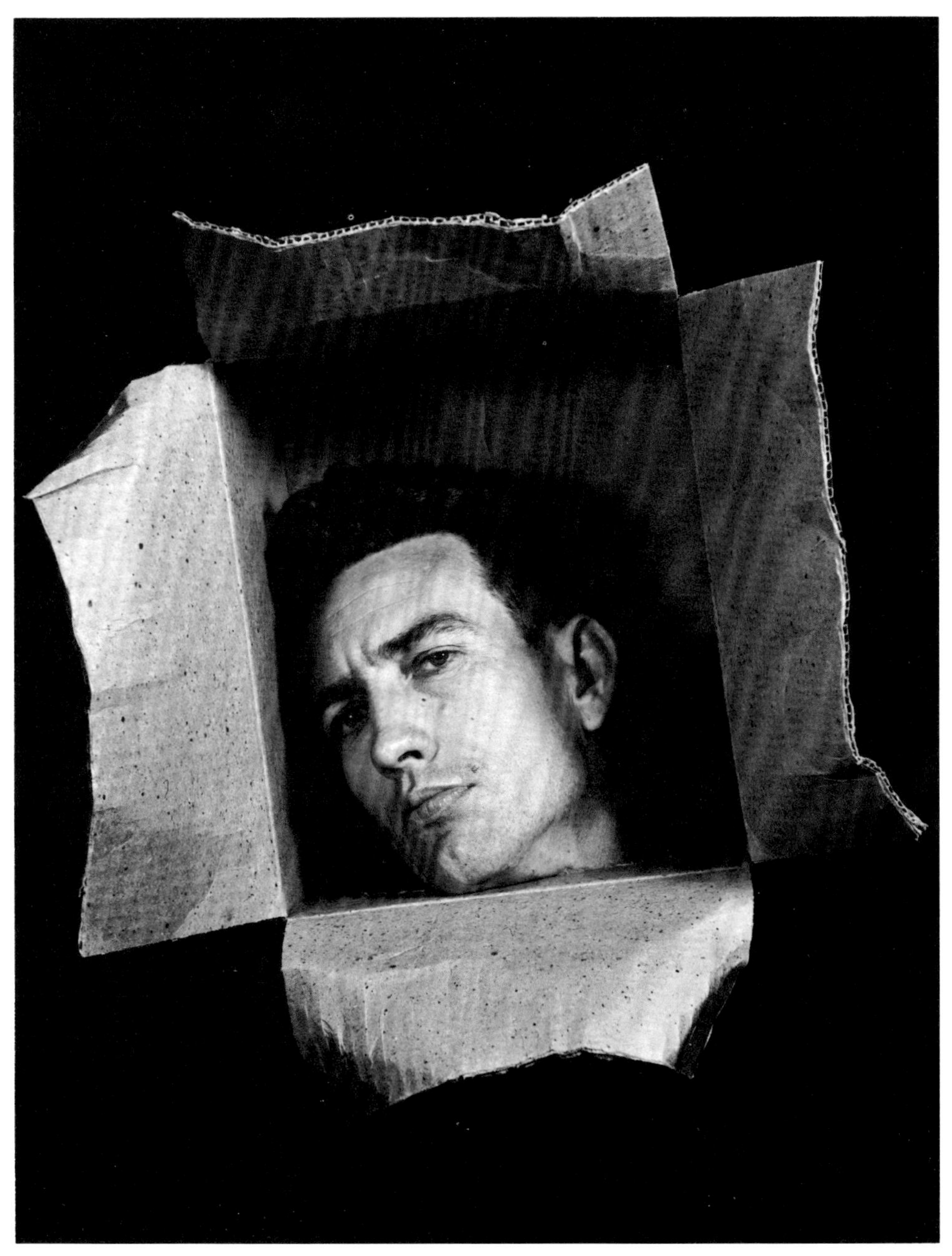

TODD WALKER
Tucson, Arizona
Self-Portrait, 1947

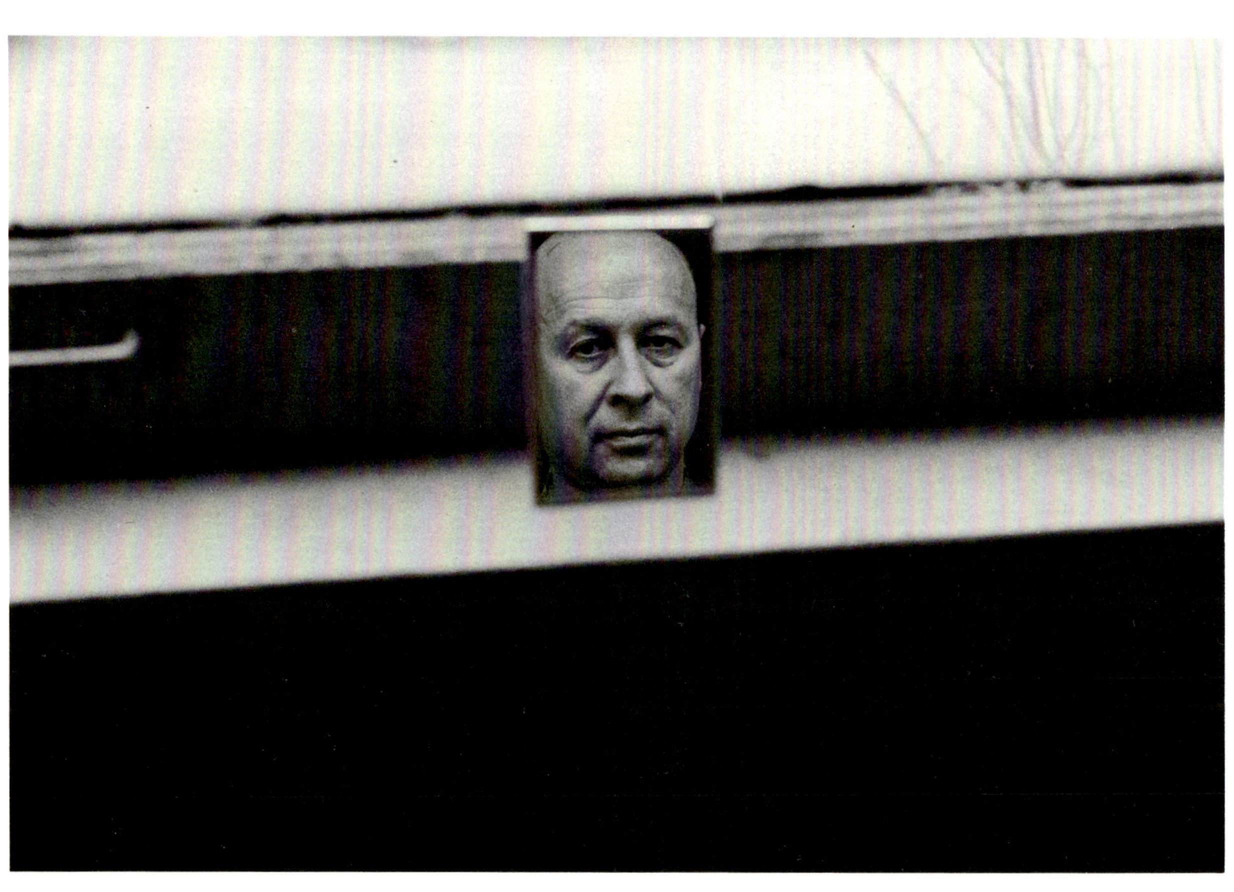

HARRY CALLAHAN
Providence, Rhode Island
Self-Portrait, 1962

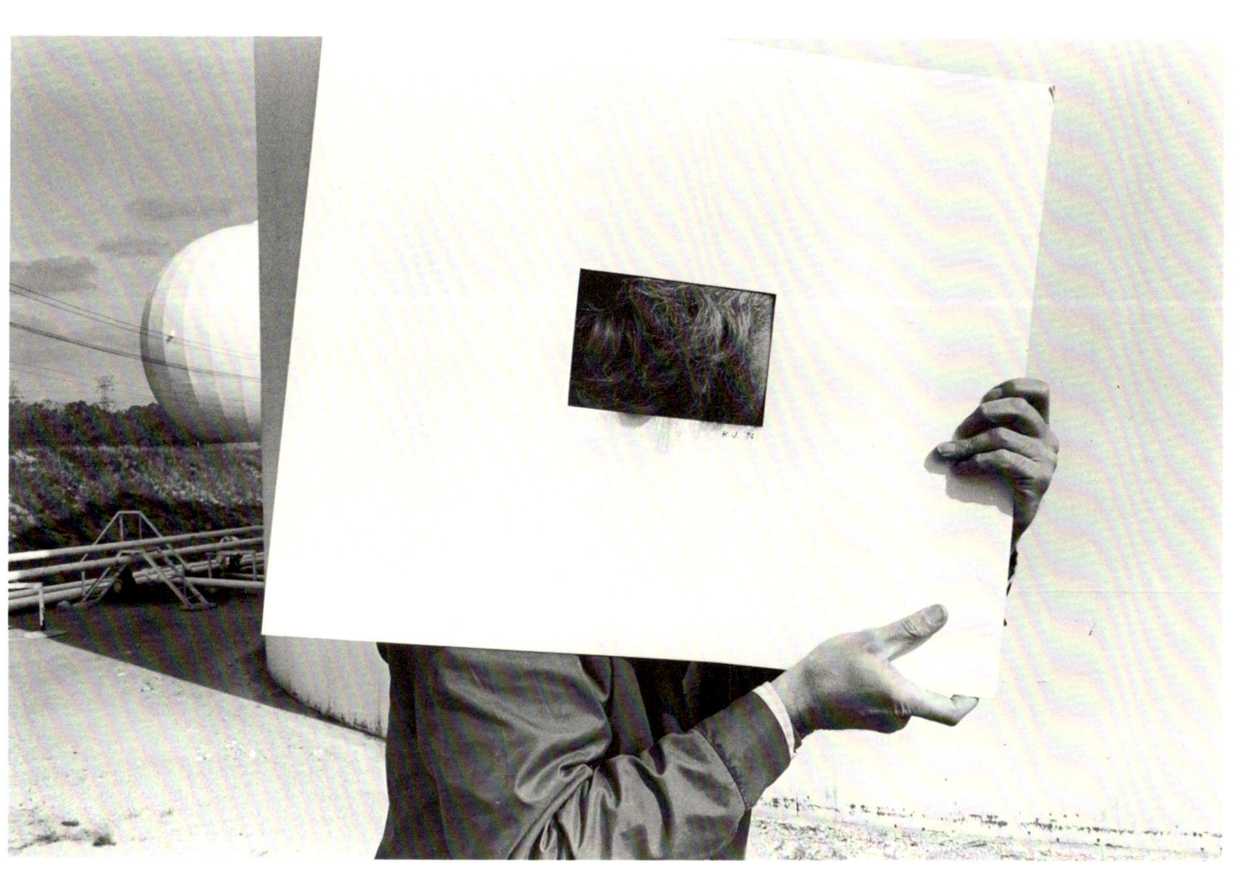

KENNETH JOSEPHSON
Chicago, Illinois
K.J., 1976

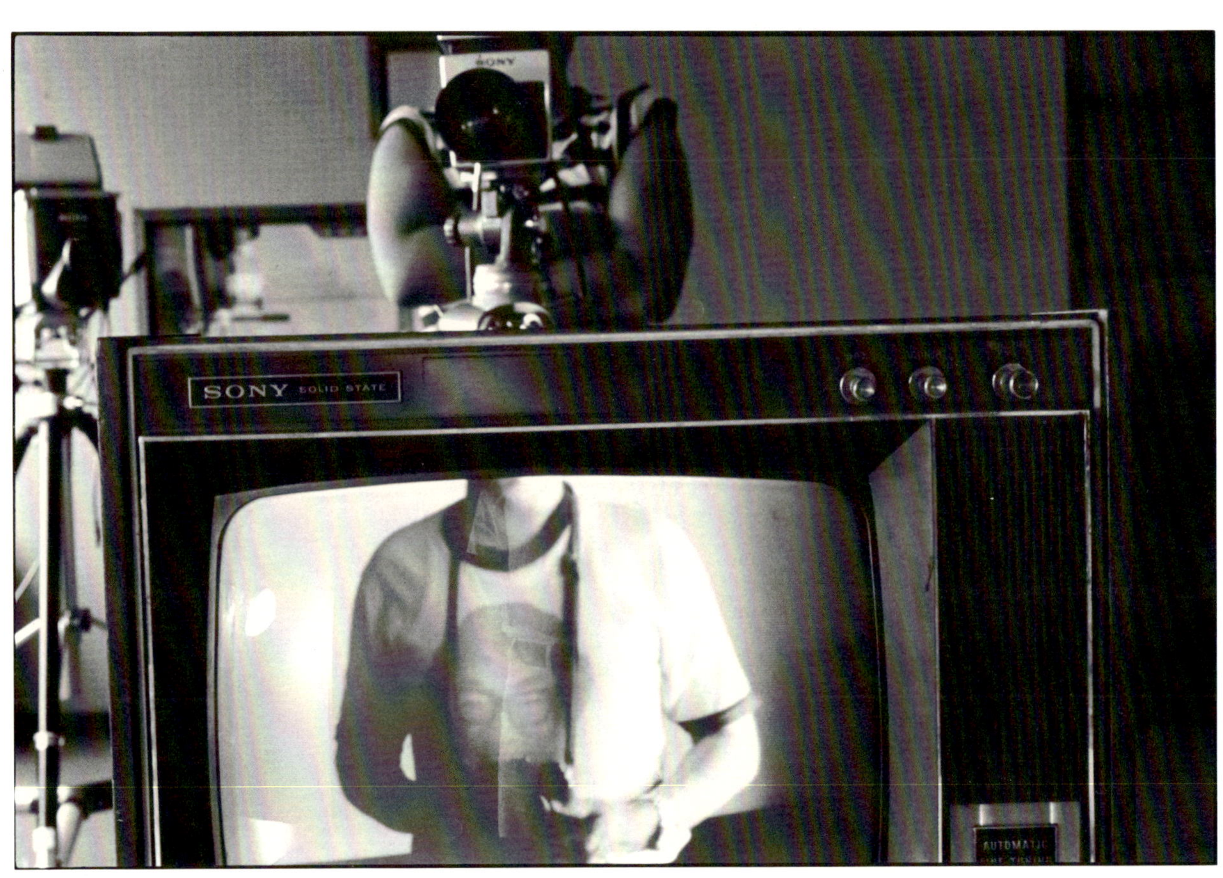

EIKOH HOSOE
Tokyo, Japan
Self-Portrait Taken on the Day of Photography, 1978

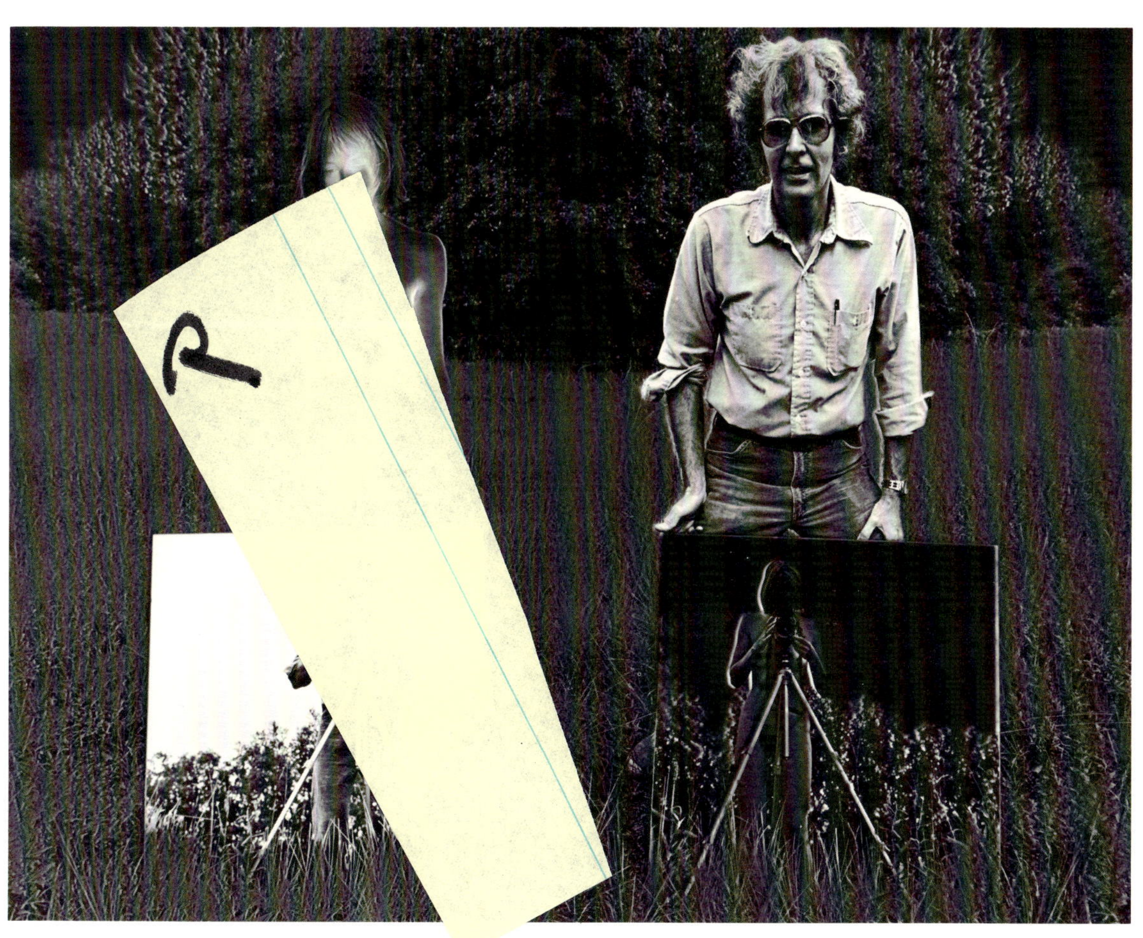

JERRY N. UELSMANN
Gainesville, Florida
Self-Portrait as Artist and Model, 1977

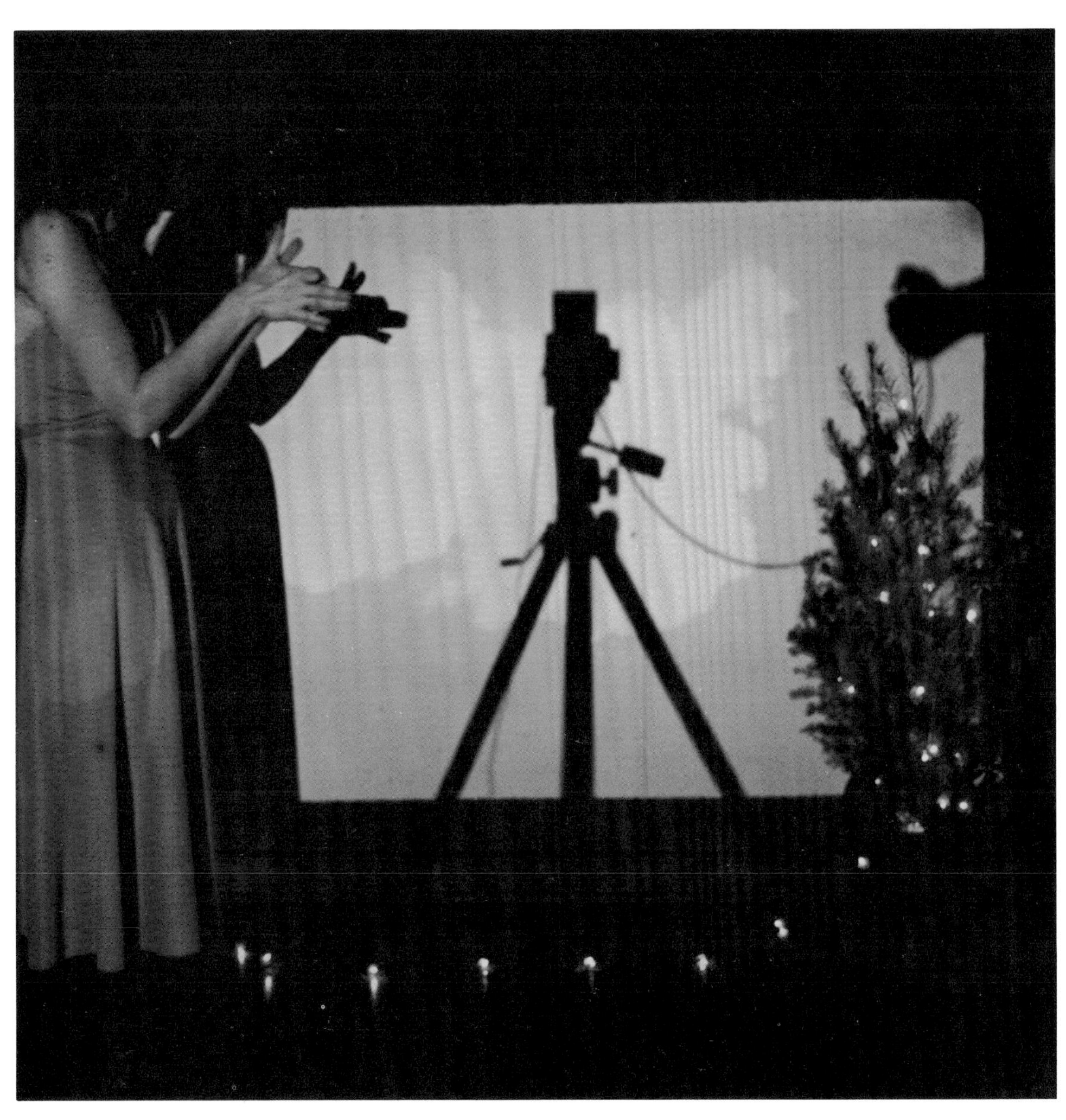

ANDRE HALUSKA
Newark, Delaware
Doghead and Shadows, 1977

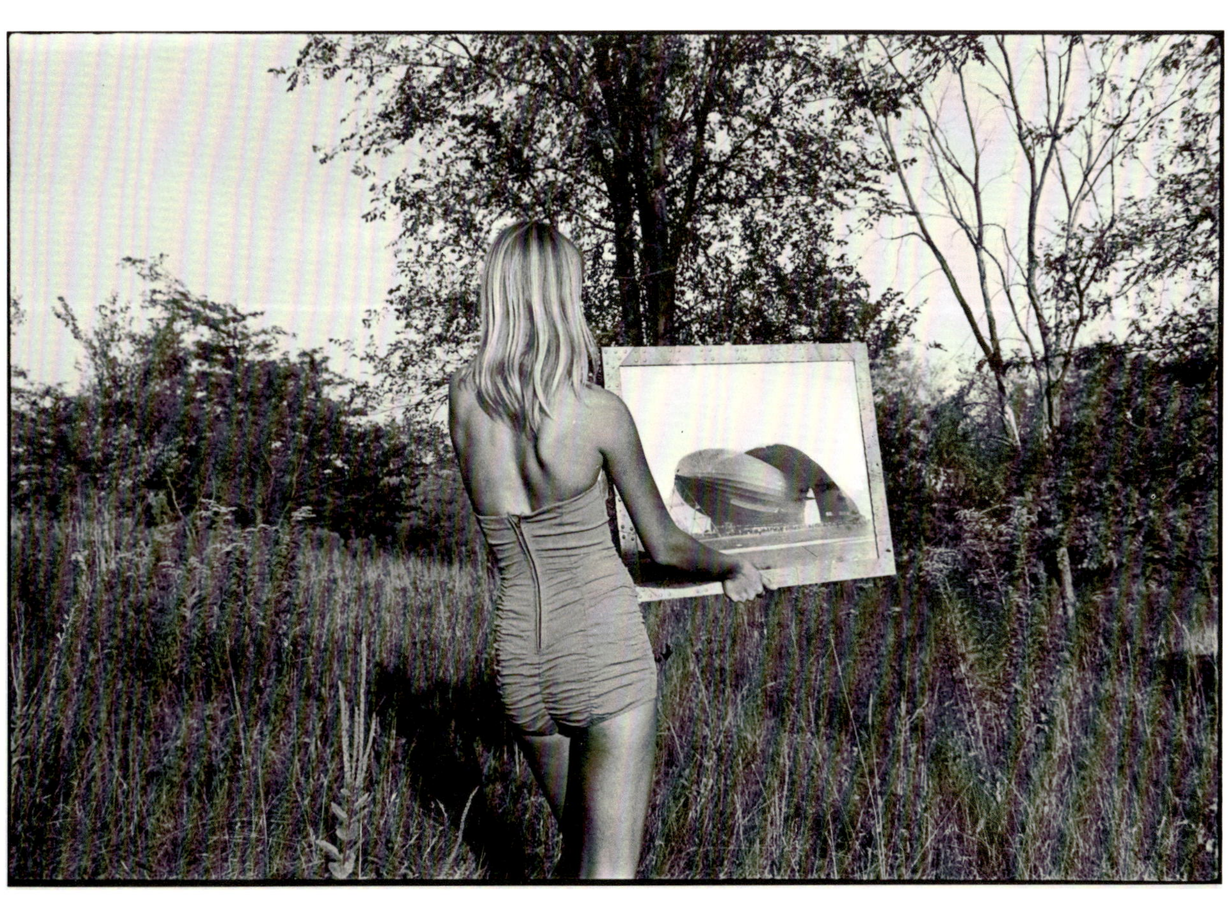

GWEN WIDMER
Cedar Falls, Iowa
Self-Portrait with Model, 1976

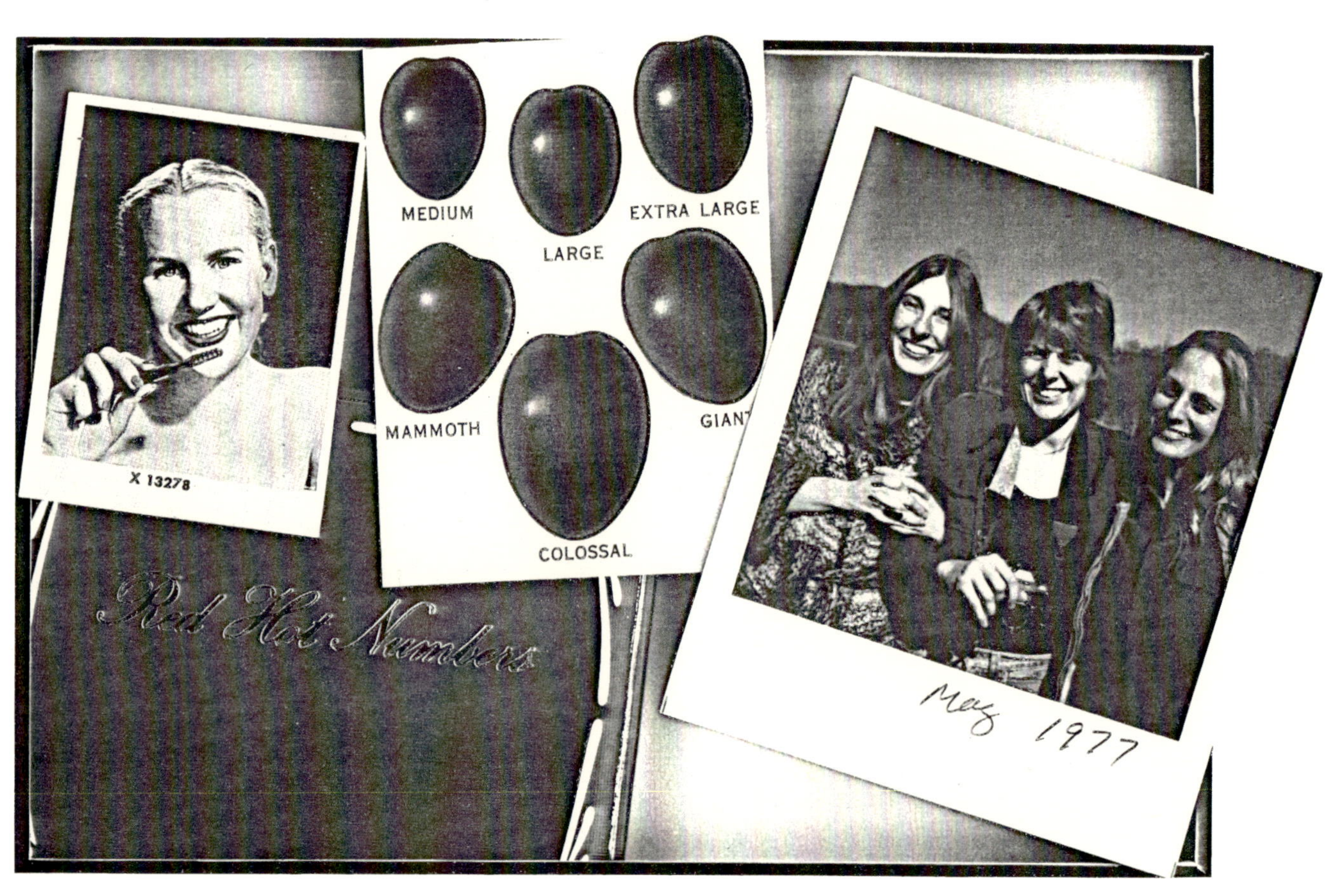

JOYCE CULVER
Rochester, New York
Red Hot Numbers, 1977

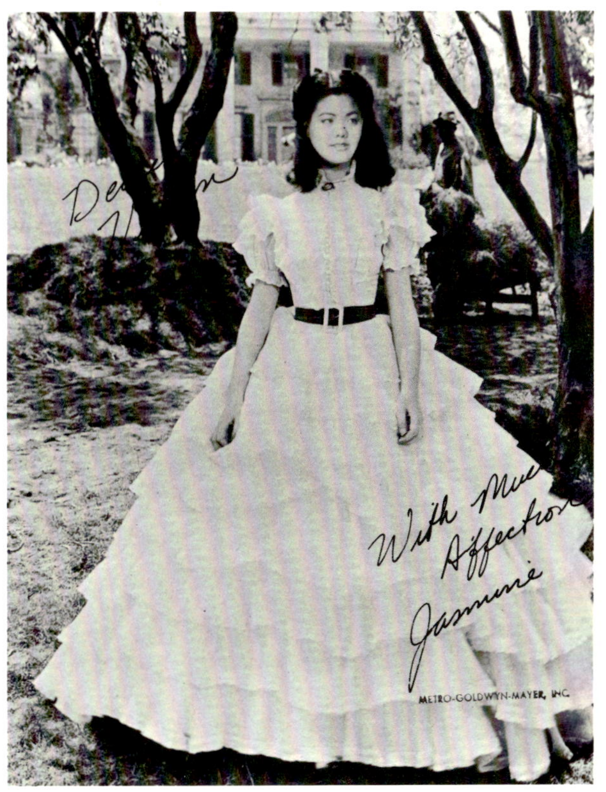

Autograph — Vivien   *Autograph — Elizabeth*

JASMINE SHIGEMURA

Pearl City, Hawaii

From the ''Transfiguration Series,'' 1978

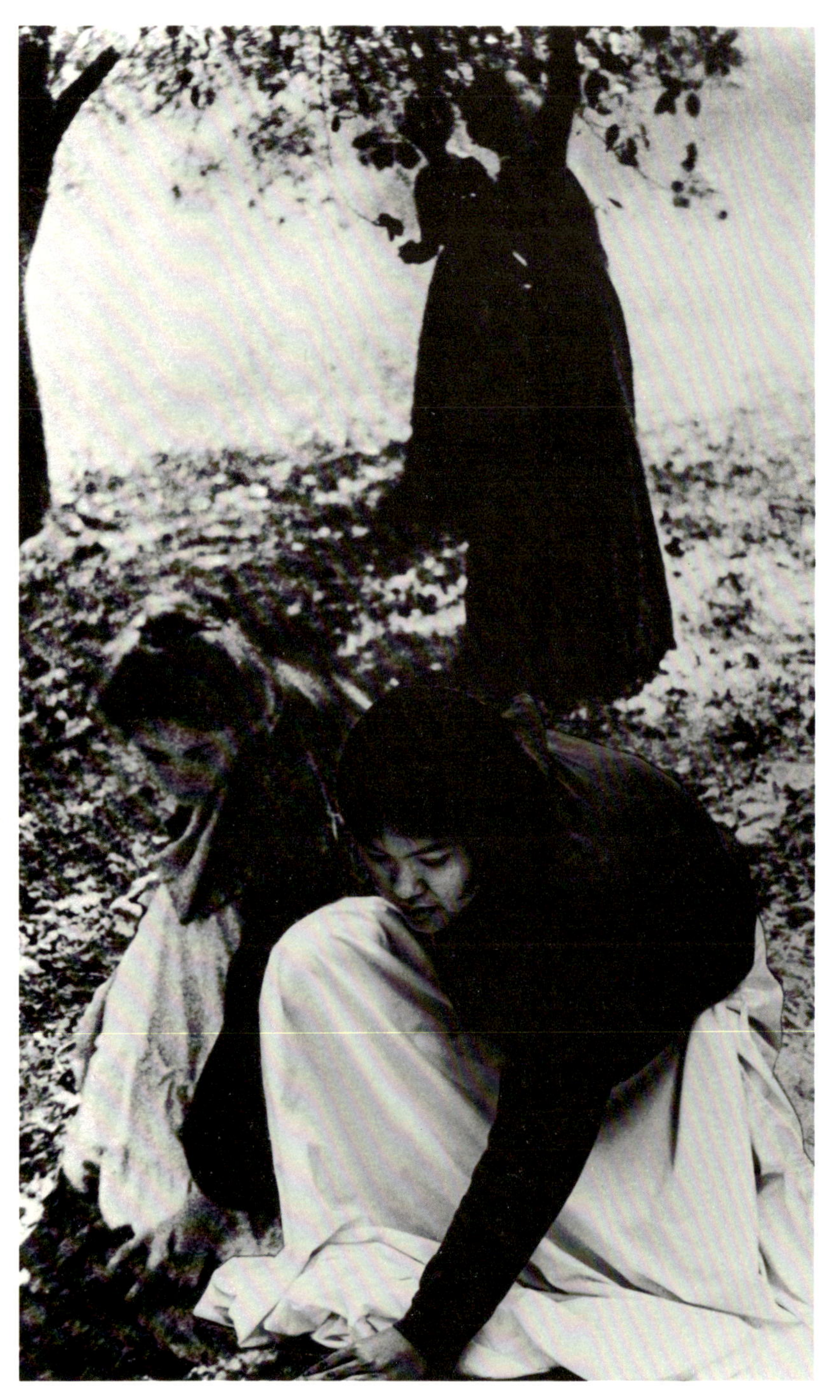

SANDRA Y. OGURO
Los Angeles, California
Pentimento #6, 1978

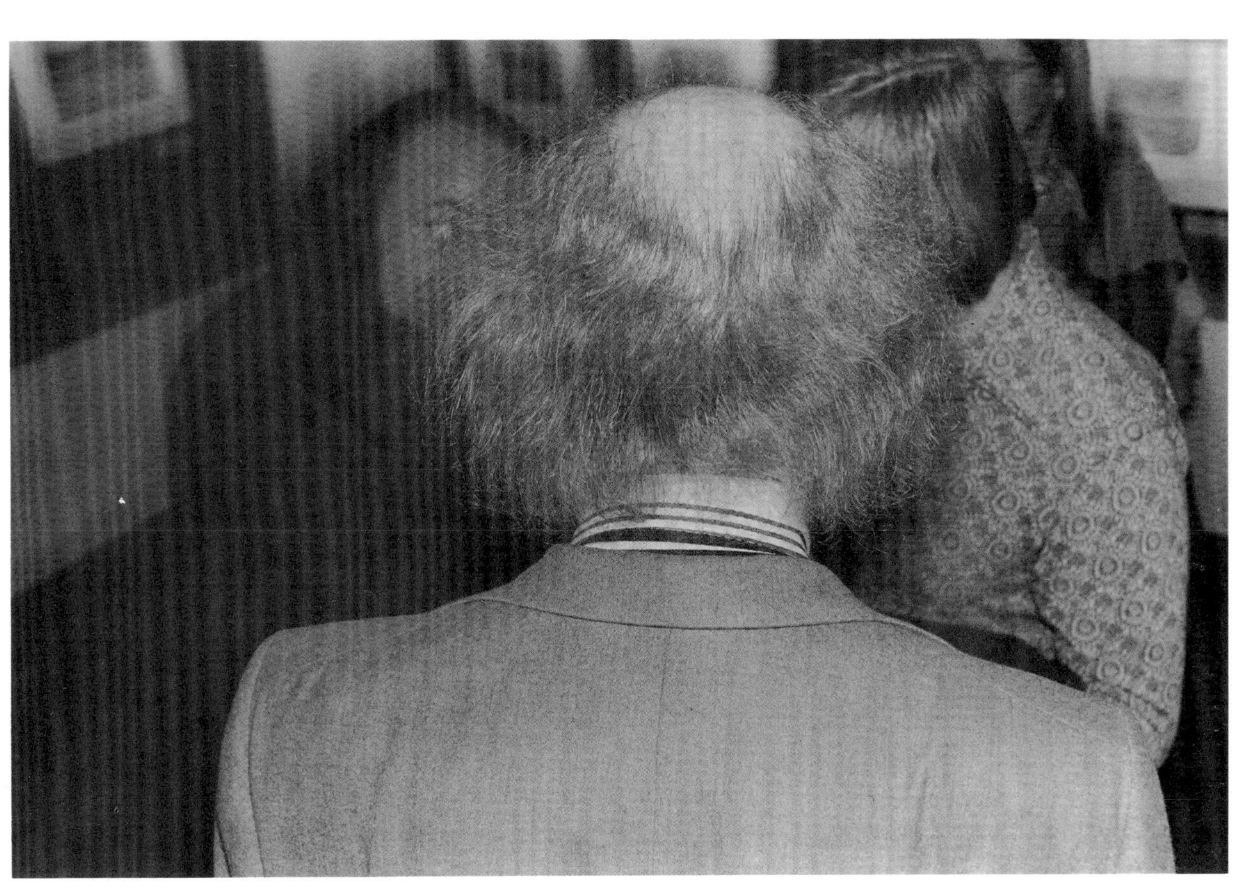

SANDY HUME
Boulder, Colorado
Manifestation of Self, Beaumont #7, 1976

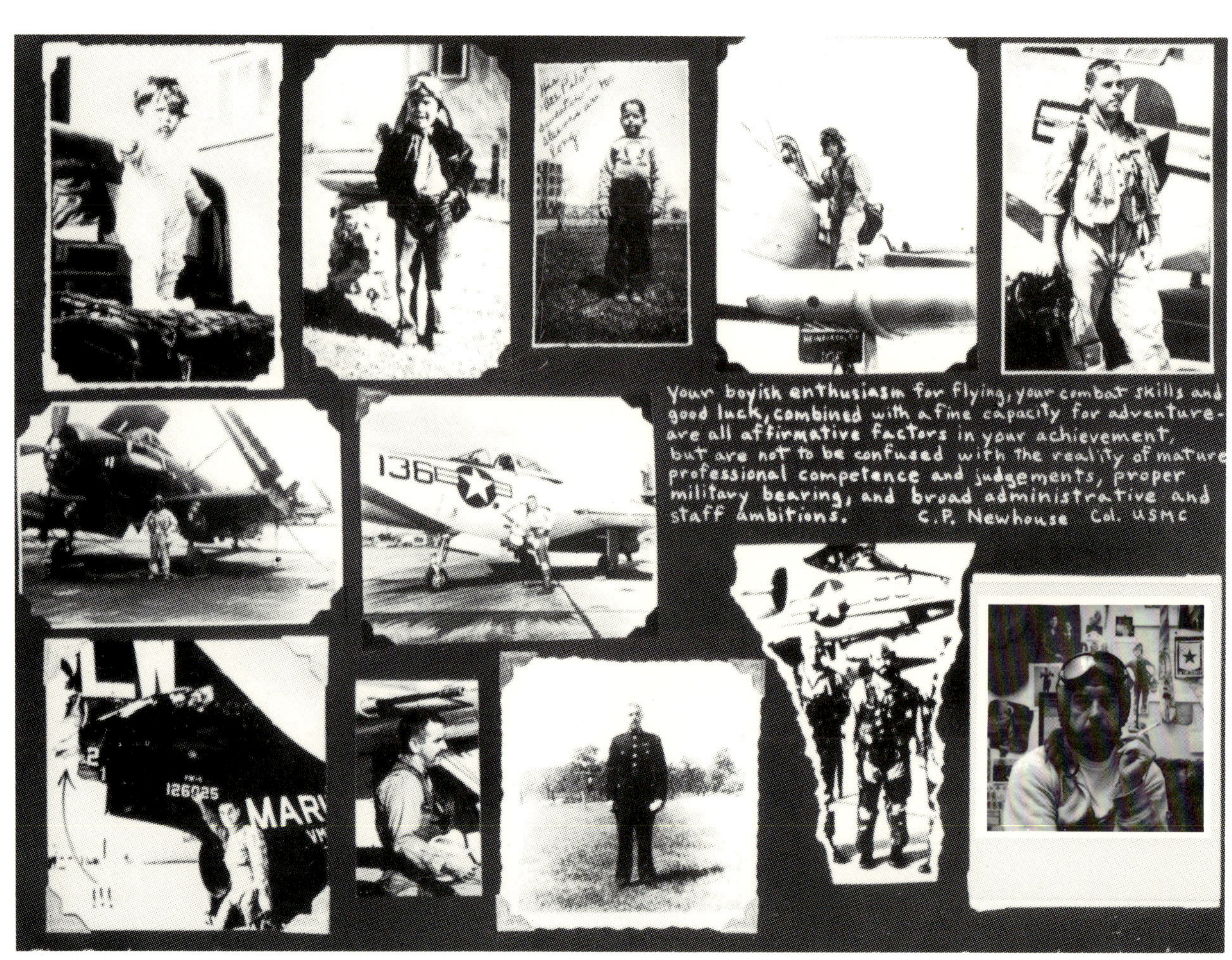

ROBERT HEINECKEN
Los Angeles, California
The Evolution of the Hair of the Artist as Aviator,
or Variations on the Frontal Pose, 1974

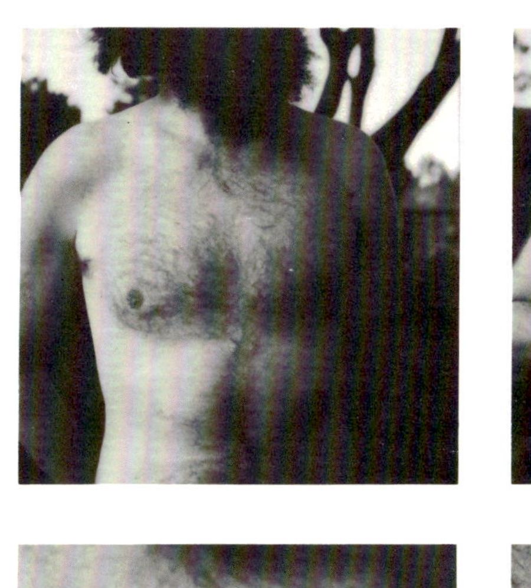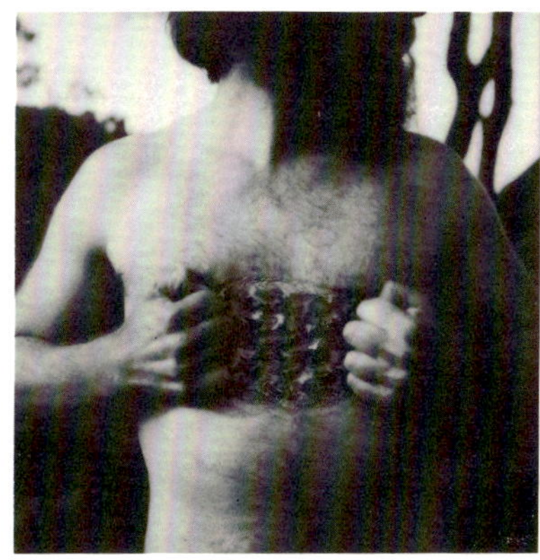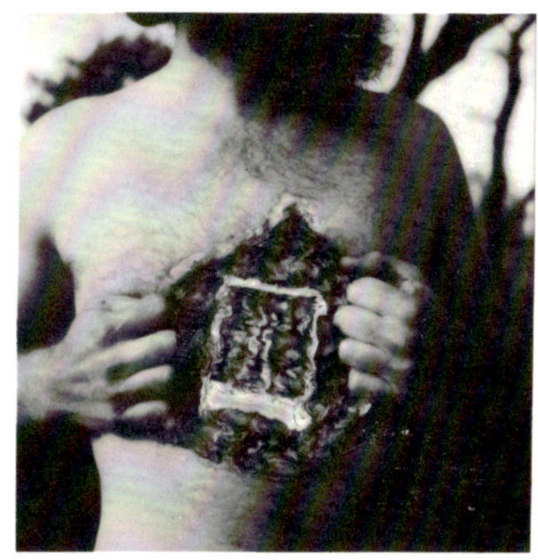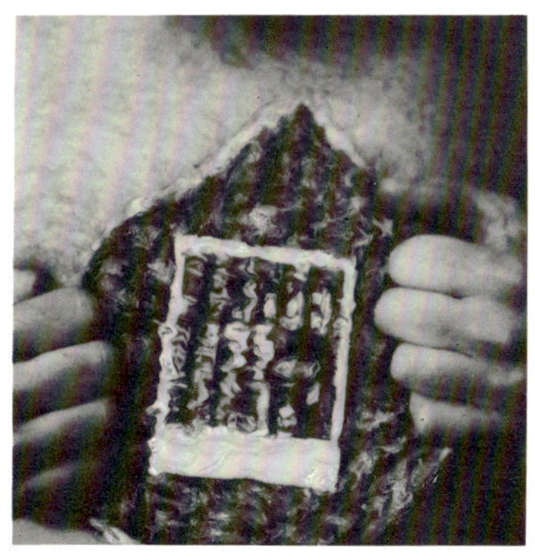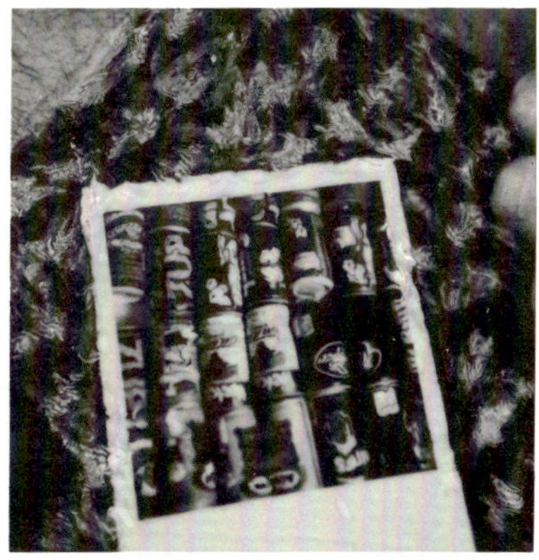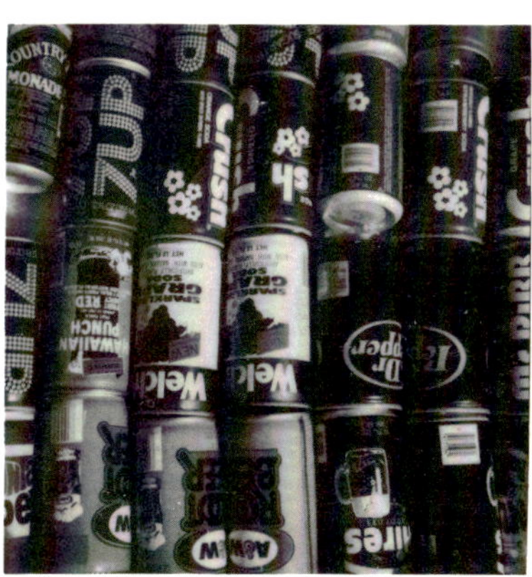

DON GRUBER
Pacific Grove, California
Self-Portrait, 1978

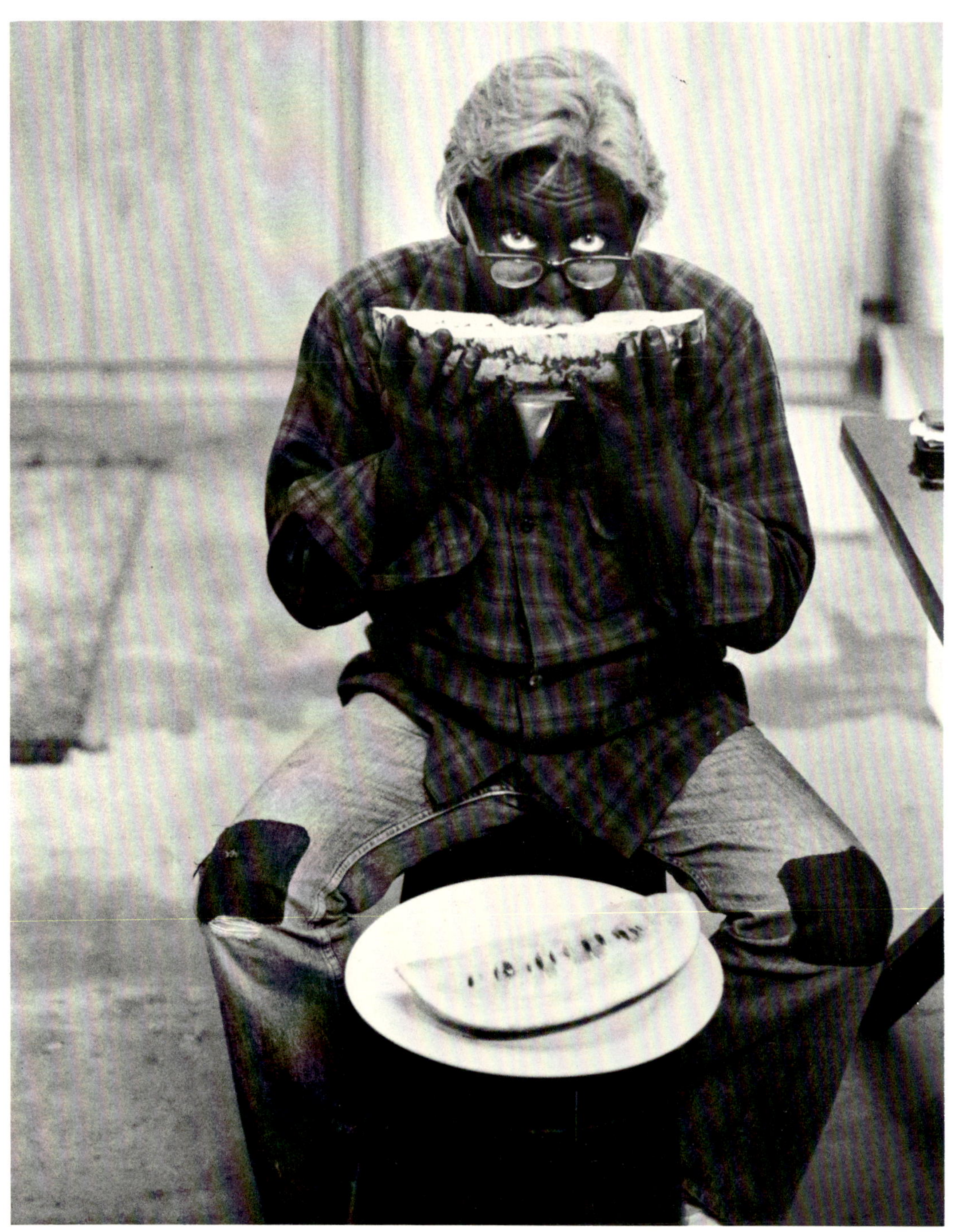

BRUCE WALLIN
Venice, California
Portrait of the Artist In Blackface, Attempting to Dislodge
Parameters of Liberalism Acquired through Middle Class Child
Rearing Practices, 1977

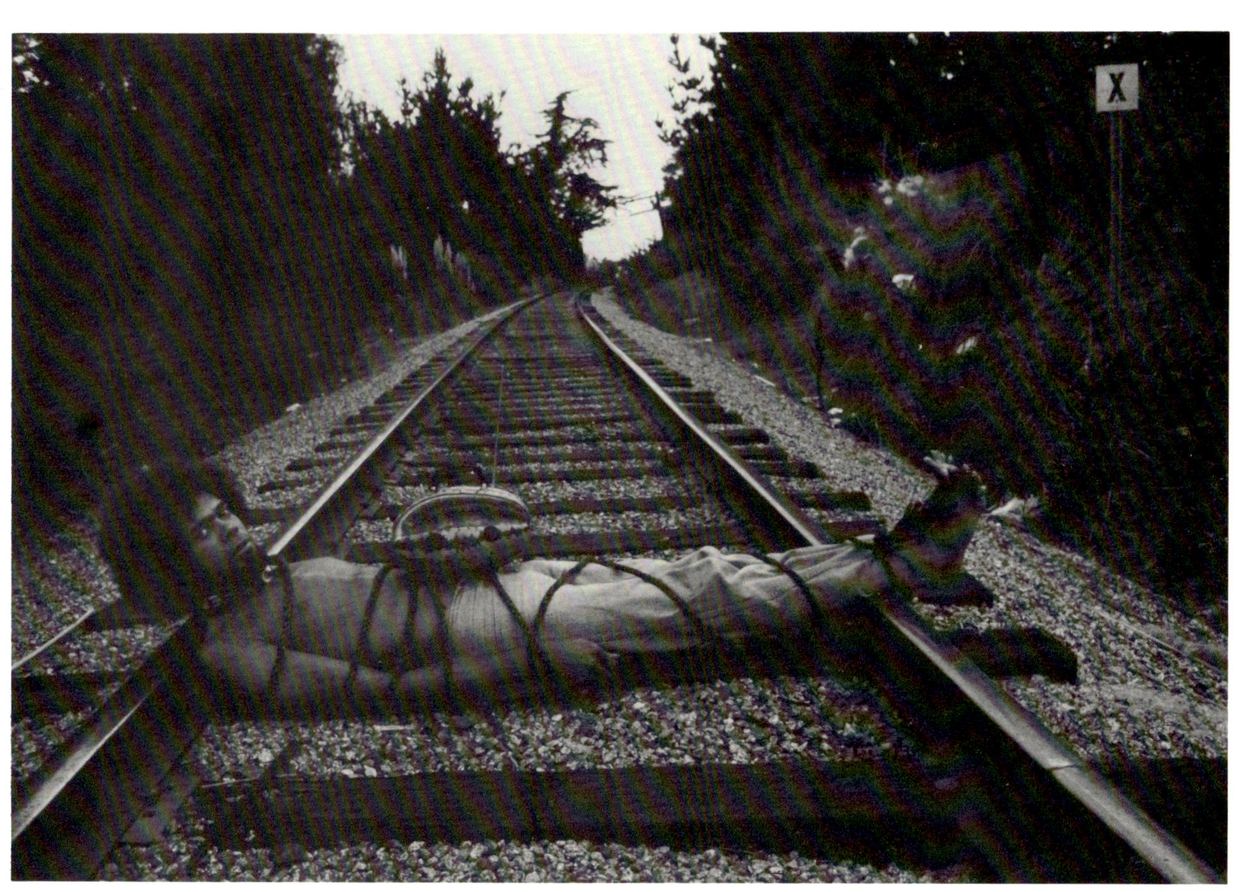

KA MORAIS
Santa Cruz, California
Radio Free Dixie, 1977

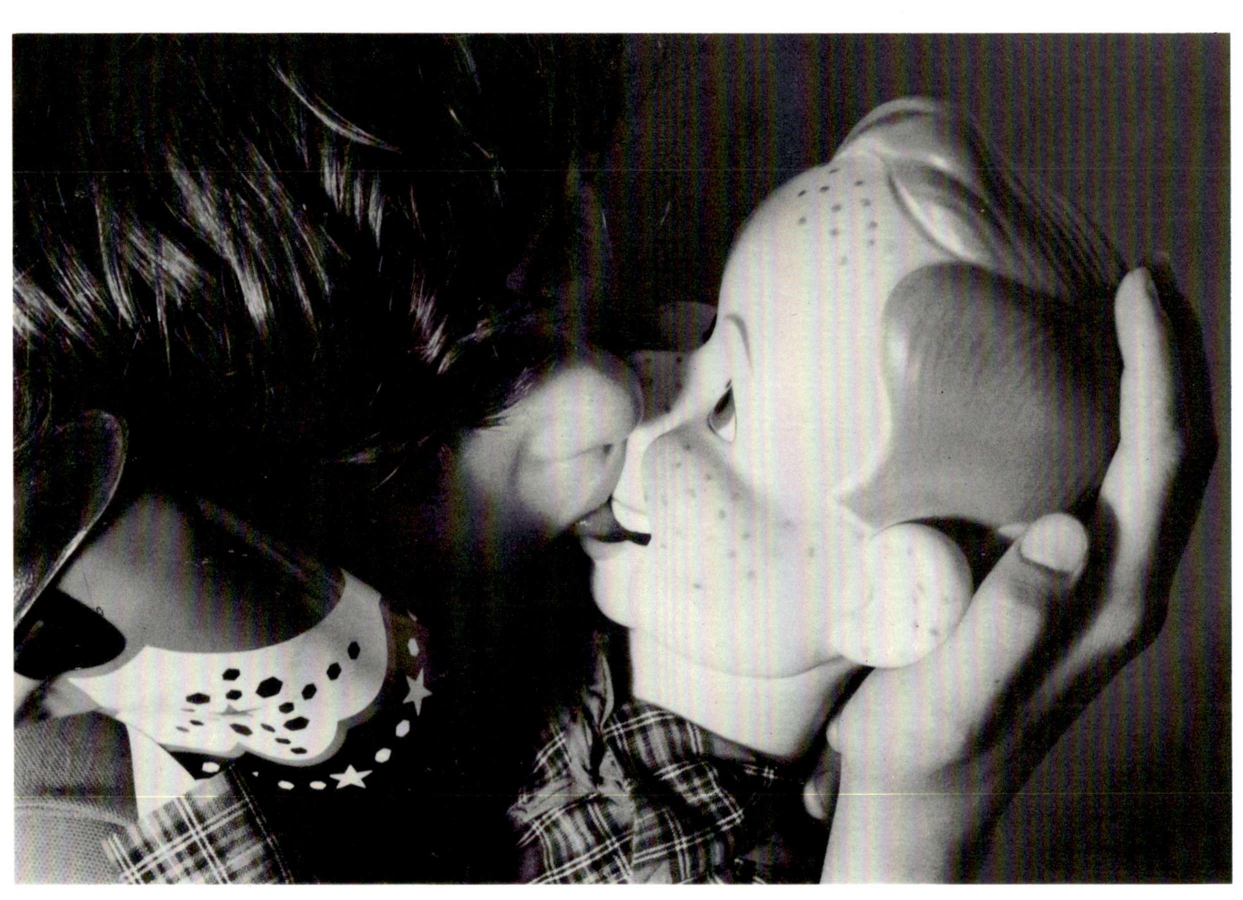

MARCIA RESNICK
New York, New York
From "Re-visions," 1978
She Secretly Lusted for Her Television Idols

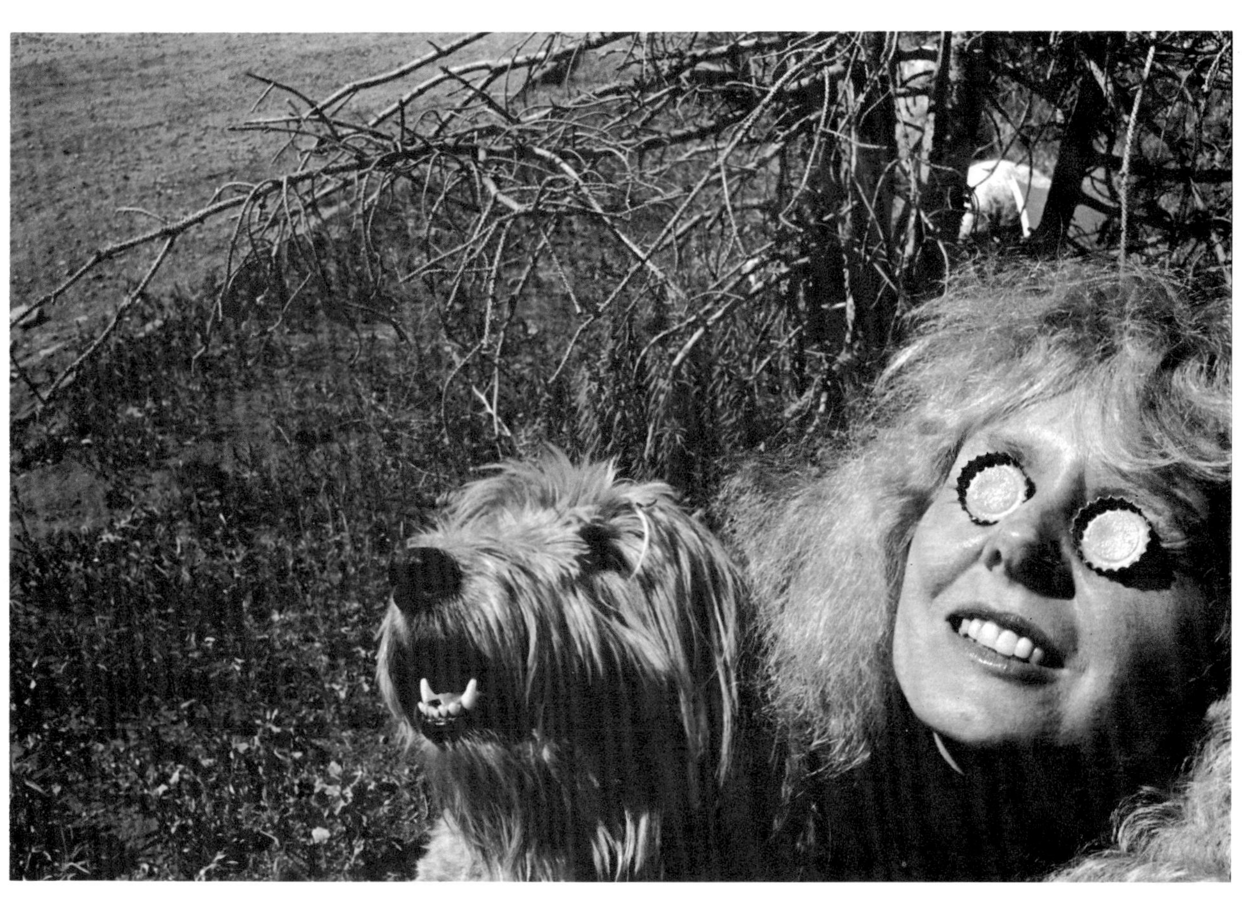

CHERI HISER
Portland, Oregon
Sandy And Annie, 1974

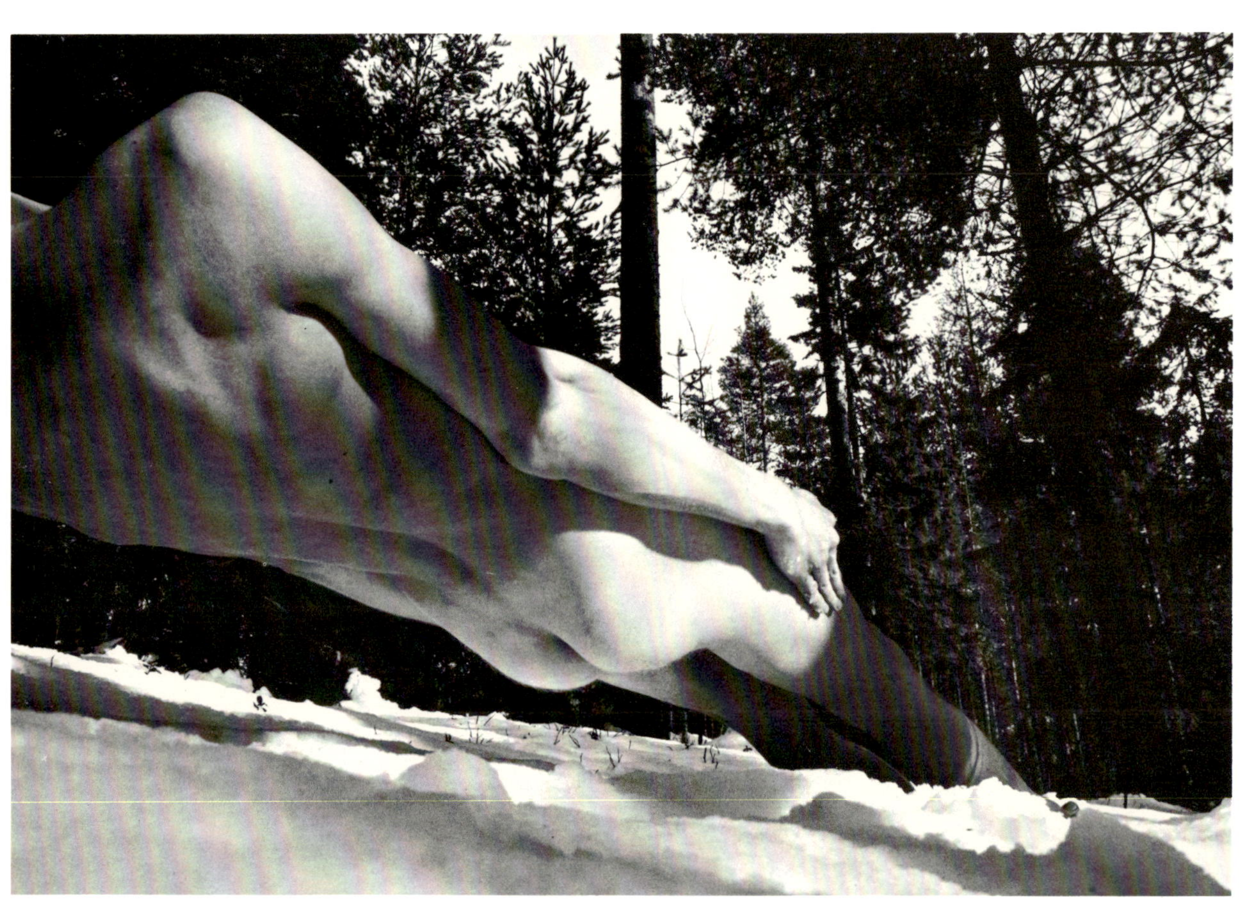

ARNO RAFAEL MINKKINEN
Andover, Massachusetts
Hyvinkää, Finland, 1976

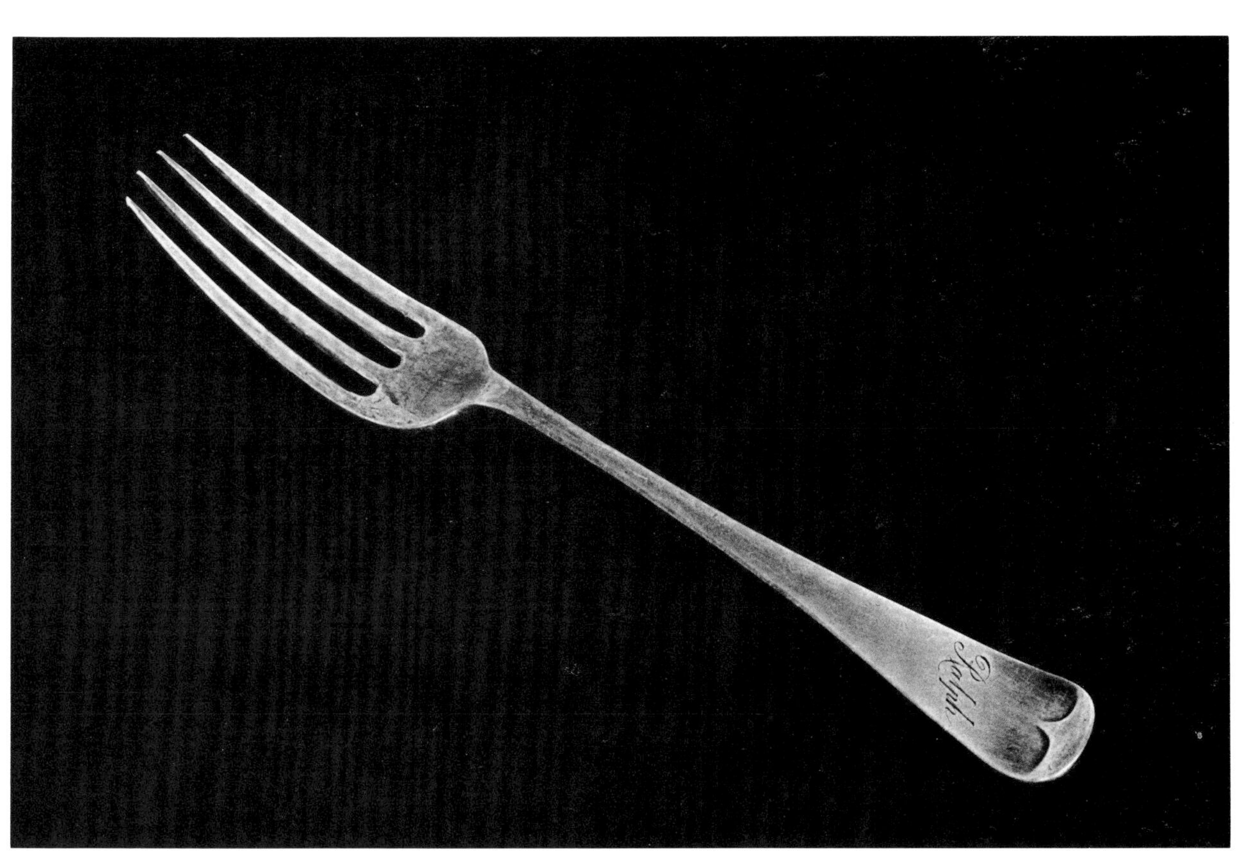

RALPH GIBSON
New York, New York
Portrait of a Fork Named Ralph, 1977

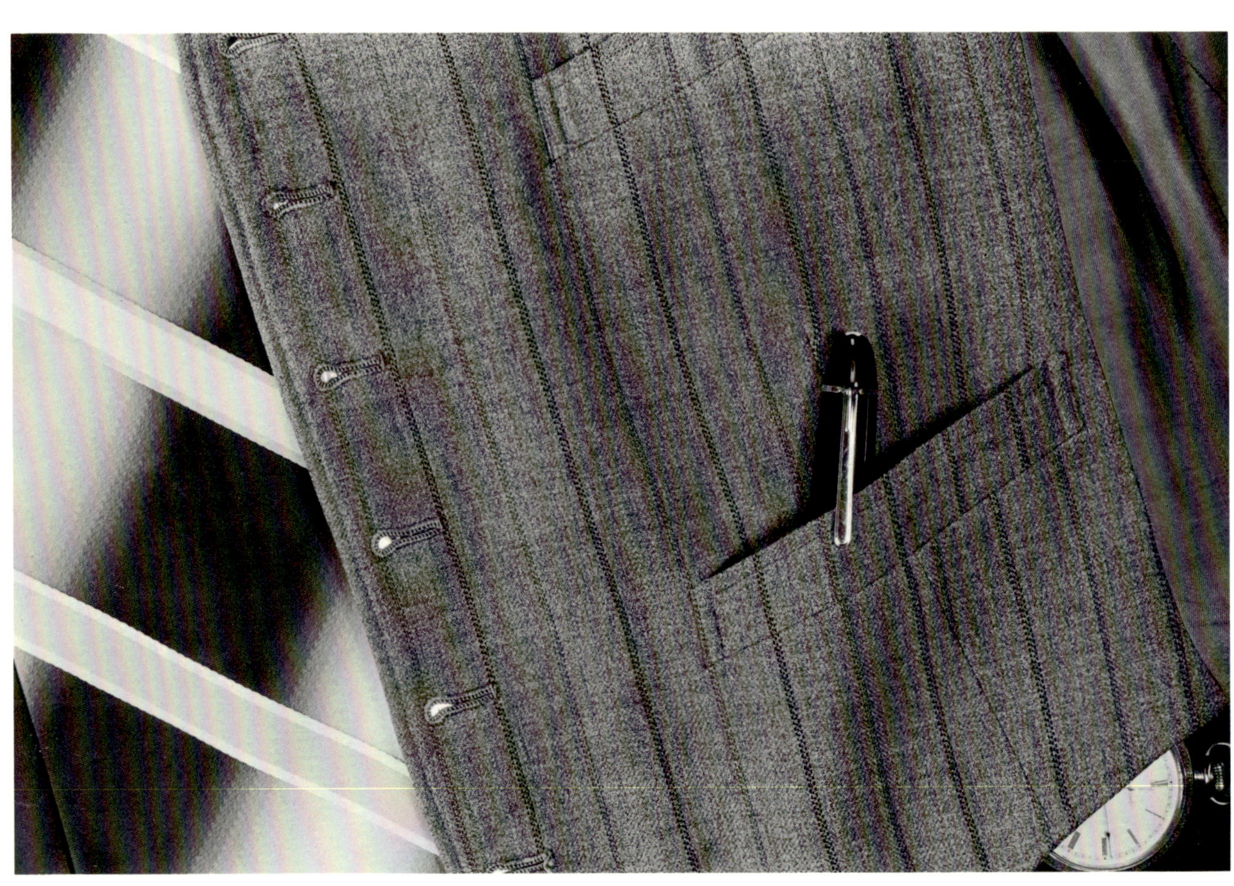

PETER DELORY
Aspen, Colorado
The Diplomat, 1978

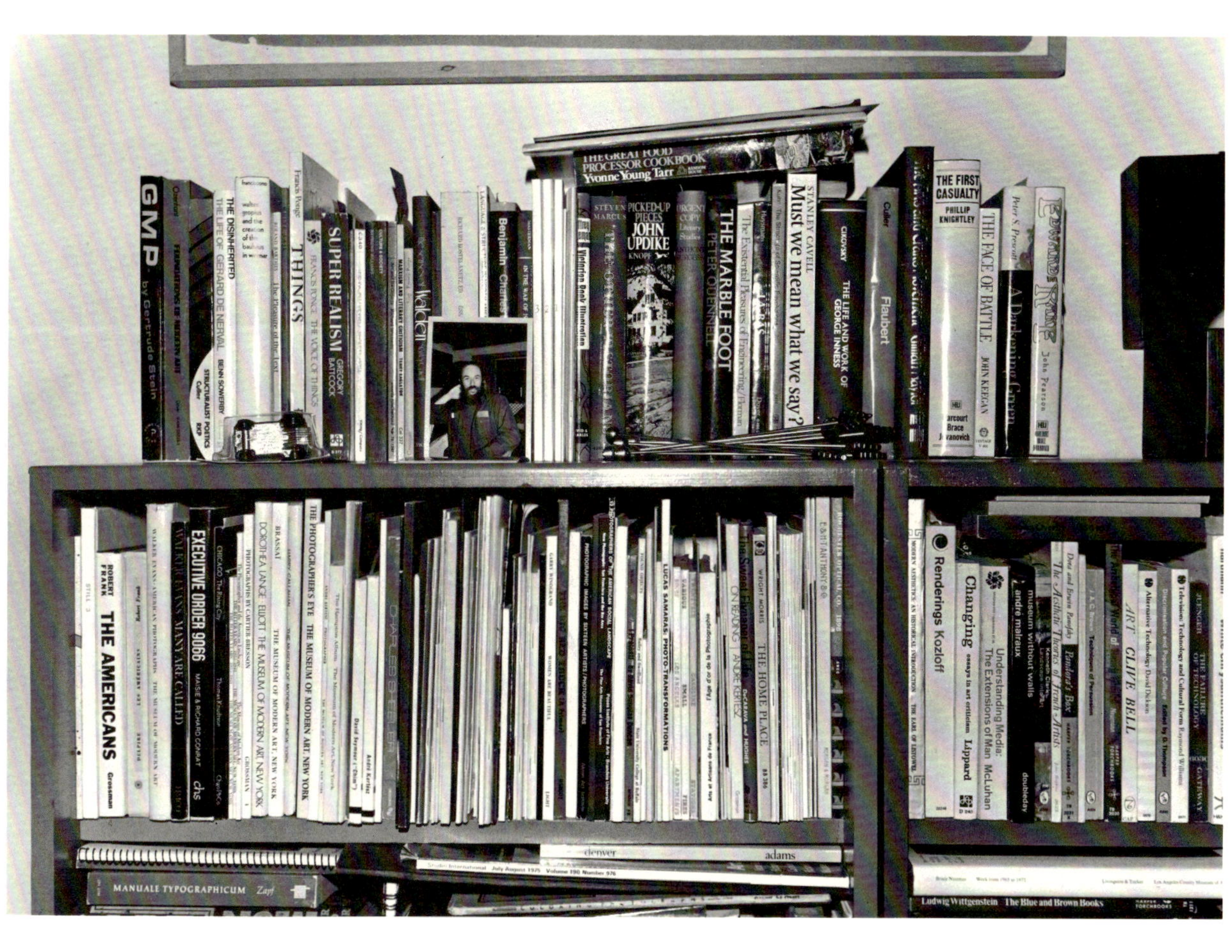

THOMAS F. BARROW
Albuquerque, New Mexico
From the series "Libraries"
TFB, Albuquerque, 1978

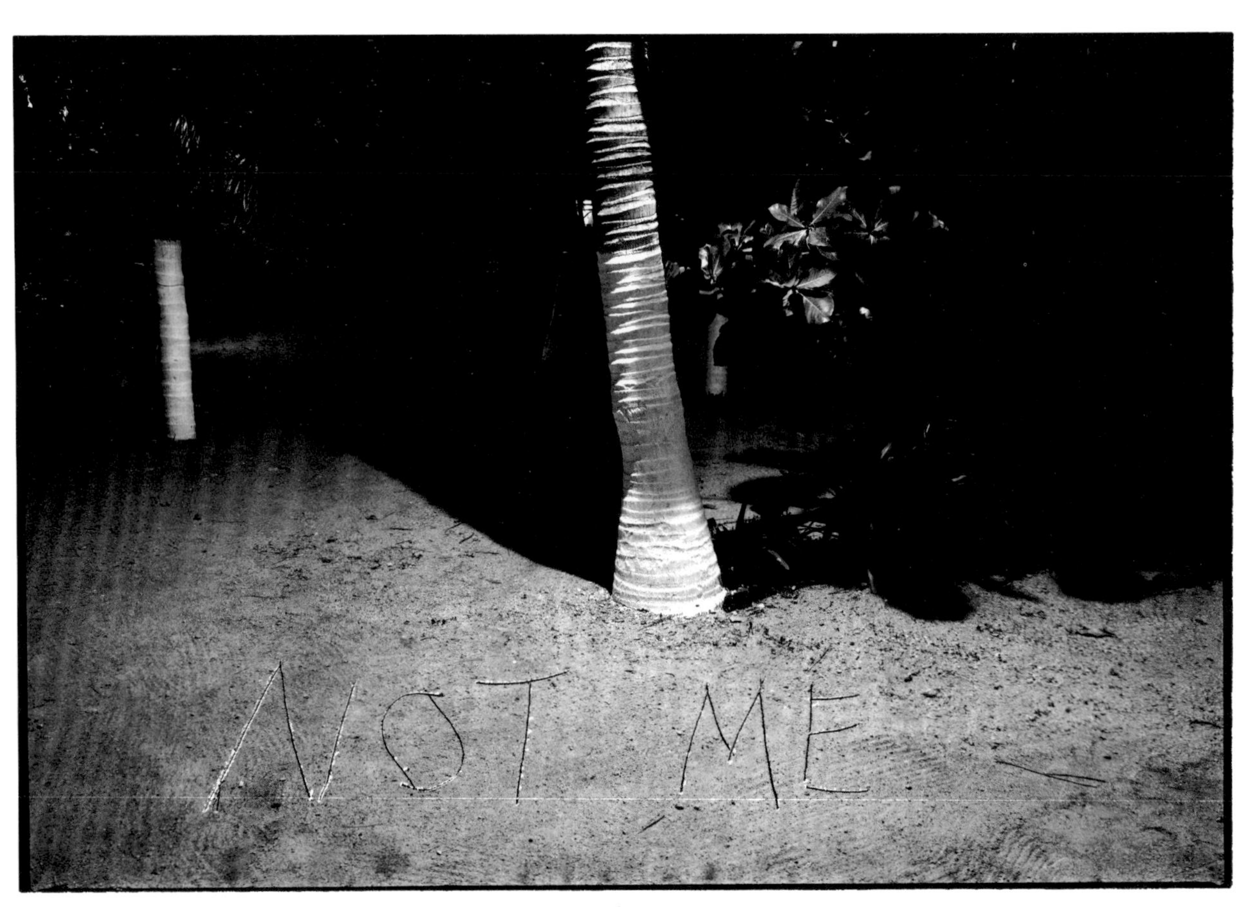

REED ESTABROOK
Cedar Falls, Iowa
Not Me, 1978

On Self-Portrayal

R. Duncan Wallace, M.D.

AWARENESS AND SELF-PORTRAYAL

The process of self-portrayal relies strongly upon the condition of awareness and the process of attaining it. The self-portrait is a physically created record of expression of the individual's awareness of the sense of self. It is a specific expression about a specific entity — the self. It creates an awareness of the self to the self-observer. It condenses time and gives us a record of our historical self-continuity. The self-portrait reveals patterns of our self, patterns of forces manifesting through structure, of forces flowing through channels of process and of forces mutually influencing and inter-relating in an eco-system of multilevel organizations.

The self is a composite of these forces. The awareness of the self, manifest in self-portrayal, is the total awareness of all previous awarenesses accumulated during the individual's existence. Awareness of the self is extremely important for fullest growth. It is integral to the growth of consciousness.

What is this important entity *awareness?* Awareness of what awareness is seems crucial. Artistic and sensitive people have awareness. Knowledgeable and understanding people have it. Any who seek new frontiers have it. They all can use it without knowing exactly what it is. But if you know what it is, you can make better use of it.

Awareness is a condition resulting from knowledge about something. It always springs from contrast. At elementary levels, awareness involves noticing and identifying the contrast. At more complex levels it also encompasses recognition, new meaning, understanding, expansion and a sensed belonging in the universe.

Closely allied to awareness is perceiving, the act of receiving an impression from the five senses, the sense of intuition, or the action of *grasping* in a knowledgeable, understanding sense. Knowing about perceiving and about what is being perceived is awareness. The ability to perceive results in new awarenesses.

HOW AWARENESS COMES INTO BEING

Awareness comes into being only in specific circumstances. There must be a contrast between at least two entities. These can be at any level, such as contrasting shapes or colors, where a distinction is recognized. The eye or mind's eye moves from one thing to the other in order to notice the contrast. With the addition of the factor of distance from the two things forming the contrast, an awareness emerges. *Movement between at least two points of contrast observed from a distance results in awareness.*

The state of mind of the observer changes the quality of the awareness. A knowledgeable person may perceive a greater awareness than a less knowledgeable person. The more knowledgeable person brings experience and previous awarenesses to mind when observing the new instance. The reverberations of contrast are greater and the sense of vision is enhanced. The new awareness can be utilized for new capability or stored in memory for future use. The new awareness may also attract further search, providing a moment of partial or complete understanding which, in turn, can fuel further search or invention.

THE LOCUS OF AWARENESS

Awareness seems to have a locus in space. Ask yourself

where you perceive your awareness sense to be. As you observe and become aware of your own awareness sense you realize you must gain distance from it to see it. That movement, to provide a contrast, gives the sense of a place in space, usually outside of yourself. Whether or not the locus of awareness is actually outside yourself, it is often perceived that way by your mind. In order for your mind to have an awareness, it must also have distance in order to create the new contrast. This constant distancing keeps providing the sense of a locus in space.

When you observe a photograph you are clear that your sense of awareness is from a place very near your point of observation. That's because the contrast lines are directly in front of you as you observe. Once you attempt to observe yourself observing the photograph, however, you then move somewhere else in a spatial mind sense in order to observe the awareness. This movement of your mind through *spaces* keeps providing contrast points for the new awarenesses.

THE AWARENESS GROWTH CYCLE

Awareness is part of a cycle of human progress. Perceived awareness leads to the sense of discovery, identification and recognition. That, in turn, leads to experimentation and to the elaboration of possibilities of technique. This leads to an increase in capability which, in turn, provides new access and application sites. The newly established capability provides an even greater awareness which starts the cycle again. Awareness leads to new capability which leads to further new awareness. And so it goes, cycling onward through history. The greater your capability and awareness, the more likely will be your capability at growth.

A knowledge of awareness is so critical to observing and understanding the process of self-portrayal that this departure has been justified. By re-weaving awareness back into self-portrayal we will have more discernible directions.

OBSERVING THE SELF-PORTRAIT

As you observe your own self-portrait or that of others, you realize you are observing a composition of many things. That's an awareness. As you become more intimately in touch with the elements within the self-portrait you gain even greater awareness of self, or of other processes. The interplay of contrasting patterns in front of you, your knowledge from living, the movement you apply with your eye and mind's eye and the distance both in terms of measurable space from the photograph and historical distance from experience bring the awareness of a new view of self into being.

From your observation, what is your awareness of the essence of the self which is composed in front of you? Where is its main life force going, the sense of the future direction? Where did it come from? What energy and capability does this self seem to rely on most strongly? What are the certainties it seems to have confidence in? What are the ingredients of your past experience that seem to come to your awareness as you play with the photographic image? What does it communicate to you? What does it kindle in you? What do you most enjoy relating to in the self-portrait? What is most meaningful? What important message or messages seem to spring out toward you? Where are the alluring and attracting points? What moods and emotions seem to show? How is all of that similar and different from former self-awarenesses? What measurable change now becomes obvious to you? What new things which you didn't realize fully are you now aware of from self-portrayal? What are your preferences, your sense of style? All of these have validity and potential for further self-growth.

THE COMPOSITION OF THE SELF-PORTRAIT

In my experience of analyzing, appreciating and understanding photographic images, those images deemed important by the photographers I have studied deeply have demonstrated some self-felt quality. The image has evoked an intimate resonance with something inside his or her mind. In that limited sense all photographs made by creative photographers are self-portrayals. In contrast, an intended self-portrait is a much *fuller* image. It has included both conscious and unconscious elements on a much grander scale. A full, as opposed to partial, self-portrait has a discernible identity of larger structures and organizations of wholes. Its levels of mastery are observable. It is a symphony of inter-related entities, orchestrated by a self-conductor and self-organizing influence.

The metaphorical states of matter and energy in the self's consciousness are present. Matter appears in structure, flexibility, flow and gaseous expansion suggestions (solid, liquid, gas). The emotions, movement, force and direction depict the energy. The source of life in the photographic image can usually be localized at a place of greatest prominence. In other words, where is the suggested source which the strongest life force seems to emanate from? From below? From above? From the foreground or background? From structure, flow or airy space? Where is that place within your own self?

The levels of awareness of the self accumulated from life experience are inferred in the self-portrait. Preferences in style and taste are present, revealing how the self likes to see itself and relate to itself. Finally, a sense of the self's repertoire of capability is suggested in the self-portrait. How powerful? How full? How confident? How open-ended? How certain? How inspiring and inspired?

The self-portrait is a composition of greater organized forces and its maker's current developed knowledge about life. It shows some of its own form of how it lives its own life. The self-portrait reveals, on deeper inspection, how it holds its own life in terms of growth, importance, self-regard, opportunity, fear and pleasure.

THE SIGNIFICANCE OF SELF-PORTRAYAL

Self-portrayal has great significance because of several areas of possible impact effect. It is much more than a simple narcissistic exercise.

First, self-portrayal provides a solidified moment of the sense of self. The fullness that can be produced in a self-portrayal is often surprising. When you look at something real and physical which you have produced, your awareness increases considerably. It's easier to have it out in front of you in an externalized and real way than inside in thought patterns only. Things are seen that were not noticed before. The sense of an entity, called the self, in front of you gives an awareness of wholeness. And yet within that wholeness are individual and other elements which have the sense of their own identity as well. What a marvelous complex composition a self really is. It provides a new sense of certainty about oneself. With this clear certainty comes greater efficiency and less waste of mind energy than results through the consumption of unclear uncertainty.

Second, the self-portrait compresses time, energy, force and motion into an identity. The expansion growth of the personality can readily be seen in the self-portrait. We have looked at those elements above when discussing how to observe the self-portrait. When you make more than one self-portrait through a period of time you have other reference points to relate to. You can compare and contrast. You can see the actual growth which you have accumulated by contrasting the two photographic records. You will be assured and convinced of your own growth movement, made real in front of you.

A bonus from the self-portrait is that you can use it to invent new possibilities from what you see in front of you. As you gain a new awareness and apply new possibilities and potentials, you can suggest to yourself new areas in which to gain capability. These will lead to new awareness. The cycle of human progress, operating through your own self, will be enhanced in its upward spiral.

Interestingly, old self-portraits take on new meaning at later times in life. Certain things not yet related to consciously will be readily apparent after the present self-portrait becomes an old self-portrait. They will require further life experience and awareness development for you to see them. Old self-portraits never die, they just change with your changed and increased awareness. In that sense the self-portrait is truly an awareness activator. Growth progress rates can be determined from them and then actively modified if desired.

Third, the impact upon photographers at seeing their self-portraits is variable. Some are embarrassed. Some are delighted. Some are secretly delighted but outwardly embarrassed. Some have a sense of new awareness and solidified being. Others may have a confusion. Whatever your response is to seeing yourself, you will definitely feel an impact. Attaching awareness and discerning the meaning of that impact upon yourself is an important action. Curiosity about why the impact was as it was is useful for increased awareness and further growth.

The biggest gain from self-impact of the self-portrait is the realization that you have an entity, your self, which you can relate to. You can utilize the self as an information source. You can utilize it as a command movement force growing in your life. You can ask it questions. You can treat it well. You will always have a relationship with your self. In that sense, you will never be alone again. As you get more thoroughly into your own sense of self, you will discover much energy and emerging, evolving movement. As a result, you will discover the desire to share or demonstrate what is inside. You will want to touch others, metaphorically speaking. You will desire to communicate. And you probably will.

Fourth, through the recognition of one's own self comes the sense of respect or awe of the self. That leads to a sense of respect for others' selves. A sense of worship or awe for other selves begins the development of a consideration ethic.

Fifth, self-portrayal hastens and expands the process of self-disclosure, which comes from the inside and moves outside. It is emergent and expressionistic. As a result it implicitly offers the desire for communication and broader understanding with other selves. That form of understanding, through considerate touch and invited expression, enhances the quality of human relationships. It increases the sense of belonging in the broad human community. It leads people to want to be facilitative, synergistic and growth-oriented. It shows your own self, eventually, that feeling threatened is no longer necessary in a psychological sense. When you are willing to be fully disclosing without the sense of threat, you can't be hurt. You realize the old sense of threat was simply hiding a now discardable vulnerability, a fear of being hurt that you have now grown beyond. What a comfortable way of living and sensing your own being this leads to. As you do this even strangers that you will never know will be touched by your act of expression. They, too, can learn to remove their fear barriers or embarrassment barriers and not withhold important evolved knowledge from our world. Evolution's fine products won't die, wasted.

Self-portrayal is an act which solidifies the sense of self. It provides a greater awareness. It facilitates further expansion and evolution of growth. It produces an emergent-expressionistic directionality. It facilitates broader understanding and broader belonging. It moves toward gracing the world with a consideration ethic. It convinces that the self is the source of its own initiating and responding forces. The self is *SOURCE*.

R. Duncan Wallace, M.D., is a psychiatrist who practices identity psychotherapy in Salt Lake City, Utah. He also conducts Accomplishment and Growth Seminars to divergent groups. He has a special interest in mind and identity growth, both generally and with respect to creativity. He has a particular interest in creative photography, has written extensively about the medium and has conducted in-depth sessions with photographers in order to learn more about the creative process.

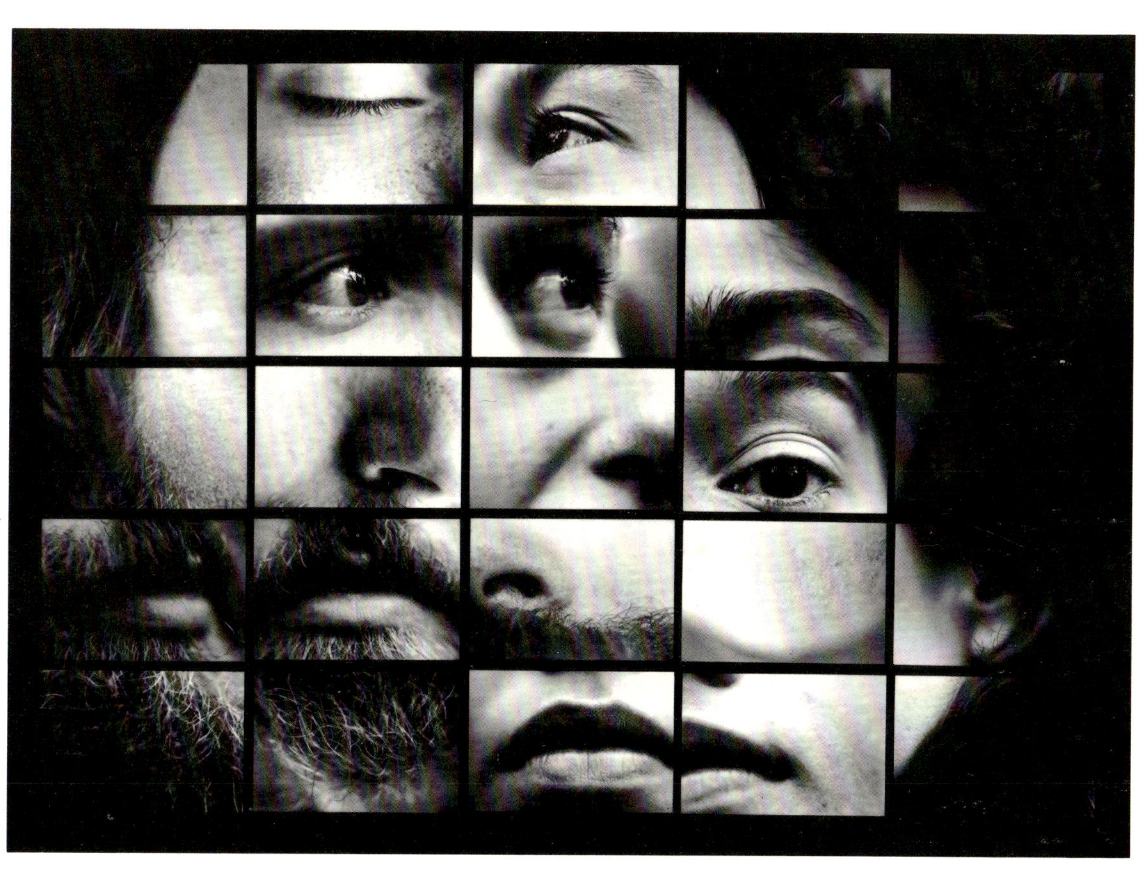

HELEN RICHARDSON
ROBERT SCHIAPPACASSE
Oakland, California
Wedding Self-Portrait

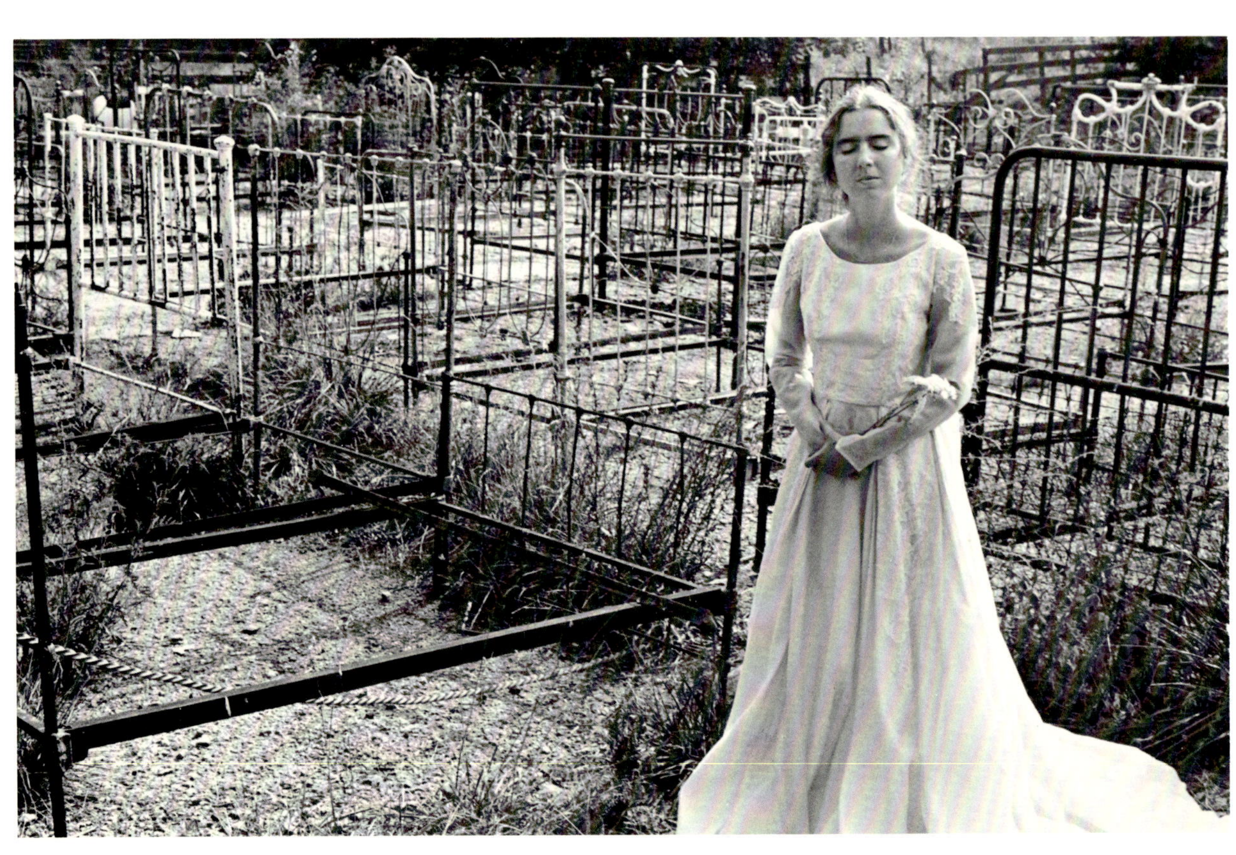

JOYCE TENNESON COHEN
Washington, D. C.
From the "Projection Series," 1973-1974

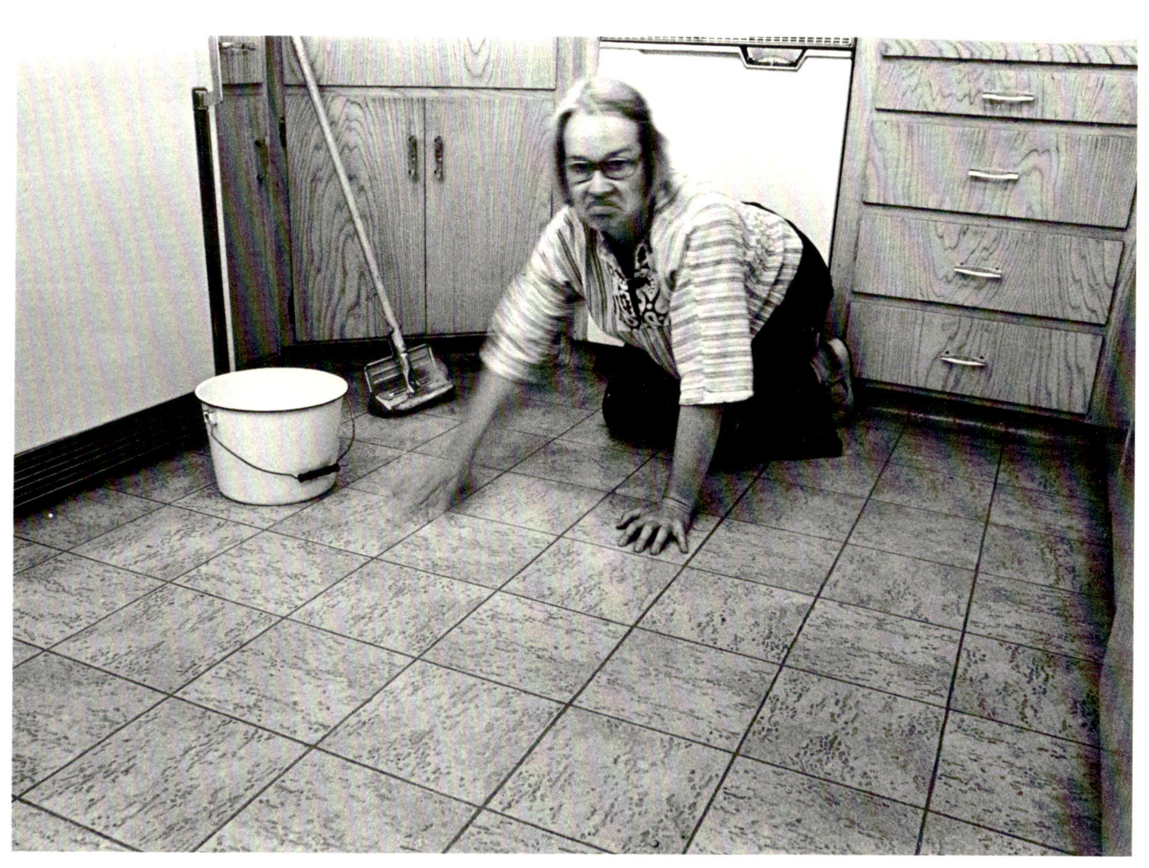

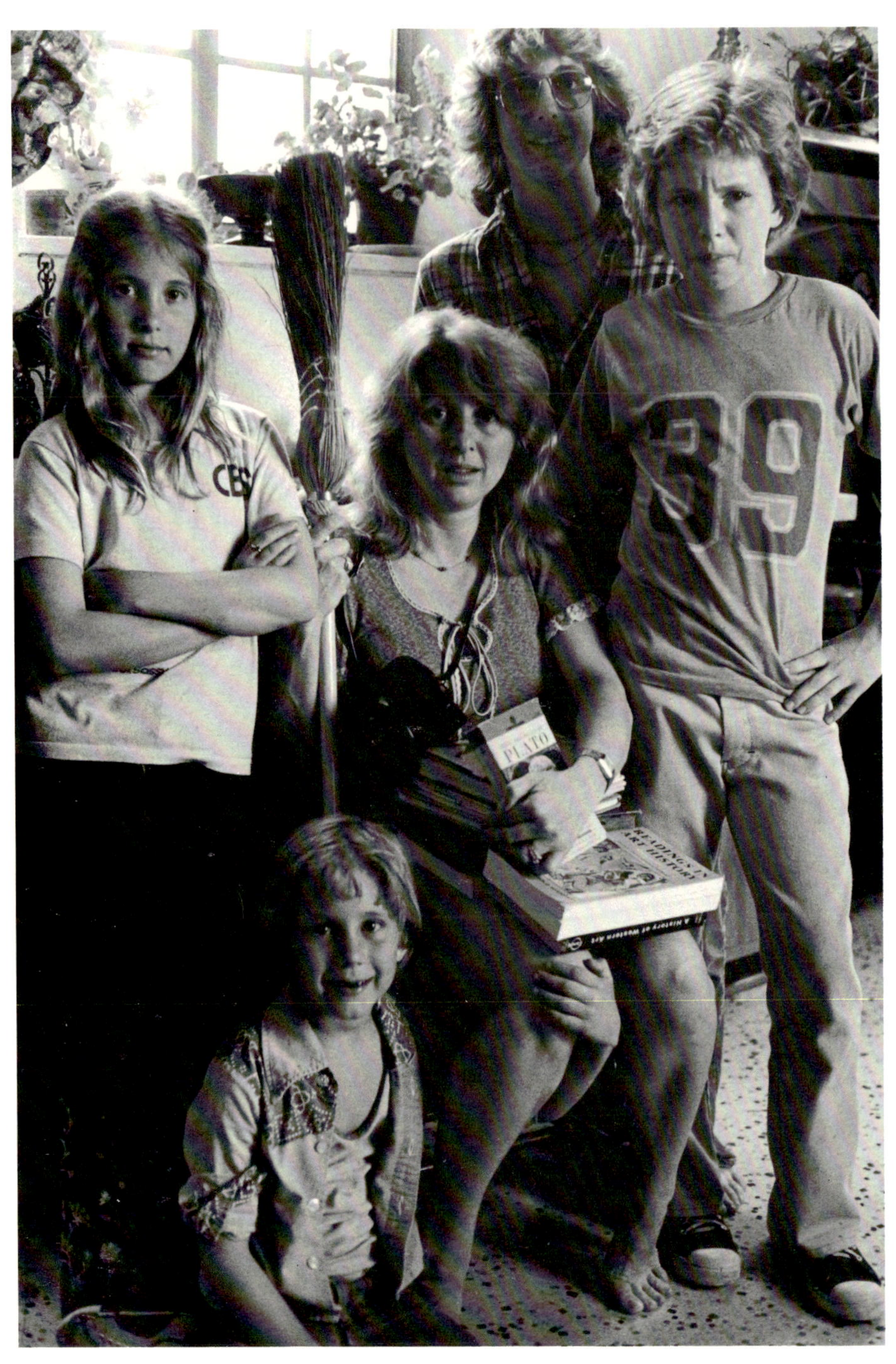

ISABELLE E. PURDEN
RAFB, Texas
The Career, 1978

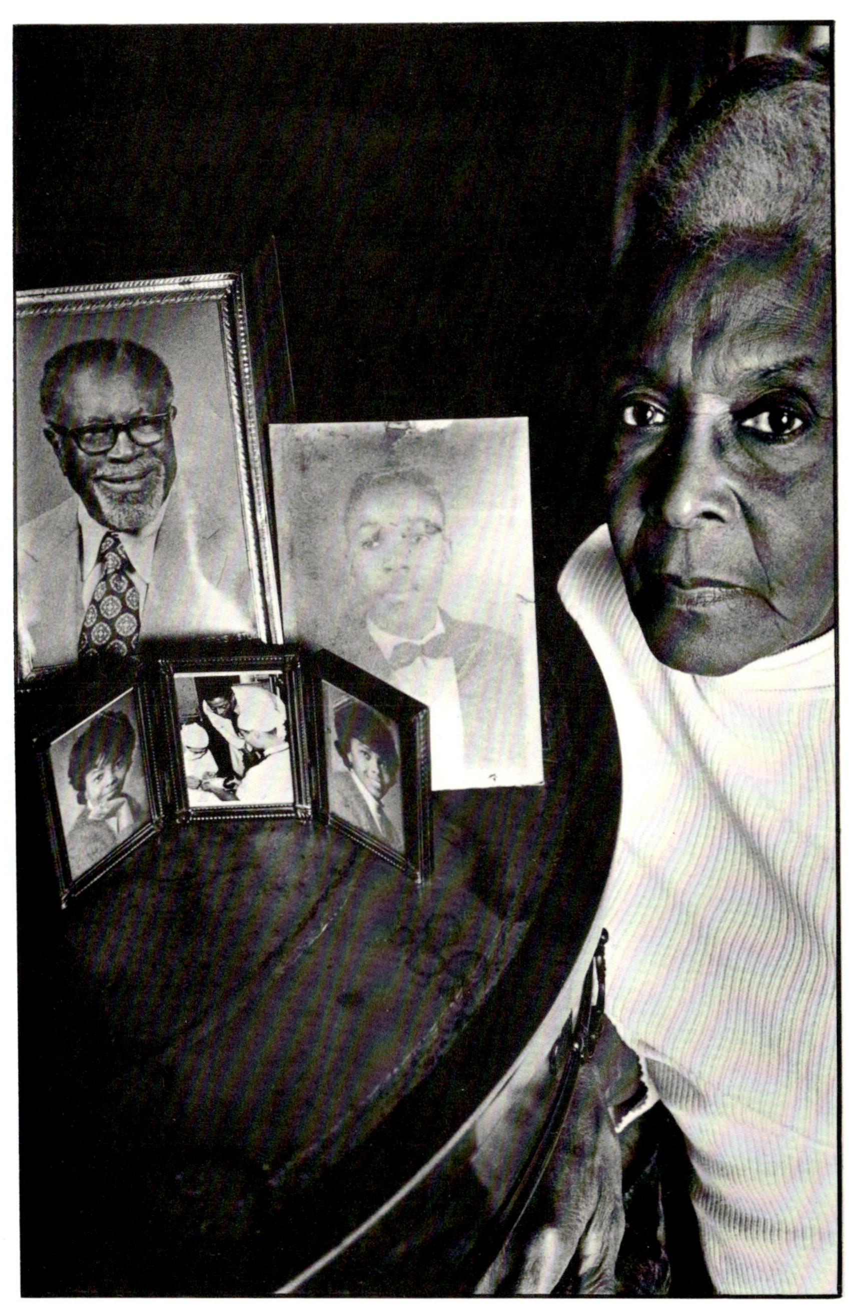

CARROLL PARROTT BLUE
Los Angeles, California
Self-Portrait, Houston, Texas
Mother with Family Portraits, 1976

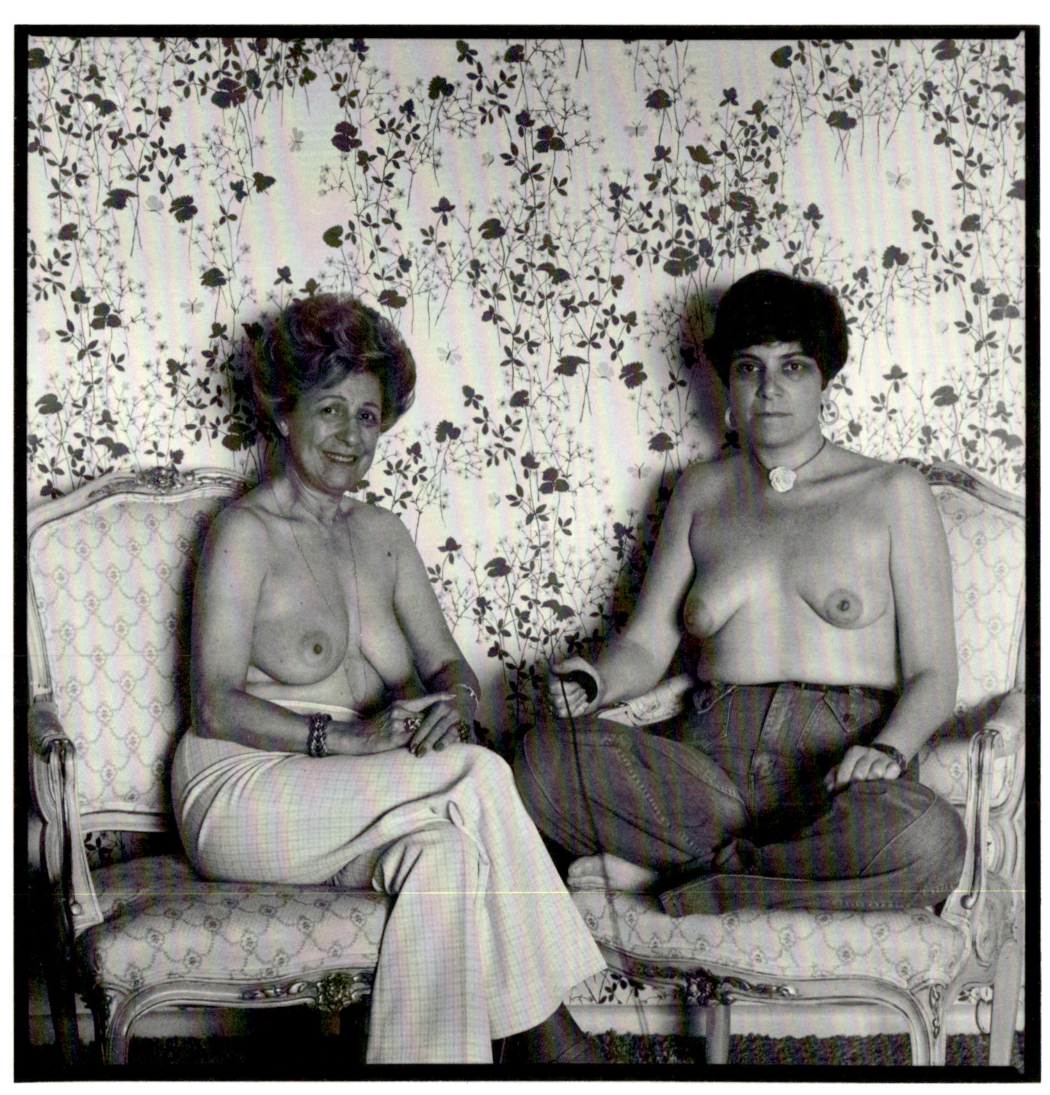

GAY BLOCK
Houston, Texas
Mother & Me, 1977

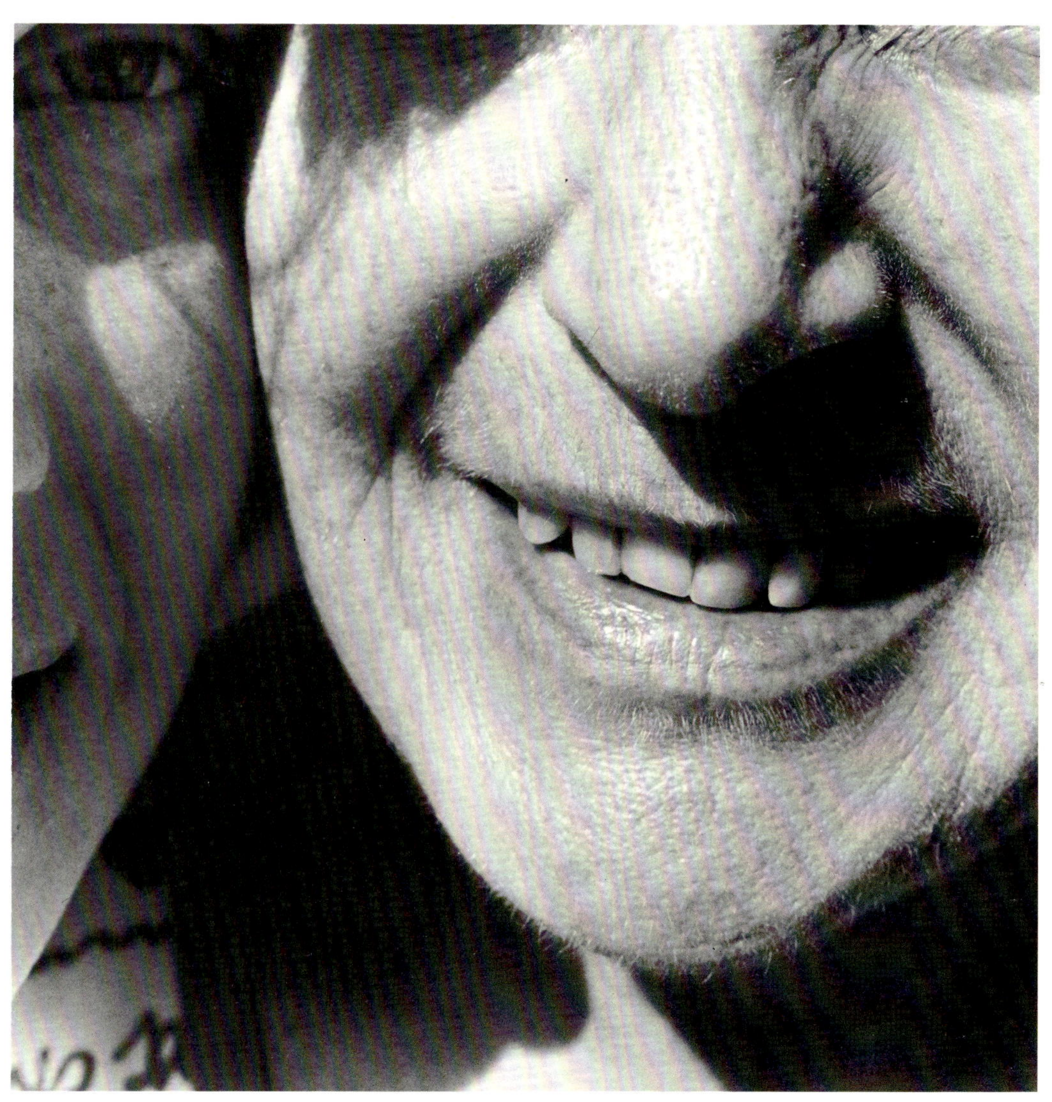

LAUREN SHAW
Belmont, Massachusetts
Self-Portrait/Mom, 1978

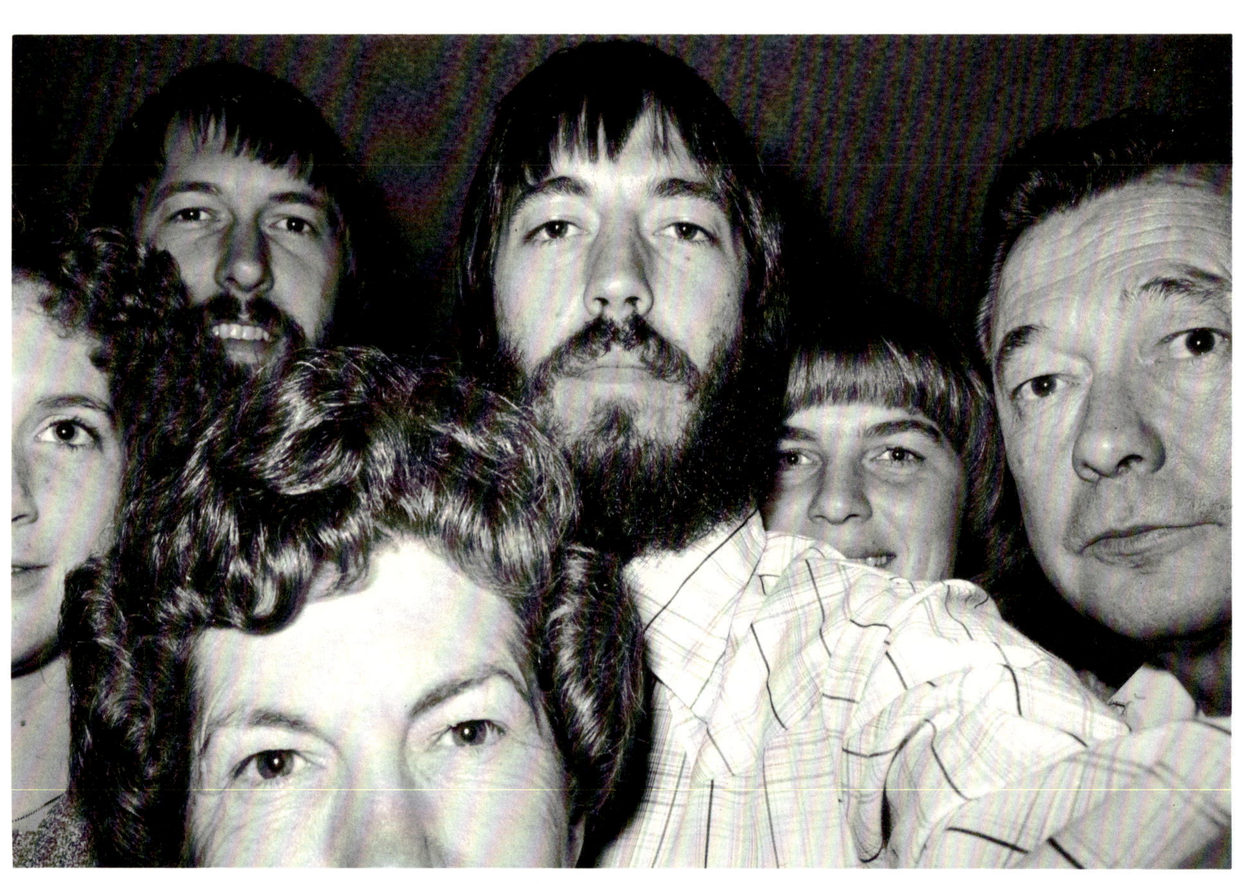

SCOTT D. ENGEL
Denver, Colorado
From the series
"What Makes Me Think I Dominate the Landscape," 1977

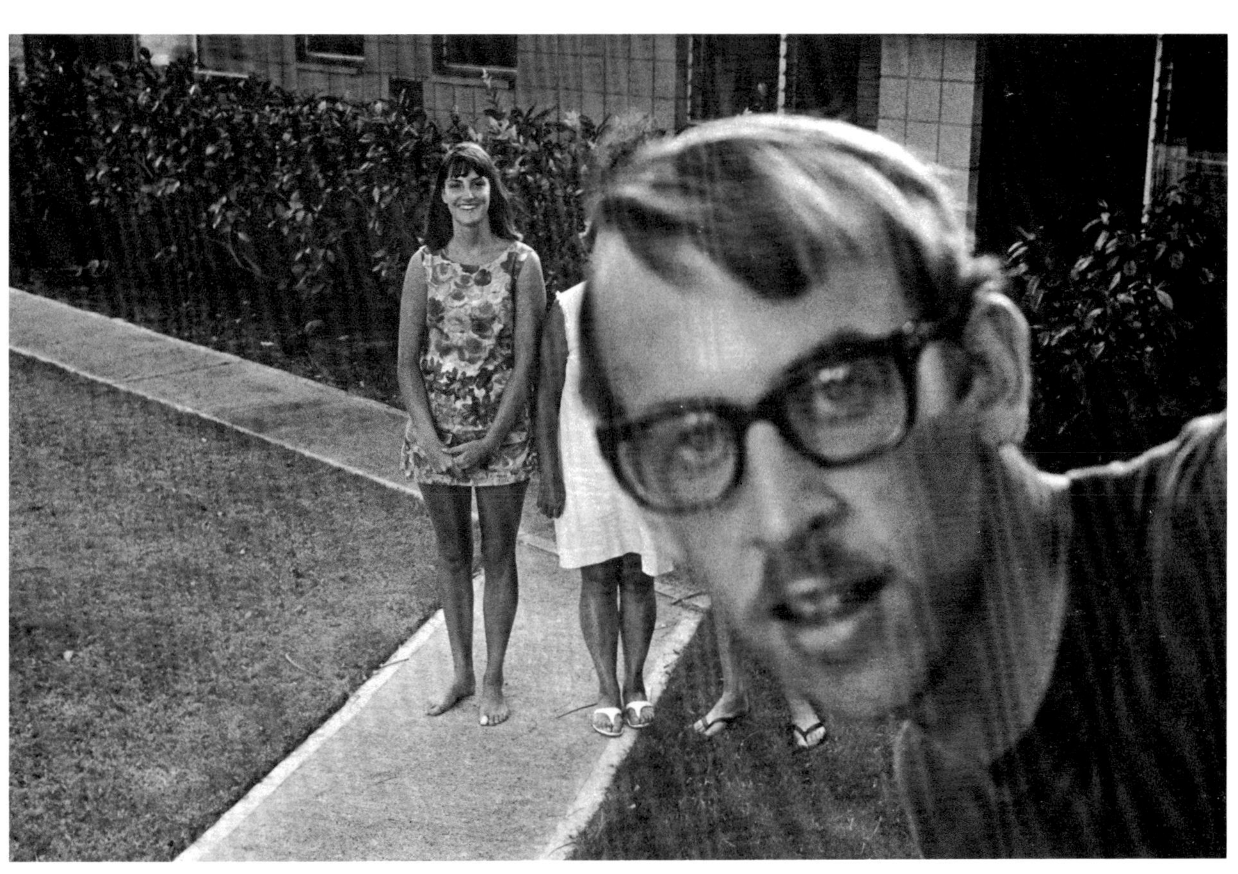

HARRY WILSON
Bakersfield, California
Kathy and Harry at Kathy's Folks, 1969

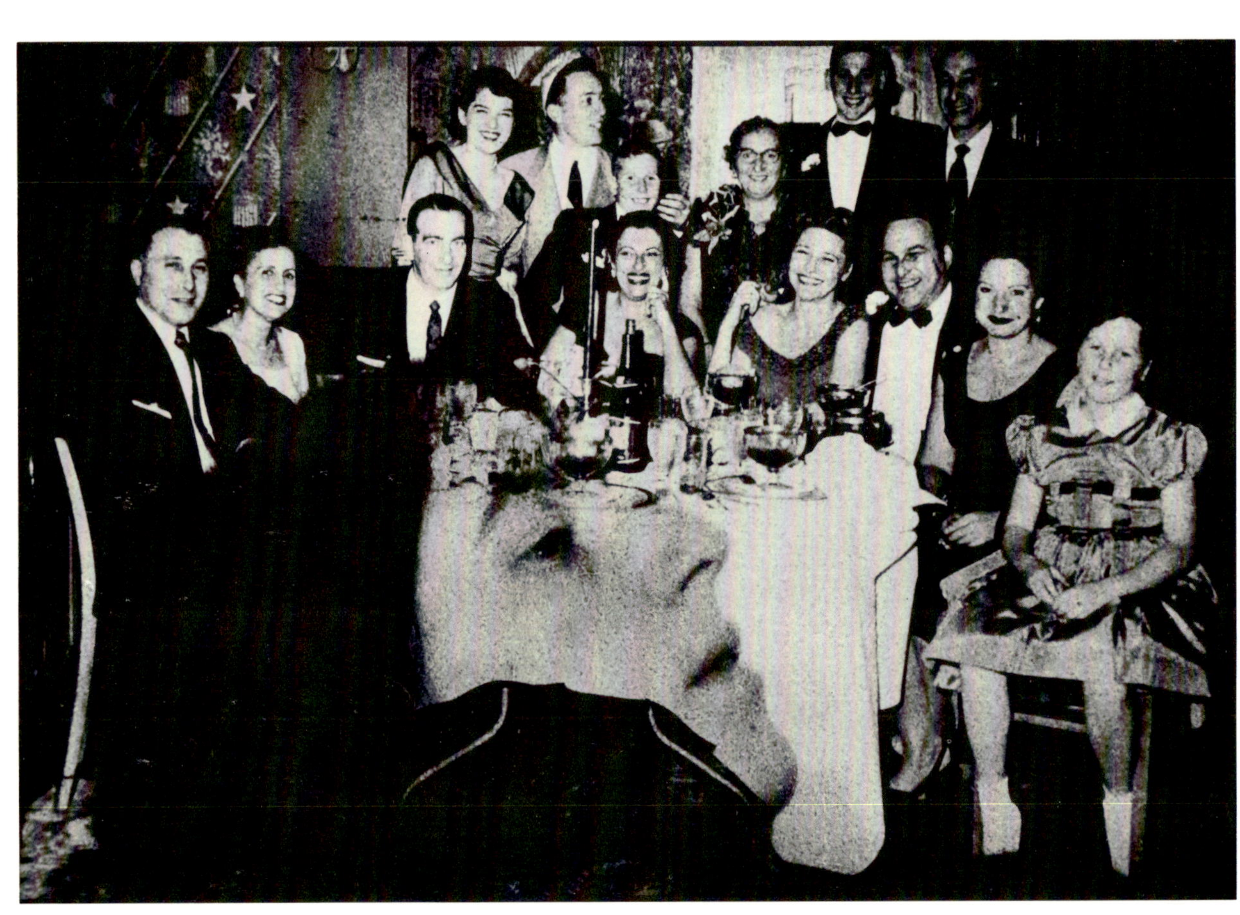

BOBBI CARREY
Cambridge, Massachusetts
Weight Watcher, 1978

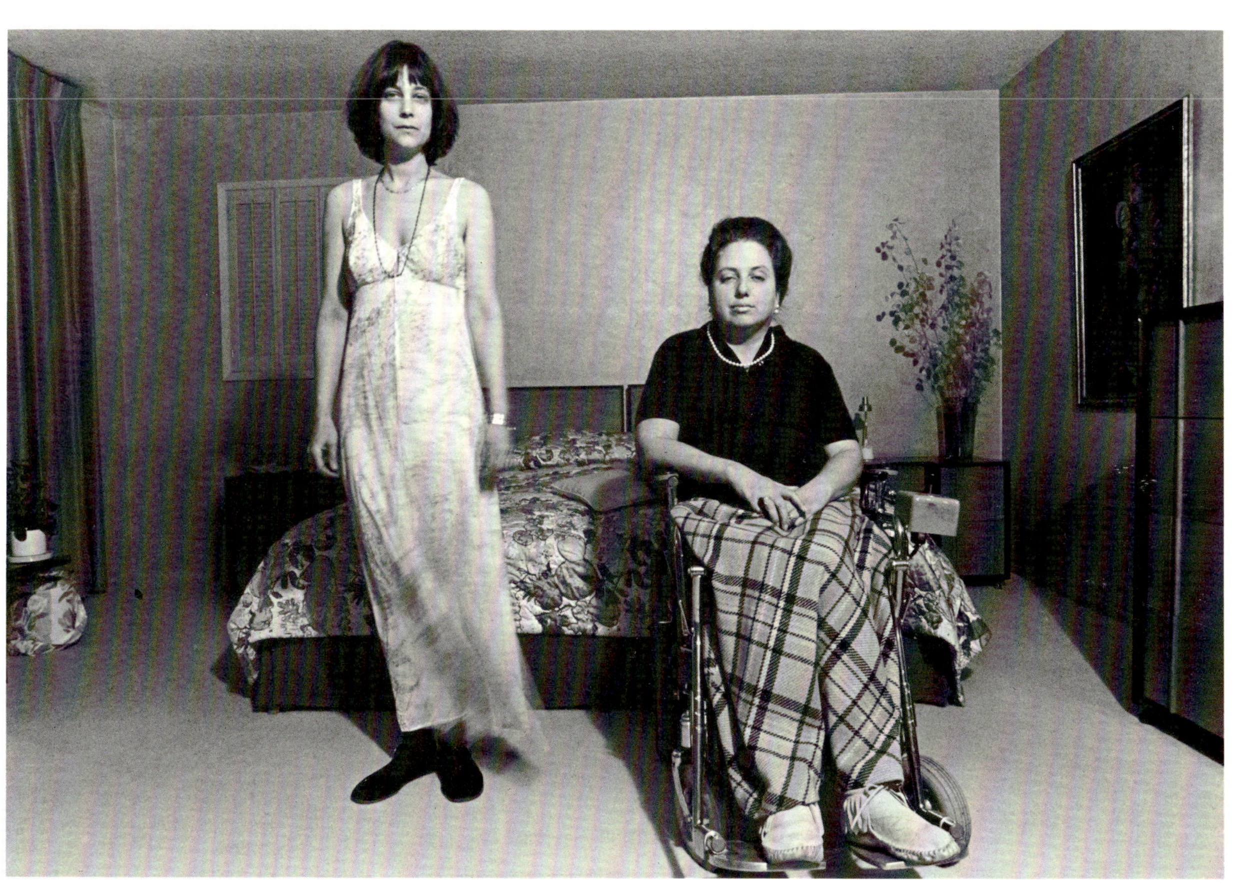

SUZANNE OPTON
New York, New York
My Sister and I and the Distance Between, 1976

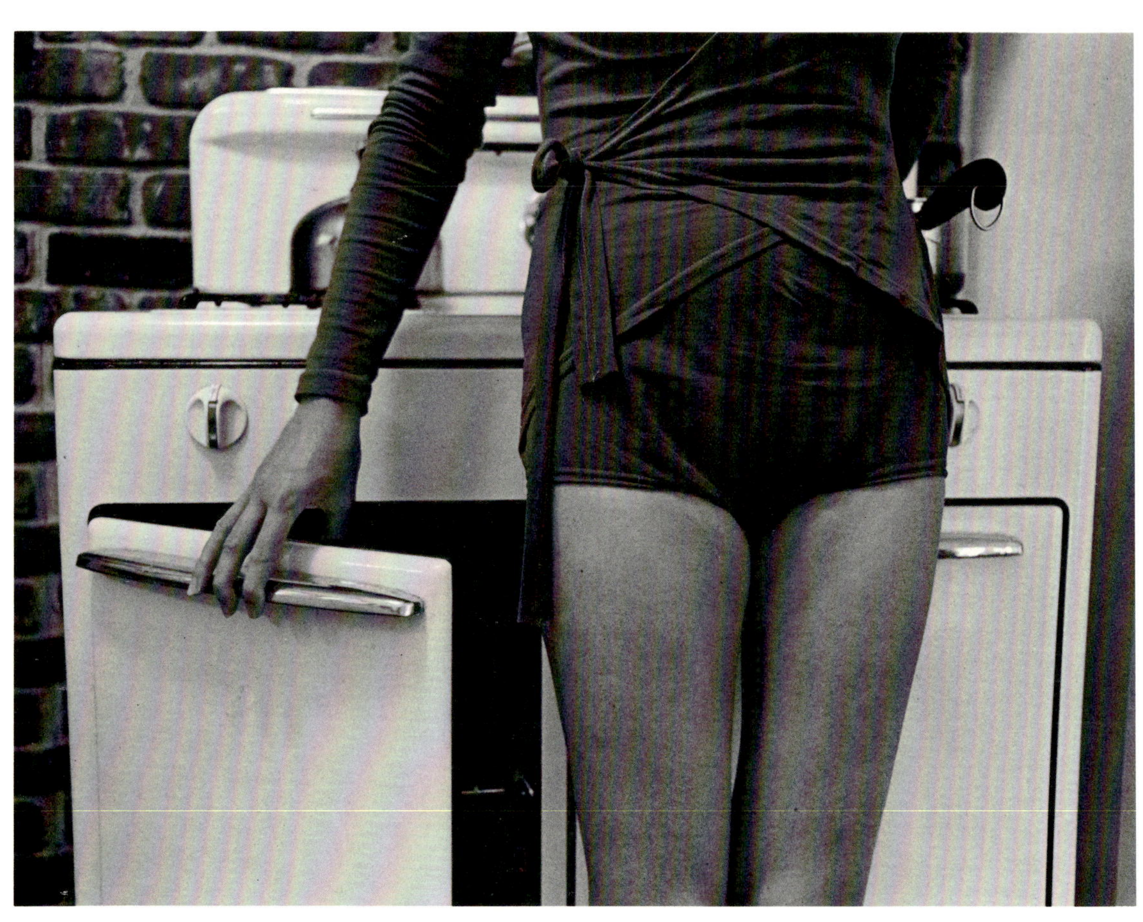

BARBARA THOMPSON
Fairfax, California
Self-Portrait

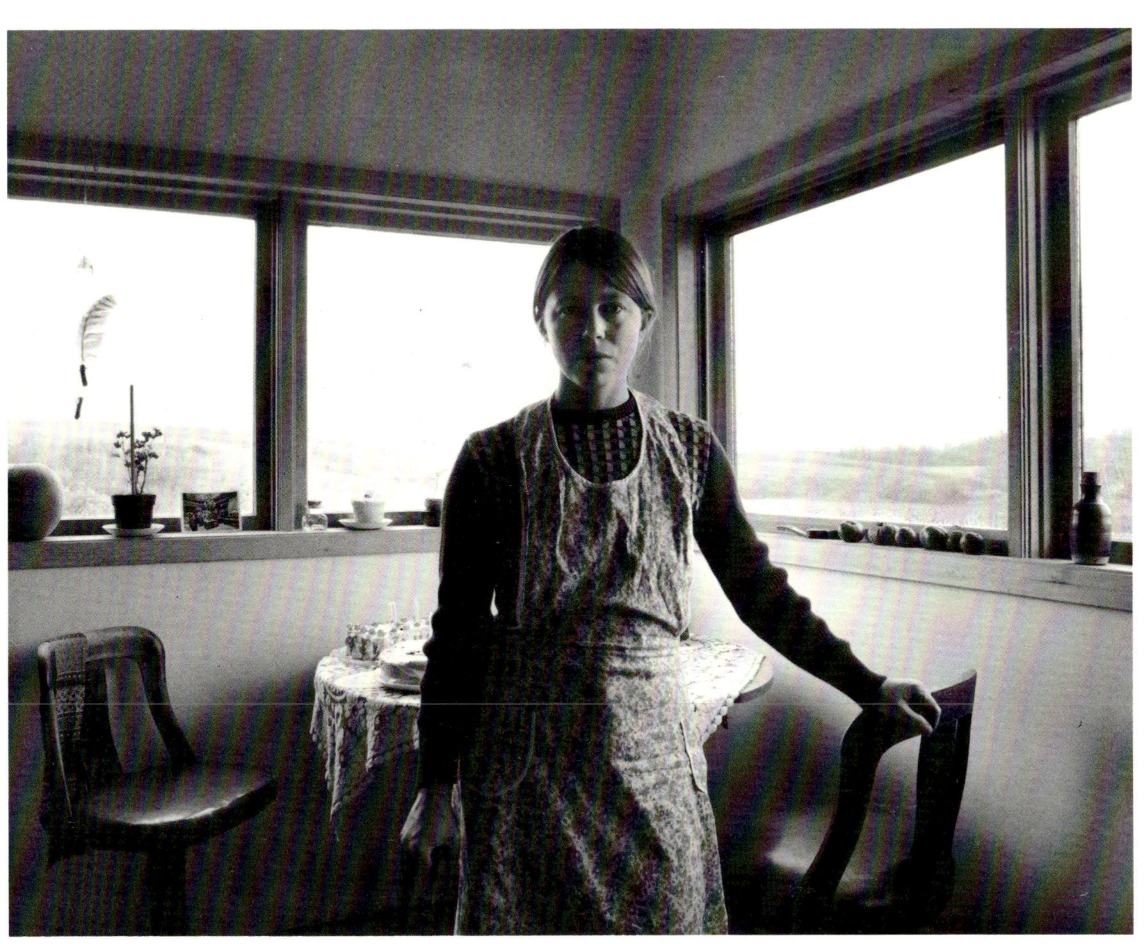

SANDRA SEMCHUK
Saskatchewan, Canada
Self-Portrait with Baba's Apron on, My Daughter's Birthday,
At Home East of Saskatoon, Saskatchewan, 1977

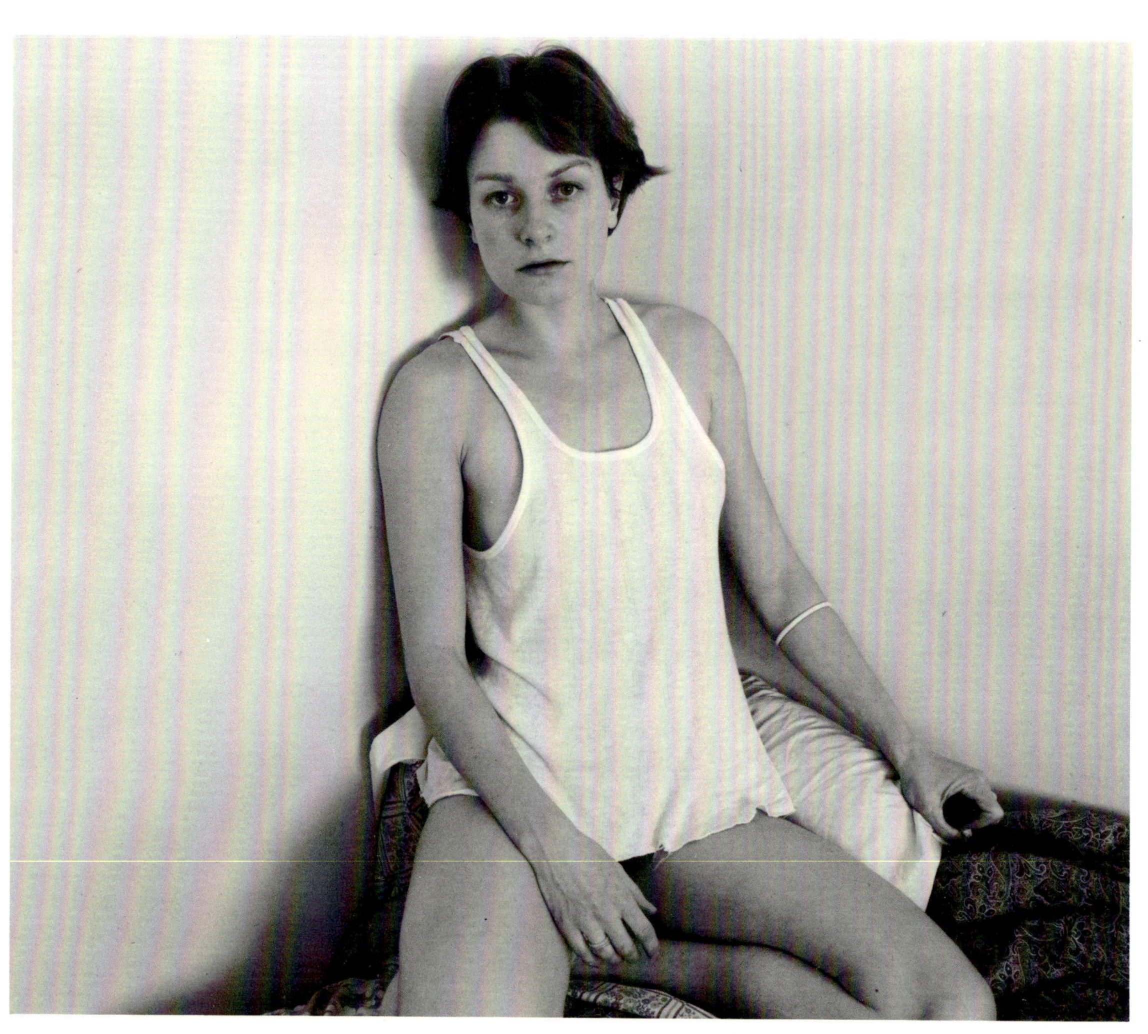

MICHAELIN MCDERMOTT
St. Boniface, Manitoba, Canada
Michaelin — Self-Portrait, 1978

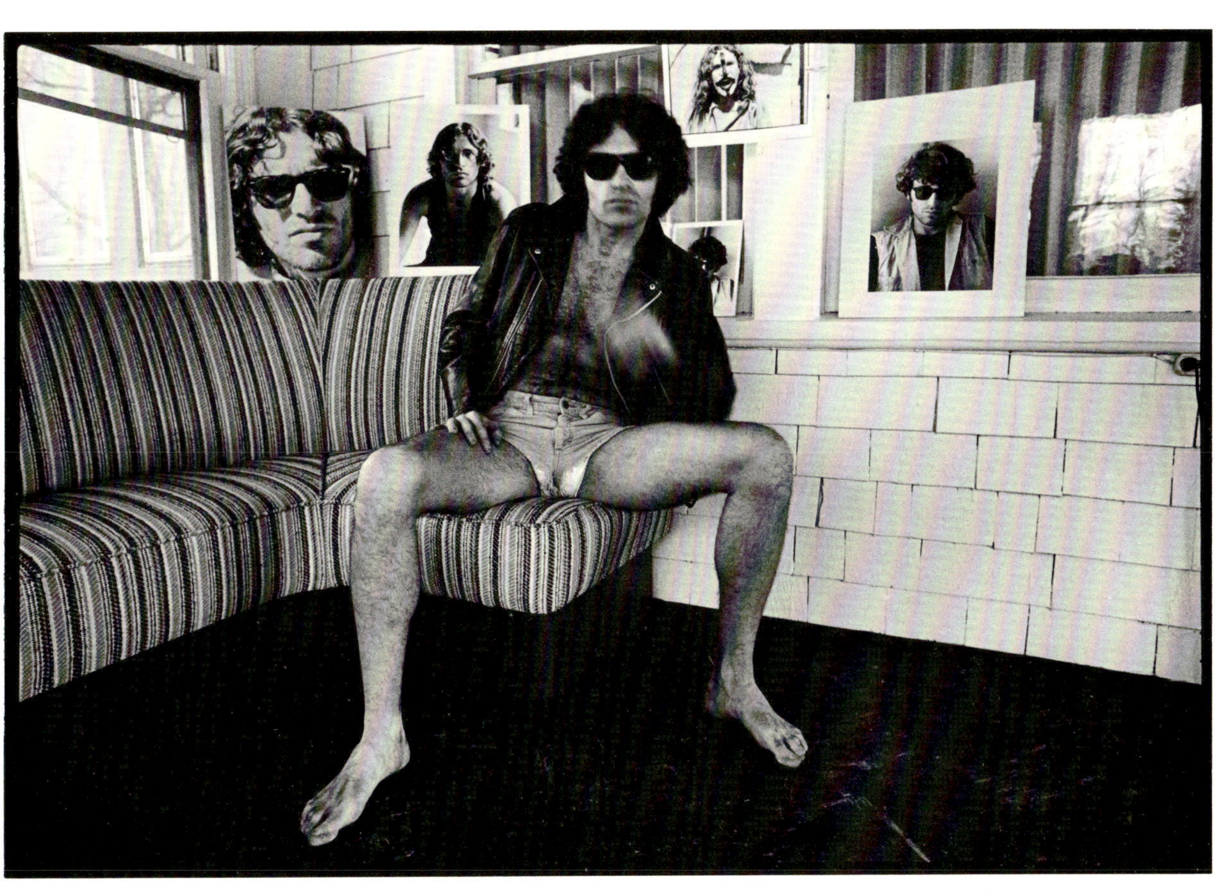

ABE FRAJNDLICH
Cleveland Heights, Ohio
Self-Portrait, Euclid, Ohio, Spring, 1976

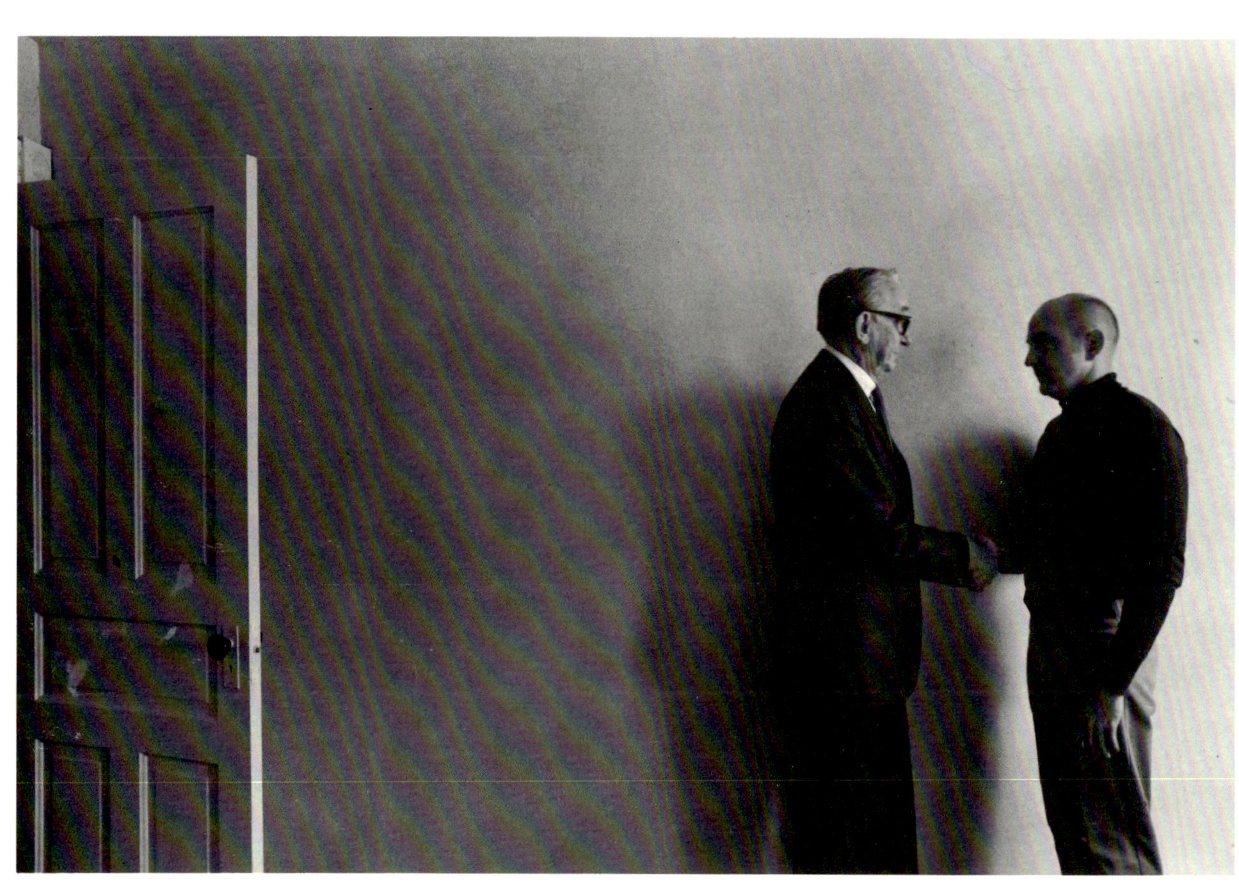

DUANE MICHALS
New York, New York
Self-Portrait Shaking Hands With My Father, 1969

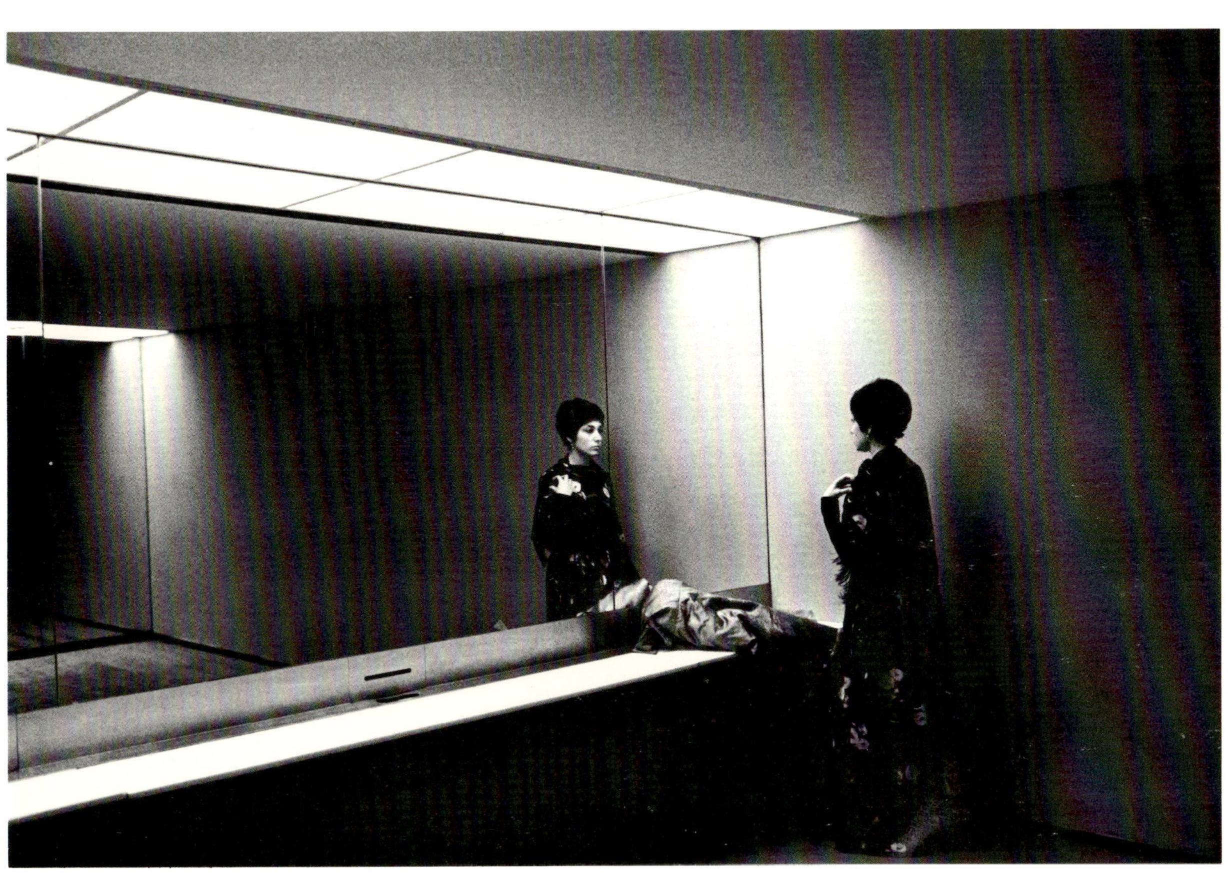

TERRY EVANS
Salina, Kansas
New York, N.Y., 1975

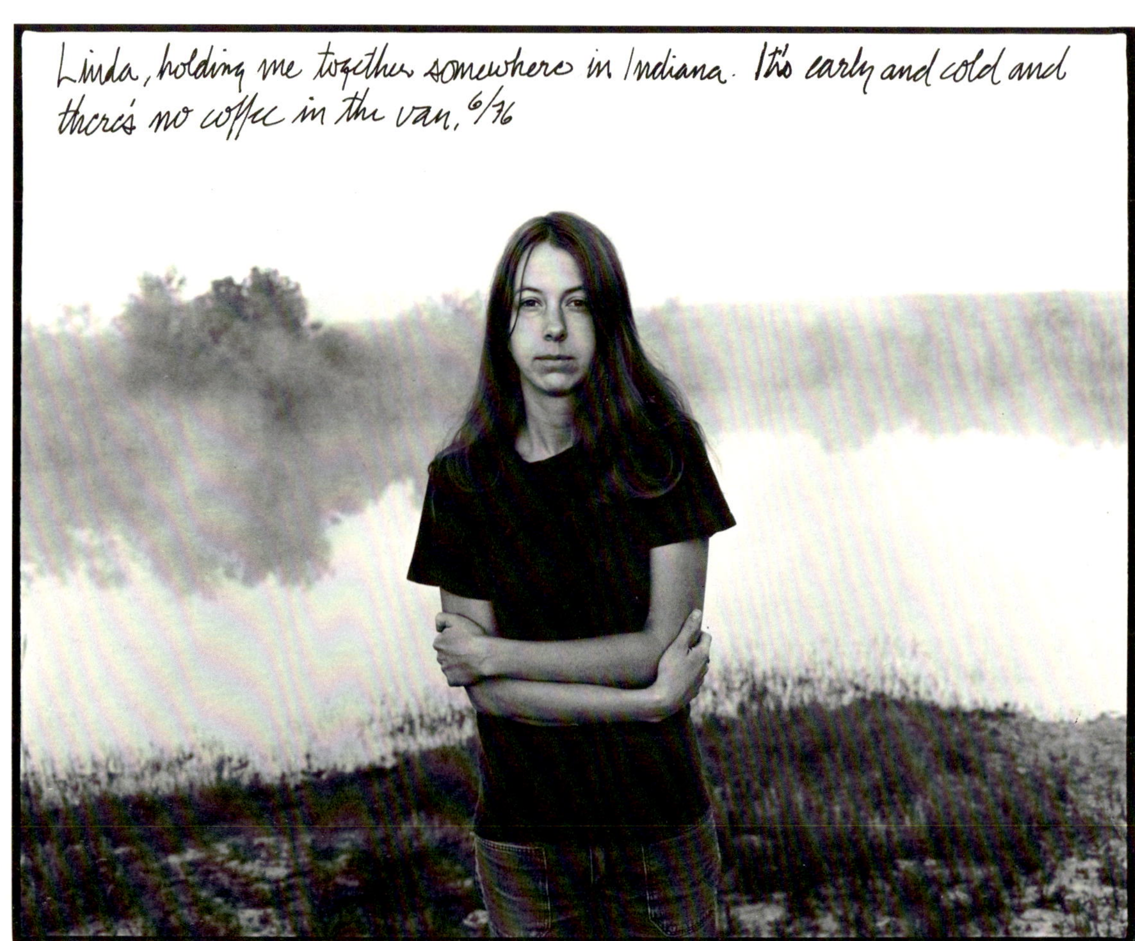

JAMES SANDALL
Whitmore Lake, Michigan
Journal Entry, 1976

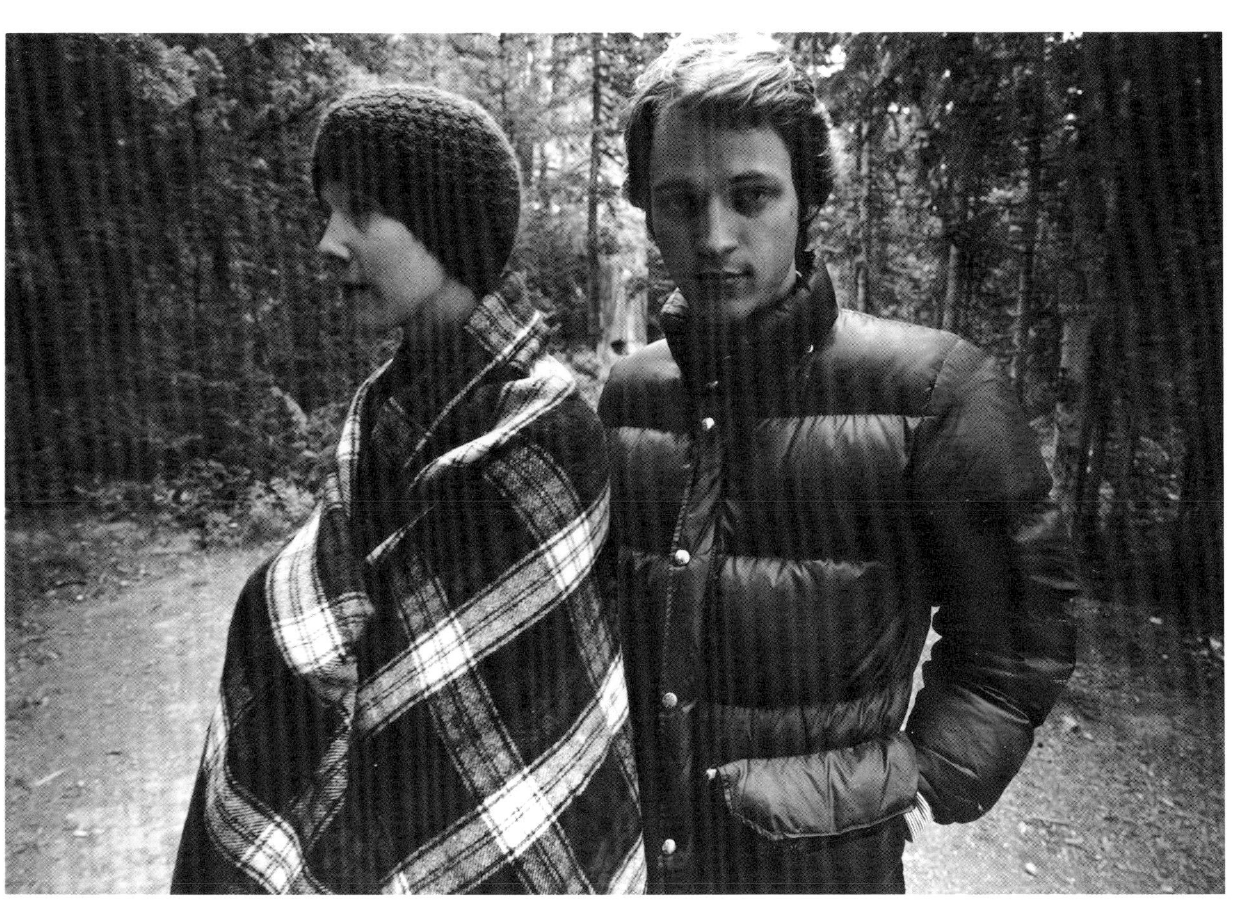

LARRY S. FERGUSON
Hastings, Nebraska
Montana, Self-Portrait With Karen Pike, 1977

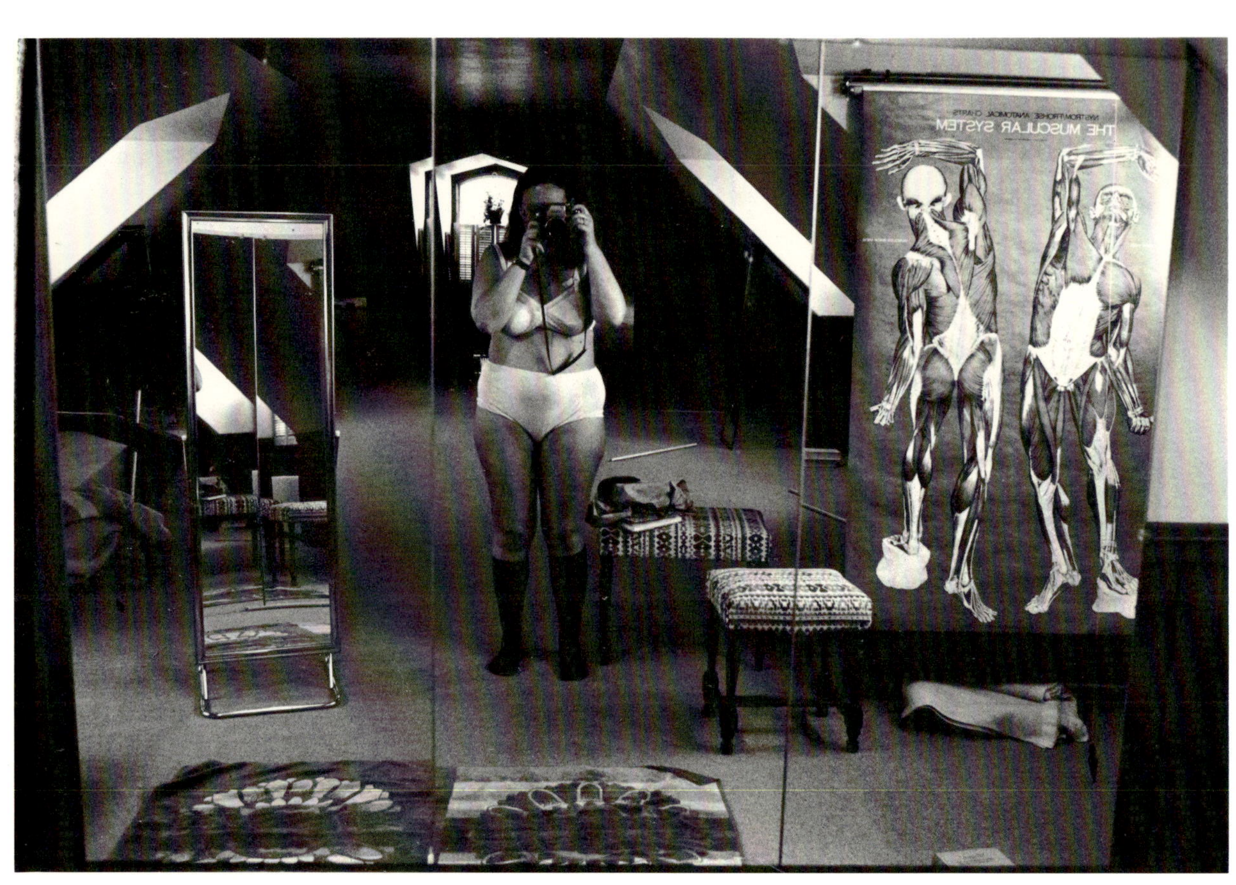

ELSA DORFMAN
Cambridge, Massachusetts
My First Exercise Class after the Birth of Isaac, 1977

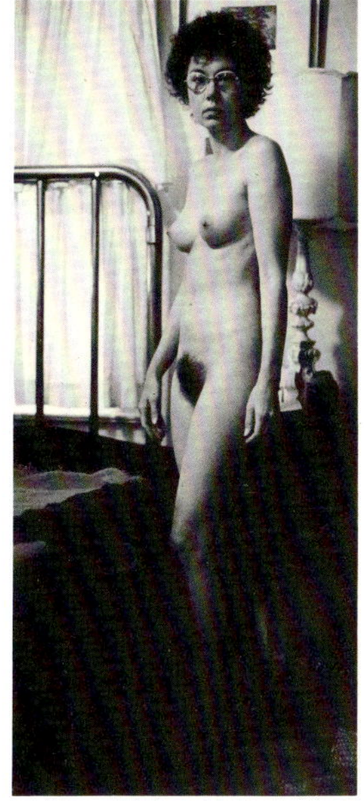

Birth Minus 240 Days

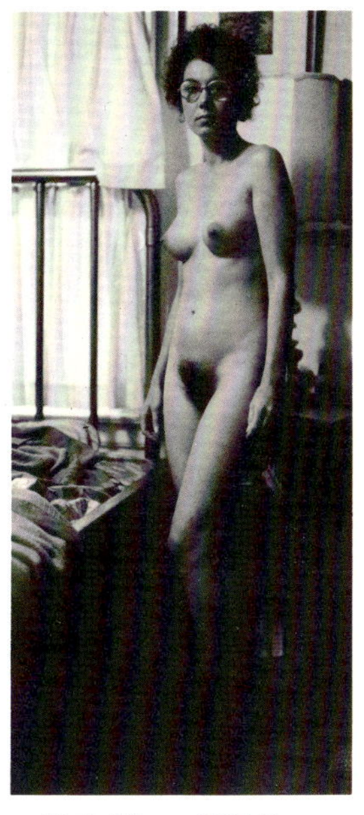

Birth Minus 208 Days

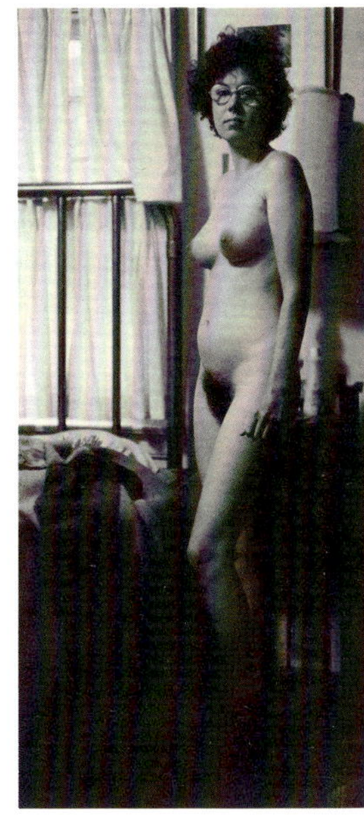

Birth Minus 176 Days

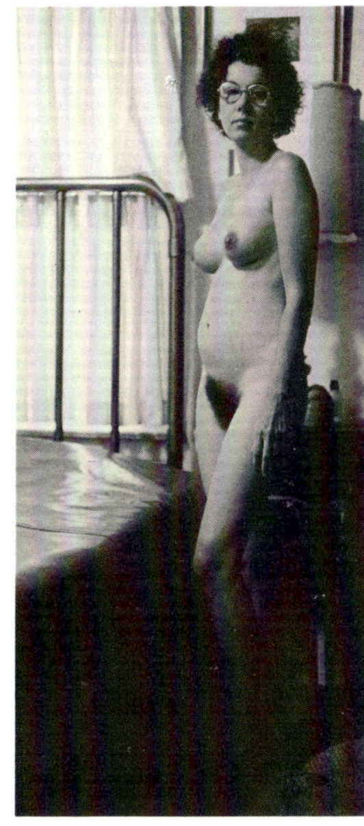

Birth Minus 148 Days

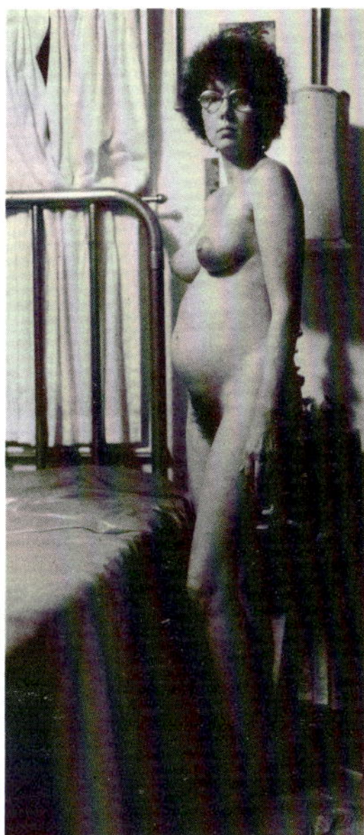

Birth Minus 116 Days

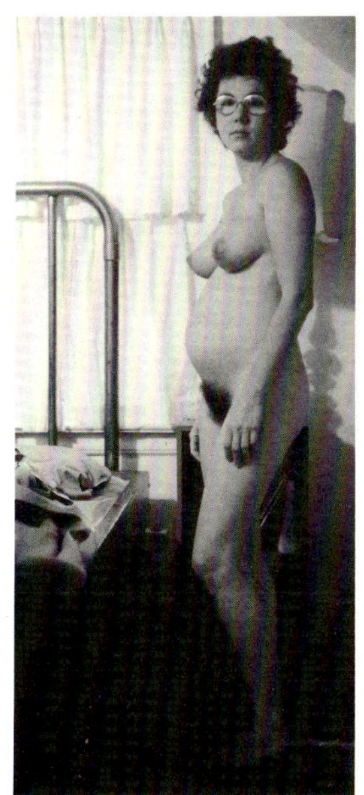

Birth Minus 91 Days

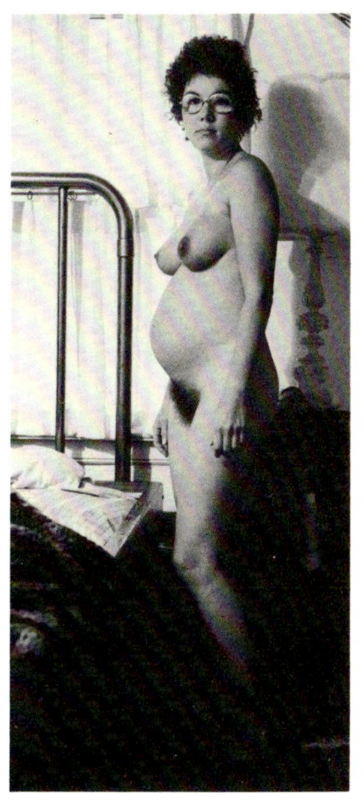

Birth Minus 55 Days

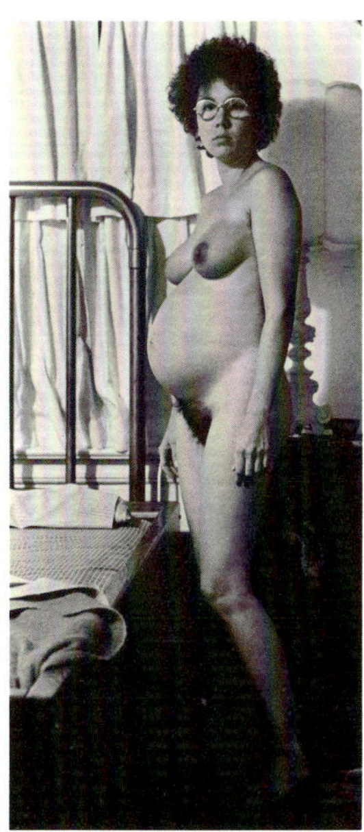

Birth Minus 27 Days

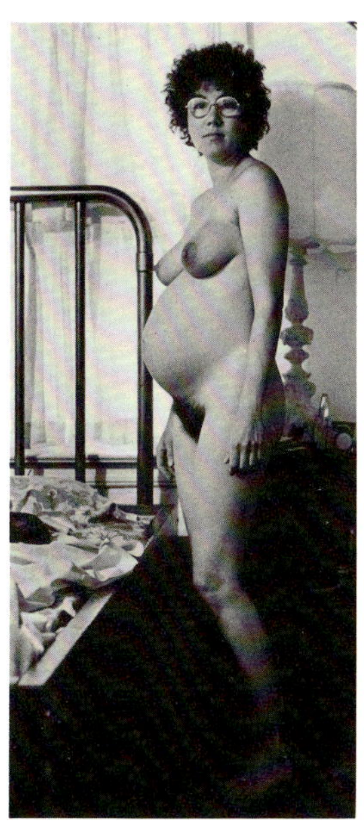

Birth Minus 9 Hours

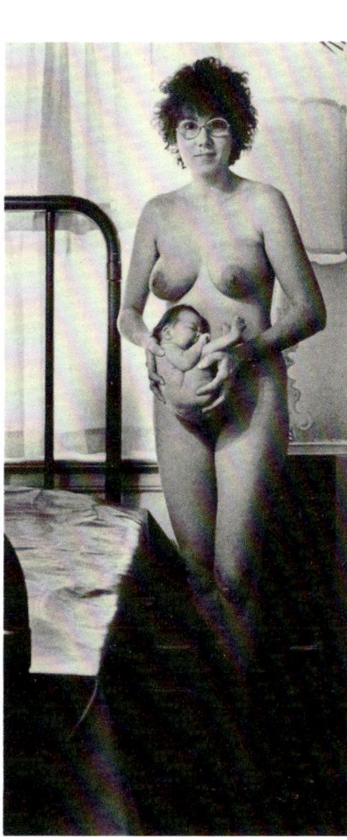

Birth Plus 4 Days

CYNTHIA CABLE
Altadena, California
Breech, 1975

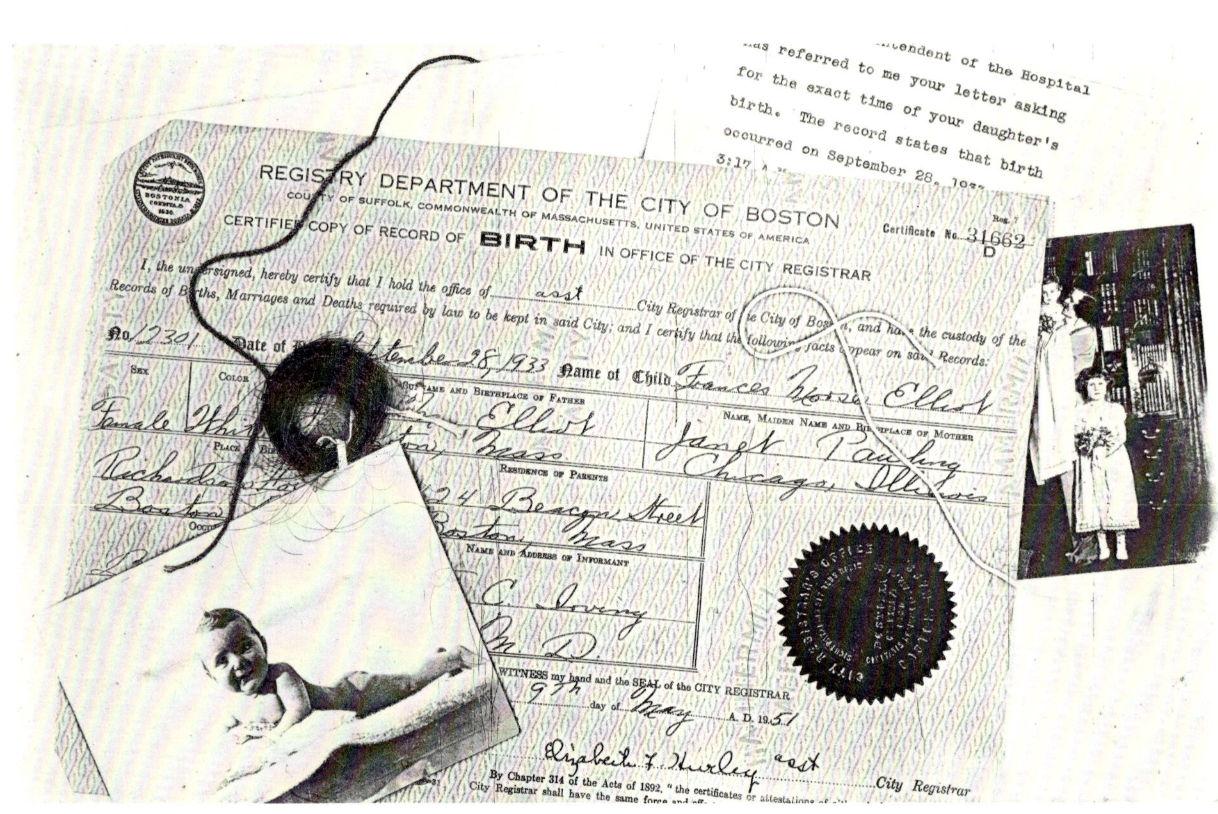

FRANCES E. STORY
Ft. Washington, Pennsylvania
Page from Autobiography, 1976